County Council

Libraries, books and more . . .

Please return/renew this item by the last due date.
Library items may be renewed by phone on
030 33 33 1234 (24 hours) or via our website
www.cumbria.gov.uk/libraries

Cumbria Libraries
Interactive Catalogue

Ask for a CLIC passw

D1349775

Reporting
from the Front

'Europe today is a powder keg and the leaders are like men smoking in an arsenal...A single spark will set off an explosion that will consume us all... I cannot tell you when that explosion will occur, but I can tell you where... Some damned foolish thing in the Balkans will set it off.'

Otto Bismarck at the Congress of Berlin 1878

Reporting from the Front

*War Reporters
during the Great War*

Brian Best

Pen & Sword
MILITARY

First published in Great Britain in 2014 by
PEN AND SWORD MILITARY
an imprint of
Pen and Sword Books Ltd
47 Church Street
Barnsley
South Yorkshire S70 2AS

ISBN 978 1 47382 117 0

Printed and bound in England by
CPI Group (UK) Ltd, Croydon, CR0 4YY

Typeset in Times by CHIC GRAPHICS

Pen & Sword Books Ltd incorporates the imprints of
Pen & Sword Aviation, Pen & Sword Family History, Pen & Sword Maritime,
Pen & Sword Military, Pen & Sword Discovery, Wharncliffe Local History,
Wharncliffe True Crime, Wharncliffe Transport, Pen & Sword Select,
Pen & Sword Military Classics, Leo Cooper, Remember When,
The Praetorian Press, Seaforth Publishing and Frontline Publishing

For a complete list of Pen and Sword titles please contact
Pen and Sword Books Limited
47 Church Street, Barnsley, South Yorkshire, S70 2AS, England
E-mail: enquiries@pen-and-sword.co.uk
Website: www.pen-and-sword.co.uk

Contents

Acknowledgements

In researching this book many hours were spent in libraries and archives, notably the British Library and the British Newspaper Archive, where the staff were unfailingly helpful. *The Times* Archive, now banished to the northern outskirts of London, was a particularly fruitful source for information and I am grateful to Anne Jensen for her knowledge and help. My special thanks, however, are reserved for Sally Baker, formerly of *The Times*, who volunteered to proof read and edit my manuscript, turning my offering into readable prose for which the reader will be grateful. Thanks also to Irene Moore from Pen & Sword.

Finally, thanks to Michael Clayton, a former BBC correspondent from the wars of Vietnam, Cambodia and the Middle East, whose advice was eagerly accepted and who has kindly contributed the Forward.

Foreword

It has been truly said that truth is the first casualty in war. In both world wars it was standard practice for the military top brass on all sides to manipulate coverage of the conflict in the media.

However, the role of the war correspondent in the First World War was distorted to a scandalous extent. The British Government and the military top brass relied on jingoism and news management to ensure a ready supply of recruits for a war whose very cause is still a subject of confusion and debate.

Having reported something of battles in Vietnam, Cambodia and the Middle East I am well aware that media coverage remains a military headache, but in the Great War 'managed' news eventually led to cynicism at home and encouraged mutiny among troops on all sides.

When conscription became necessary to reinforce mightily the British Expeditionary Force after catastrophic early losses, it was deemed even more necessary to keep the full truth about trench warfare from the public at home.

Brian Best has performed a considerable service in describing the 1914–18 war from the viewpoint of correspondents who were at first forbidden even to visit the front line. Taking 'unauthorised' pictures of battle was punishable by a firing squad.

Correspondents worked under excruciating censorship and other pressures from the senior military and politicians. Only years later did some correspondents write truthfully of what they had seen – and apologise for their reports during the war. Many of their published accounts were so distorted that correspondents were often despised by those serving in the trenches.

Brian Best rightly apportions considerable blame to the newspaper proprietors. He is fair in emphasising the work of a few correspondents who were prepared to buck the system, and produced truthful reports, especially from the disastrous Gallipoli campaign. His narrative of the Great War through the press coverage which helped to prolong it provides a clear guide to the conflict from an important aspect often overlooked.

This is a fascinating contribution to 1914–18 literature offering valuable lessons on the conduct of war reporting which are still relevant.

Michael Clayton

Prologue

With the passing of the Victorian age, so also passed the so-called Golden Age of war reporting. In a period of about fifty years, stretching from the Crimean War to the Second Anglo-Boer War, the 'specials', as the war reporters were known, enjoyed a freedom and popularity which made them the stars of their newspapers. It was a time when war reporting actually sold newspapers. Often armed with little more than a bag of sovereigns, a notebook and a revolver, the special was free to wander the battlefield and, in some cases, become involved in the fighting.

In the Crimean War and the Indian Mutiny, it was William Howard Russell of *The Times* who inspired other adventurous spirits with a literary bent. Men like Archibald Forbes of the *Daily News*, who rode 110 miles in 20 hours through enemy-infested territory to be the first to file the news of the Zulus' defeat at Ulundi in 1879. This kind of determination to be first with the news began to sow the seeds of resentment among many senior military officers who felt that their triumphs were being trumped by the newspapers.

General Sir Garnet Wolseley, who benefitted from exposure by the press, confided in his wife: *'Confound all this breed of vermin – Shall I never be strong enough to be honest and tell these penny-a-liners how I loath them and their horrid trade.'*

One officer in particular harboured a visceral hatred of the press and for over fifteen years did all he could to keep reporters away from the action and force them to report only what suited the army. He was Field Marshal Horatio Herbert Kitchener, Lord Kitchener of Khartoum. During the Sudan War of 1898, he famously snapped at a group of reporters standing outside his tent: *'Get out of my way, you drunken swabs.'* He also imposed a news blackout which foreshadowed what was to come.

In the first decade of the twentieth century, the war correspondent could still accompany the army on minor expeditions but increasingly had to adhere to guidelines that did not allow the reporting of poor morale, bad conditions for the troops or cruelty towards the native population.

The final fling before the curtain came down for ever was the Balkan War of 1912–13. This heralded the descent into the horrors of the Great War. For the war correspondent it saw the end of freedom to write reports on what he had seen in the name of patriotism. It effect, war correspondents evolved into the mouthpiece of the military, enjoying the flattery they received from the generals, wearing smart uniforms and turning a blind eye to the reality of what the ordinary soldier endured. In doing so, they turned what had been a noble profession into one to be reviled.

After the First World War most of them had pangs of conscience and wrote books about their part in the war with a genuine regret that they had masked the truth. It was to be many years before the public and, more particularly, servicemen would believe what was published in the newspapers.

As the term implies, the Great War was to be on a world-wide scale with many front lines from which war correspondents would report. All would, however, be subject to censorship, some more stringent than others, but there was still scope for a determined war correspondent to go digging for a story. Another aspect of reporting the First World War was that after 1915, all the fit younger reporters had either volunteered or been conscripted into the armed forces. Those left were, in the main, middle-aged veteran reporters with a sprinkling of physically rejected younger men. Some were short-sighted, like Lester Lawrence of Reuters, who could see little of the fighting going on before him. Some were very deaf, like Henry Tomlinson, who displayed no fear of incoming shells, as he could not hear them. There was even a one-armed reporter, Edmund Candler, who typed single-handed reports from the uncomfortable Mesopotamian Front.

The reporters may have been castigated for following the official line, but their powers of observation and descriptive accounts have left with us an invaluable source of material from the aspect of a close observer.

Chapter 1

Sunset of the Golden Age

W hen Queen Victoria died in 1901, many things passed with her. Small-scale colonial wars and a certain amount of press freedom became 'Victorian'. Wars were about to become more far-reaching and destructive. The reporting of them became increasingly more restricted and frustrating. Although there were many things that made a correspondent's job easier, like the portable typewriter, the camera, the telephone and, soon, the radio, officially controlled censorship and the sheer scale of modern conflicts made reporting a constant round of struggle and obstruction. The Boer War was both the last of the old-style and the first of the new-style conflicts.

War correspondents, as long as they were accredited, had still been free to wander around during a battle to observe what they liked. What the censor did not like was the reporting of morale (unless good), troop dispositions and future plans. Despite the censor, the reporters generally felt that they had done the best they could in the circumstances.

This was all about to change.

After the Boer surrender in 1902, Britain, generally, was at peace. She had been involved in a unique multi-national expedition in China during the summer of 1900. A secret society called 'Righteous Harmonious Fists', or Boxers as they were known by Westerners, came into prominence with a call to exterminate all 'foreign devils' in China. They backed up this call by killing missionaries, businessmen and Chinese Christians. The Western embassies in Peking appealed to the Dowager Empress to use the Imperial Army to suppress the uprising. Instead, they found that there was considerable royal sympathy for the Boxers and that they could not rely on the Chinese authorities to supply protection of the foreign legations.

With the surrounding country in an uproar and communications being cut, the foreign diplomats sent for troops and sailors from their coastal bases.

A total of 430 marines and sailors from eight different countries arrived and set to building a defensive perimeter in the Legation Quarter of the city. This had to house 353 civilian men, women and children, in addition to which there were about 2,700 Chinese Christians. From the beginning of June until their relief on 14 August, they were cut off by thousands of fanatical Boxers.

Among the civilians was Dr George Ernest Morrison, *The Times'* man in China. He, like Mark Twain, became one of few people to have had the interesting experience of reading his own obituary. After the first fierce attack, the *Daily Mail* reported that the Legations had fallen and everyone was slain. *The Times* assumed that Morrison had died and printed a glowing three column obituary.

Happily Morrison survived, although he was wounded. He was even mentioned in despatches by the British Minister:

> *'Dr Morrison,* The Times *correspondent, acted as Lieutenant to Captain Strouts and rendered most valuable assistance. Active, energetic and cool, he volunteered for every service of danger and was a pillar of strength when matters were going badly. He was severely wounded on 16th July by the same volley that killed Captain Strouts and his valuable services were lost for the rest of the siege.'*

After peace returned, Morrison resumed his post for *The Times* until his death in 1920.

The paper had sent John Cowan as his replacement and he joined other reporters as they accompanied the relief force of 20,000 troops made up of units supplied by Britain, Japan, Russia, United States, France, Germany, Italy and Austria. George Lynch of *The Illustrated London News*, who had attempted to escape through the Boer siege of Ladysmith only to be captured, was also on hand. He wrote critically of the brutal treatment of Chinese civilians meted out by the Russians, French and Germans. On one occasion, British soldiers rescued a couple of women who had been thrown down a well by Russian soldiers. Overcoming stiff resistance, the Alliance fought its way to Peking and successfully relieved the Legations.

Another example of multinational co-operation occurred in 1909 during the aftermath of the Messina earthquake in southern Italy, in which 200,000 died. The ships of six navies brought relief and the crews helped look for survivors.

Sadly these two examples of international co-operation and goodwill were soon forgotten as all of the nations involved were about to become locked together in the most cataclysmic of all wars.

In 1903, Britain undertook a minor expedition in Somaliland which prompted Melton Prior and Bennet Burleigh to be diverted on their return from reporting the Delhi Durbar proclaiming Edward Vll, Emperor of India. It was just thirty years since Prior had accompanied Edward during his first trip to India. Although the old friends did not see any action, Prior found the climate good for his increasing health problems, particularly emphysema and asthma. Burleigh, in his droll way, concurred by writing: *'It is very healthy, plenty of sun, plenty of sand but the shortest road to a public house is a thousand miles long!'*. The campaign was short with little fighting but plenty of hot and thirsty marching. It also produced the awards of three Victoria Crosses, all for the same action. One of the recipients was Major Johnnie Gough, leader of the column that was attacked. Also accompanying the column was the *Daily Graphic* special correspondent, William Theobald Maud, a fellow Ladysmith veteran, with whom Johnnie enjoyed a good relationship. When the column came under attack, Gough and two other officers went to the rescue of a mortally wounded officer in charge of the rearguard some half a mile distant. In the absence of any officers, it was Will Maud who took charge of the column, directing fire and keeping formation, while sketching and making notes.

Maud was instrumental in Gough being awarded the Victoria Cross by ignoring the officer's efforts to play down his part in the rescue and sending a glowing report back to his paper. Johnnie was greatly saddened by the news that Will Maud had died of fever in Aden while on his way home to his pregnant wife. He asked his father to write to the editor of the *Daily Graphic* to suggest a public subscription to which he would contribute anonymously. Given the general suspicion in which the military held war reporters, this was an unusually generous gesture.

In 1904, the British provoked a regrettable confrontation in Tibet. Without wishing to occupy the country, they sought a treaty with the Tibetans but, when they received no response, crossed the border and marched on the capital, Lhasa. Led by Sir Francis Younghusband, who had acted as correspondent for *The Times* during the Chitral Relief of 1895, 3,000 British and Indian soldiers crossed the Himalayas to this remotest of countries. In several skirmishes, some 2,100 primitively armed Tibetans were killed. One of the few casualties suffered by the British was Edmund Candler of the *Daily Mail*. In bitterly cold weather on a mountain pass between Tuna and Guru, the two sides confronted each other in a close quarters stand-off. A misunderstood gesture led to the Tibetans reacting violently. Candler, who was standing on the end of the front rank, was hacked at by a swordsman and wounded in twelve places. Fortunately his thick *poshteen¹* saved his life but his right hand was badly mutilated, resulting in amputation.

The British reacted with a couple of minutes of sustained close-range rifle and machine-gun fire which left over 600 tribesmen dead. Despite his wounds, Candler remained with the expedition until its successful conclusion. Teaching himself to write with his left hand, he went on to report in the First World War.

In the same year, 1904, Japan and Russia went to war over each other's claims of influence in Manchuria and Korea. A war involving a giant power like Russia and a swiftly modernising country like Japan attracted the world's press. The British were well represented with veterans like Prior, Burleigh, Frederick Villiers of *The Graphic*, William Maxwell of the *Daily Mail* and the newly left-handed Edmund Candler, as well as some newcomers like Ellis Ashmead-Bartlett of the *Daily Telegraph*.

The Times sent Lionel James to Hong Kong where he attempted a 'first'. The paper hired a boat, the SS *Haimun*, installed the newly-invented wireless and went looking for news. On 14 March, he was rewarded. Off the Russian-held Port Arthur, he saw and reported the sinking of the Russian flagship by a Japanese mine. He was able to say over the airwaves: *'In the history of journalism, the first time that a message has been sent direct from the field of war activity.'* His triumph was short-lived, however, for he also reported two Japanese ships sunk in the same minefield. This new style of news gathering was too uncontrollable for the censor-conscious Japanese, and James's operation was banned. James concluded that there was no future for wireless as a means of reporting wars. The Japanese, on the other hand, saw its potential and used it during their operations against the Russians.

The Japanese were found to be masters of polite procrastination as the correspondents fretted in their Tokyo hotels and awaited the elusive press pass that would take them to the front. As Burleigh put it: *'(we) ate the bread of idleness'*. Melton Prior, in particular, seems to have suffered the most from the inactivity. He arrived on 7 February and kicked his heels for six months. With nothing to report, except a severe earthquake that shook the city in May, his health deteriorated. Worry and depression caused him to lose weight and his asthma attacks became more frequent.

Finally, he and Burleigh did get to Manchuria but were not allowed to get nearer the front than four miles. This final frustration and his poor health finally broke him and he returned home, never to travel again.

His increasing despondency was heightened when his first wife, whom he adored, was knocked down and killed by a tram. He still occasionally called into the offices of the *Illustrated London News* and, during a conversation with the new editor, was persuaded to commit to paper the story of his adventurous life. The result was a manuscript of 400,000 words! Sadly it was the last thing he did, for he died in November 1910. His funeral was a lavish and well-attended affair that befitted the passing of one of the truly great old-time 'specials'.

Bennet Burleigh's campaign ended not soon after as he tried to free himself from the stranglehold the Japanese had imposed on the foreign reporters. He travelled to Tientsin and attempted to get permission from the Russians to cover events from their side. Once the Japanese found out, they withdrew his accreditation and complained to the British Government until he was recalled home.

Frederic Villiers was also frustrated by the months of waiting but he was finally part of a group of ten who were chosen to observe the siege of Port Arthur. These included Richmond Smith of *Associated Press*, Benjamin Norregaard of the *Daily Mail*, Richard Barry of the *San Francisco Chronicle* and a newsreel cameraman named 'Rosy' Rosenthal of the Bioscope Company. Although he and his comrades had to travel six miles each day from their billet, he was able to see much of the bombardment and some of the Japanese attacks.

He shared a mess with the *Telegraph* reporter, David James, and a 50-year-old photographer named James Ricarlton. Villiers was both amused and irritated by the behaviour of the young Ellis Ashmead-Bartlett, who had served as a subaltern in the Boer War and was the son a wealthy baronet. Later he was to become a considerable correspondent but he gave the first impression of being a condescending snob. Villiers heard him say to a Japanese officer: *'There's my card, sir – the Junior, don't you know and you can take it from me, as an officer and a gentleman, that what I tell you is correct.'* To Villiers and the other specials he became known as 'The Toss'.

During the three months they were in Port Arthur they were offered every courtesy by their hosts but ended up seeing and reporting only what the Japanese wished them to see. As Villiers later wrote: *'the correspondents are practically prisoners, held, of course, with a silken cord.'* Although the Boer War had been censored, the reporters had been free to wander where they liked. The Japanese took measures to prevent this happening and put all foreign reporters virtually under strict surveillance and, in so doing, invented the modern military censor.

William Maxwell of the *Daily Mail* saw the beginning of the Battle of Laio-Yang but was prevented from witnessing anything more than the artillery exchanges. He did, however, admire the Japanese control of the newsmen, something he drew from when he was acting as military censor in the First World War. One reporter who managed to evade his 'minders' was *The Times* correspondent, Lionel James, now back on dry land. Tiring of watching shrapnel bursting in the distance, he hid out in the millet fields and, for five days, witnessed the Battle of Liao-Yang.

Being an ex-military officer, he avoided describing the battle as a personal adventure and sent an accurate report from a purely military aspect. After a gruelling journey, he managed to reach a telegraph office and file his detailed and uncensored account, the only eye-witness report of the battle. This, however, was a minor success for the Japanese had gone a long way towards crushing the most romantic trade in journalism – the war correspondent.

Having said that, there were still some small colonial wars in North Africa to cover that gave the impression that things were unchanged.

In 1909, Spain was involved in a fierce six-month fight with Rif tribesmen in Spanish Morocco, which took the lives of thousands and led to unrest in Spain itself.

In 1911 the French-held city of Fez in French Morocco was twice besieged by Berber tribesmen before reinforcements arrived from France. It took weeks of hard marching and fighting in the desert to subdue the tribes.

Italy was anxious not to be left behind in the slicing up of the crumbling Ottoman Empire. She went to war in late 1911 over the area which is now modern Libya. In a nasty and cruel war, Italy finally overcame all opposition and the Turks lost their last African province. The young British war correspondent, Ellis Ashmead-Bartlett, fell foul of the Italians when he revealed that unarmed Arabs had been killed at Tanguira Oasis in what was the world's first aerial bombing.

In 1912–13, there was yet more trouble in the Balkans, with the Turks losing more of their Empire. This was the first war assignment for Philip

Gibbs of the *Daily Graphic*, who recalled meeting the old brigade of war correspondents:

'Among the British contingent was H.W. Nevinson...a hater of war, though a lover of liberty, passionate in his championship of the little nations and the underdogs everywhere...Another man...who had been through the South African war and other campaigns was Bennet Burleigh – a bluff, boisterous man, who greeted Nevinson with a heartiness received rather coldly. The fact was that the old war correspondents had conducted their campaigns with ruthless rivalry to get a "beat" on the news at all costs. Burleigh had once thrown Nevinson's baggage out of a train to prevent his getting ahead. Nevinson never forgot that episode.'

This turned out to be Burleigh's last war, for he returned home sick and died the following year at his home in Bexhill. He may not have been the greatest writer journalism ever had, but he was certainly one of its most colourful.

Frederic Villiers was determined to explore all possibilities of the moving image and equipped himself with a new system called Kinemacolour. He did, however, draw the line on what he felt was suitable fare for the public. When the Bulgarians hanged a couple of Turkish spies, dozens of cameramen augmented the howling crowd of spectators. Sickened by this morbid circus, Villiers packed up his equipment and returned home.

The *Daily Mail* sent out a new reporter named G. Ward Price, who was still reporting when the Korean War ended. He teamed up with Lionel James of *The Times* and they were the only correspondents to have a close-up of the decisive Battle of Lule-Burgas. Ward Price described the campaign as: *'the last of the nineteenth century type of war, in which correspondents would be dependent on horse-transport, and accompanied by a staff of interpreters, grooms and batmen.'* In this short and vicious war, Bulgaria and Serbia defeated the Turks and thus ended their centuries-long power in Europe. It was also a prelude to a catastrophic war that would forever change the political and social structure of the world.

When war with Germany broke out in August 1914, the British authorities were prepared with, if nothing else, an effective censorship system in place. The next four years changed irrevocably the relationship between the press and the military and the public's acceptance of what it reads in the newspapers. This radical change came about in a climate of great patriotism, national security and a need to maintain the public support for the war.

British military observers of the Russo-Japanese war had been impressed by the control the Japanese exerted over the press through their strict censorship. Learning from this, a Bill was proposed but, due to much opposition, was not enacted. The framework, however, was established so when war was declared, it was a simple matter to put it into action. As early as August 1914, the War Office, under the control of the reporter's nemesis, Lord Kitchener, established the Press Bureau with the express purpose of excluding war correspondents from the Western Front. All news would be controlled and supplied by the military. In a candid statement, the Lord of the Admiralty, Winston Churchill, told a journalist that: *'the war is going to be fought in a fog and the best place for correspondence about the war is London.'* How ironic that the old press-hater Kitchener and the shameless publicity-seeking war correspondent Churchill should now both be dancing to the same tune. There was to be no question of allowing war correspondents to wander around the front line, observing conditions and discussing tactics with senior officers as they did in Victoria's time.

Other reporters decided to quit their profession to contribute to the war effort. Lionel James had been an officer in the Yeomanry for many years and entered the war as commander of King Edward's Horse, which fought in the battles of Passchendaele and Cambrai.

George Lynch, the would-be escapee from Ladysmith, indulged in his hobby of 'taking out patents' and came up with a widely-used glove to handle barbed wire.

The Golden Age of war reporting had ended, never to return.

Notes

1 A poshteen is an Afghan sheepskin coat (wool on the inside) much favoured by the military in cold climes.

Chapter 2

Mons and the First Weeks

The long anticipated war with Germany broke out in August 1914. Colonel Charles à Court Repington, *The Times* military correspondent, wrote in his diary:

'During the first ten days of August 1914, it positively rained ultimatums and declarations of war, and very soon all the great Powers of Europe, except Italy, were at war. Though war had often been expected, it had been expected for so long, and so many crises had been successfully overcome by diplomacy, that it came in the end like a thief in the night, quite unexpectedly.'[1]

The assassination of the heir to the Austro-Hungarian Empire, Archduke Franz Ferdinand and his wife, Sophie, in Sarajevo on 28 July by a weedy teenager named Gavrilo Princip, a Serbian terrorist, set in motion events that swiftly pushed the Great Powers into the catastrophe of the first global war. In Britain, the newspapers reported it as yet another outrage from Europe's most notorious trouble spot, the Balkans, something that was of passing interest. After all, the newspapers had only just finished reporting yet another war in the region and there were more pressing domestic matters like women's suffrage and the eternal Irish question, to occupy the nation. David Lloyd George, the British Chancellor remembered:

'that some time in July, an influential Hungarian lady called upon me at 11 Downing Street and told me that we were taking the assassination of the archduke much too quietly; that it had provoked such a storm throughout the Austrian Empire as she had never witnessed – and that unless something was done immediately, it would certainly result in war with Serbia, with incalculable consequences

9

which such an operation might precipitate in Europe. However, such official reports as came to hand did not seem to justify the alarmist view she took.'[2]

As Colonel Repington inferred, the following few days involved a fever of threats and mobilisations. Austria-Hungary responded to the murder of the royal couple by declaring war on Serbia. Russia began mobilisation, to which Germany demanded that she cease immediately. Germany mobilised and France followed. On 1 August, Germany declared war on Russia and the following day, on France.

Germany believed that Britain would remain neutral, along with The Netherlands and Belgium. She did, however, make a demand that brought Britain into the conflict. Germany declared that she would treat Belgium as an enemy if she did not allow free passage of German troops across her lands. Britain, more concerned with the spectre of Germany occupying the Channel ports of Belgium and north-west France than the violation of Belgium's neutrality, declared war on 4 August.

The Germans had already implemented the Schlieffen Plan which involved attacking the French through Belgium calculating that they could knock their rival out of the war in six weeks. Employing seven armies, the Germans made short work of the tiny Belgian army, whose valiant but short display of resistance was soon swept aside.

The reporter who first alerted the British public that Belgium had been invaded was an American freelance journalist named Granville Fortescue, who was living with his family near Ostend. He was a cousin of the former president, Theodore Roosevelt, with whom he had served in the Rough Riders in Cuba. With war threatening, he packed his family off to London and made his way to the American Embassy in Brussels. Using a journalist's knack of keeping his ears open, he learned that German troops had appeared in the east of the country near Liège. Fortescue contacted the *Daily Telegraph* and filed his story, which was published on 3 August under the headline 'COUNTRY INVADED BY GERMAN TROOPS'. The adverse reaction in London when no other paper mentioned the story and the Foreign Office's denial of its truth, led to Fortescue being castigated by the *Telegraph*. Twenty-four hours later, the news was confirmed and the paper apologised and offered Fortescue a roving commission.

When war was declared, the British newspapers already had reporters in Europe including the *Daily Chronicle*'s 21-year-old Geoffrey Pyke, on his first assignment. Armed with a passport obtained from an American sailor, Pyke entered Germany through neutral Denmark. Wandering around Berlin, he was able to learn through conversation or just eavesdropping that German life was nothing like as grim as portrayed in the British press. He also witnessed the mobilisation for war with Russia as dozens of trains packed with soldiers and equipment journeyed east. His life as a reporter lasted just six days when he was arrested and threatened with execution as a spy. After several weeks, he was transferred to the internment camp at Ruhleben, just west of Berlin, where he spent the winter suffering from food poisoning and nearly dying of double pneumonia. When he was sufficiently recovered, Pyke and a fellow inmate managed to scale the wire and make their way to neutral Holland. His escape was hailed as one of the scoops of the war, certainly by the *Daily Chronicle*, and his memoir, *Ruhleben and Back*, published in 1916 was a best seller. As an escaped prisoner of war, Pyke was exempt from conscription.

The American journalist Albert Rhys Williams, of the magazine *Outlook*, was in Belgium when it was invaded. Although his career as a war correspondent was also brief, it was remembered for a 'joke' photograph that was later used as a propaganda subject. Preparing to leave Belgium, a fellow photo-journalist asked Williams if he would like to have a souvenir photograph of himself in war-surroundings. After rejecting several ideas, the photographer suggested: *'I have it. Shot as a German spy. There's the wall to stand up against and we'll pick a crack firing-squad out of these Belgians.'*

Williams recalled that he was led over to the wall, and a handkerchief was tied over his eyes. The photographer then directed the five-man squad of Belgian soldiers who took aim, but thankfully did not fire. It did cross Williams's mind that: *'I was reposing a lot of confidence in a stray band of soldiers. Some of those Belgians, gifted with a lively imagination, might get carried away with the suggestion and act as if I were a German spy...'*

The un-named photographer, having given a print to Williams, then sold another to the *Daily Mail*, who printed it on 10 October with the caption:

'The Belgians have a short, sharp method of dealing with the Kaiser's rat-hole spies. This one caught near Termonde and, after being blindfolded, the firing-squad soon put an end to his inglorious career.'

When Britain's first Continental war since Waterloo broke out, there was a less than enthusiastic response from both newspapers and the public. Nevertheless, having kept itself aloof from the power struggles in Europe for a century, Britain could no longer be a spectator as a complexity of treaties and alliances found her allied to her old enemy, France, against the Central Powers of Germany, Austria-Hungary and soon Turkey.

In July, Field Marshal Horatio Herbert Kitchener had returned from Egypt, where he was consul-general, to receive an earldom from a grateful government. He was on the point of returning to his post when, on 3 August, he was recalled from Dover and offered the position of War Minister. Busy as he was with organising troop and equipment movements, he still had time to impose a strict embargo on news correspondents reporting the war in France. One of his first acts was to appoint Colonel Edward Swinton to be the official spokesman for the military. His reports, signed 'Eyewitness', would still be vetted by Kitchener before being passed to the newspapers for publication.

The newspaper proprietors had not been idle. Alfred Harmsworth, later Lord Northcliffe, was determined to make the *Daily Mail* the official newspaper of the British Army and to have copies of the paper delivered to the Western Front by military cars. He also intended to use front-line soldiers as news sources and for them to submit articles written about their experiences. Not surprisingly, Kitchener put a stop to these plans. Lloyd George took a different view and was active in persuading the newspapers to support the war and to champion patriotism.

The government sent a small well-trained regular army called the British Expeditionary Force to cover the hard-pushed French Army's left flank. The BEF, without any accompanying 'specials', arrived at the French ports on 14 August and advanced into Belgium. They comprised two infantry corps numbering about 70,000 with 300 guns, marching east from Boulogne and north from Le Havre to meet and face an overwhelmingly superior enemy numbering 160,000 and 600 guns.

The Germans were both surprised and scathing that Britain had sent their token force to support the French, referring to it as a 'contemptible little army'. This was enough to enrage the British Army, who then took a perverse pride in calling themselves the 'Old Contemptibles'. As it turned out, they punched well above their weight, slowing and eventually halting the German advance. In doing so, they suffered huge losses that would take a long time to fill.

On 23 August they confronted the German army at the coal mining town of Mons. The BEF's Commander-in-Chief was General Sir John French who deployed his two infantry corps, commanded by General Horace Smith-Dorrien and General Douglas Haig, respectively, east and west of Mons across a 40-kilometre front. Roughly following the south bank of the Mons-Condé canal, the BEF took up defensive positions. One of the important canal crossings was the railway bridge at the village of Nimy where men of the Royal Fusiliers set up a defensive position. Despite being heavily outnumbered, the Fusiliers put up a determined defence and held the Germans at bay for hours. Two men, Lieutenant Maurice Dease and Private Sidney Godley, were the first of the Great War's recipients of the Victoria Cross. All along the front the heavy and accurate fire from the British riflemen convinced the German commander, General von Kluck, that his troops were facing machine-guns. The fight, in the end, was little more than a holding action. The French on their right flank had started to fall back and the BEF was in danger of being outflanked. So began the BEF's epic fighting retreat to the Belgian border, harried all the way by the pursuing enemy.

With his two infantry corps widely separated and suffering from exhaustion, General French ordered his command to retire to the Somme. On 26 August, General Smith-Dorrien disobeyed this order and decided that his Second Corps would engage the Germans at Le Cateau. It was a disastrous decision and the British suffered huge casualties, losing a third of their number and most of their guns. But they also inflicted enough casualties to give the rest of General French's command some breathing space as they continued their retreat.[3] In fact, they were unmolested by the Germans for a further five days. All this action went virtually unreported as Lord Kitchener banned war correspondents with dire threats to those who disobeyed. There were, however, still some in place who took their chances.

Two correspondents, William Arthur Moore of *The Times* and Henry Hamilton Fyfe of the *Daily Mail*, managed to be in the right place to alert the public to the facts. In Rouen, Fyfe had previously interviewed wounded soldiers from Mons and learned of the on-going retreat. He was anxious to reach the remnants of the retreat and, accompanied by Arthur Moore, he drove his Rolls Royce around the lanes near Amiens, until they found themselves amongst the scattered remnants of the British Army. All was confusion and they were free to interview men who were only too willing to discuss their experiences in the retreat and the Battle of Le Cateau.

Hamilton Fyfe recalled:

'Driving from Boulogne we saw British soldiers and we heard the whole story. Orders had been given for a hasty retreat of all British troops in and about Amiens. What had happened? They shrugged their shoulders…There was nothing to keep us out of Amiens now. In less than two hours we were there, listening to the sound of not very distant guns. We drove around all day seeking for news and realising every hour more and more clearly the disaster that had happened. We saw no organised bodies of troops, but we met and talked to many fugitives in twos and threes, who had lost their units in disorderly retreat and for the most part had no idea where they were.

'That Friday night, tired as we were, Moore and I set off to Dieppe to put our messages on a boat which we knew would be leaving on the Saturday morning. They (the reports) reached London on Saturday morning.'

Ulsterman Arthur Moore of *The Times* had been recalled from an assignment in Serbia and ordered to fish for news about the BEF. None of what he learned was anything like the official Press Bureau bulletins fed to the newspapers which issued bland up-beat accounts which concealed the terrible losses suffered.

Moore wrote his report from Amiens dated 29 August with a plea to his editor, Henry Wickham Steed:

'I read this afternoon in Amiens this morning's Paris newspapers. To me, knowing some portion of the truth, it seemed incredible that a great people should be so kept in ignorance of the situation which it has to face. The papers read like children's prattle, gleanings from the war talk of their parents a week ago. Not a word of the fall of Namur and considerable talk about new successes on the Meuse.

'This is not well. I would plead with the English censor to let my message pass. I guarantee him that as regards the situation of troops I have nothing to say that is not known and noted already by the German General Staff. There is no reason, either in strategy or tactics, why every word I write should not be published. And to get my information I have broken no promise and no obligation…'

He then went on to write:

'First it has to be said that our honour is bright. Amongst all the straggling units that I have seen, flotsam and jetsam of the fiercest fight in history, I saw fear in no man's face. It was a retreating and a broken army, but it was not an army of hunted men...

'Since Monday morning last the German advance has been one of almost incredible rapidity. As I have already written you, the British Expeditionary Force fought a terrible fight – which may be called the action of Mons, though it covered a big front – on Sunday. The German attack was withstood to the utmost limit, and a whole division was flung into the fight at the end of a long march and had not even time to dig trenches. The French supports expected on the immediate right do not seem to have been in touch...

'The British force fell back through Bavai on a front between Valenciennes and Maubourge, [Maubeuge] then through Le Quesney [Le Quesnoy], where desperate fighting took place, southwards continually. Regiments were grievously injured, and the broken army fought its way desperately with many stands, forced backwards and ever backwards by the sheer unconquerable mass of numbers of an enemy prepared to throw away three or four men for the life of every British soldier...

'Tonight I write to the sound of guns. All the afternoon the guns were going on the eastern roads. A German plane flew over us, and was brought crashing down...

'Our losses are very great. I have seen broken bits of many regiments. Let me repeat that there is no failure in discipline, no panic, no throwing up the sponge...The men are battered with marching, and ought to be weak with hunger, for, of course, no commissariat could cope with such a case, but they are steady and cheerful, and whenever they arrive make straight for the proper authority, report themselves and seek news of their regiment...

'Apparently every division was in action. Some have lost nearly all their officers. The regiments were broken to bits, and good discipline and fine spirit kept the fragments together, though they no longer knew what had become of the other parts with which they had once formed a splendid whole...

'To sum up, the first great German effort has succeeded. We have

to face the fact that the British Expeditionary Force, which bore the
great weight of the blow, has suffered terrible losses and requires
immediate and immense reinforcement. The British Expeditionary
Force has won indeed imperishable glory, but it needs men, men, and
yet more men...We want reinforcement and we want them now...'

His strong and truthful account, when read by the editorial staff, caused alarm as they felt sure it would fall foul of the censor at the Press Bureau. Before submitting it to the censor, *The Times* toned down some of the statements. To their complete surprise the censor, Captain Frederick Edwin Smith (later Lord Birkenhead), passed the report in its entirety, even reinstating the editor's deletions. He had an agenda which was to force the government to recognise the shortages of men and materials. To emphasise the message, Smith added his own plea that the BEF: *'has suffered terrible losses and requires immediate and immense reinforcement...'* and echoing Moore's words: *'it needs men, men and yet more men. The investment of Paris cannot be banished from the field of possibility...We want reinforcements and we want them now.'*

Moore's report, which came to be known as the 'Amiens Dispatch', was headlined BROKEN BRITISH REGIMENTS BATTLING AGAINST ODDS –UNTARNISHED HONOUR OF OUR TROOPS – MORE MEN NEEDED. The reaction to this report was predictable. Kitchener denied it and the rival papers accused *The Times* of being unpatriotic. The *Daily Mail* also printed the similar report by Henry Hamilton Fyfe, who interviewed wounded BEF men in Rouen, and headlined it GERMAN TIDAL WAVE, OUR SOLDIERS OVERWHELMED. Censor Smith also added his request for immediate reinforcements.

Fyfe was made a scapegoat and threatened with arrest if he remained in France. He got around this problem by joining the French Red Cross as a stretcher-bearer and managed to send many despatches to his paper. He later wrote of his experiences:

'I had no experience of ambulance or hospital work, but I grew
accustomed to blood and severed limbs and red stumps very quickly.
Only once was I knocked out. We were in a schoolroom turned into
an operating theatre. It was a hot afternoon. We had brought in a lot
of wounded men who had been lying in the open for some time; their
wounds crawled with lice. All of us had to act as aids to our two

surgeons. Suddenly I felt the air had become oppressive. I felt I must get outside and breathe. I made for the door, walked along the passage. Then I found myself lying in the passage with a big bump on my head. However, I got rid of what was troubling my stomach, and in a few minutes I was back in the schoolroom.

'What caused me discomfort far more acute – because it was mental, not bodily – were the illustrations of the bestiality, the futility, the insanity of war and of the system that produced war as surely as land uncultivated produces noxious weeds: these were now forced on my notice every day. The first cart of dead that I saw, legs sticking out stiffly, heads lolling on shoulders, all the poor bodies shovelled into a pit and covered with quicklime, made me wonder what the owners had been doing when they were called up, crammed into uniforms, and told to kill, maim, mutilate other men like themselves, with whom they had no quarrel. All of them had left behind many who would be grieved, perhaps beggared, by their taking off. And all for no purpose– for nothing.'

After a couple of months, the British military caught up with Fyfe and he was banned from entering France again. He spent the next two years covering the fighting on the Eastern and Italian fronts before being allowed to return to the Western Front in 1918. While Fyfe was in Russia in 1915, he had a scoop when he reported the murder of Rasputin.

During these early days there was much fluid movement as the Germans advanced and then, as they outstripped their supply lines, retreated. Shortly after he had written his Amiens Dispatch, Arthur Moore was captured by a German cavalry patrol but soon released. Hamilton Fyfe experienced something similar while driving his Rolls. He was caught by a patrol of Uhlans (German lancers) and told to drive towards the main body of Germans. Taking the advice of a peasant, Fyfe left the road and drove across a ploughed field and took cover in a wood as a large force of German cavalry rode by.[4]

The Mons battle, which compared with the subsequent battles was more like a skirmish, was one of what became known as the Battle of the Frontiers. It was the French plan to recapture Alsace-Lorraine, attack the Germans through the southern Ardennes and halt the Germans at the Belgian border. The battles took place at Mulhouse, Colmar, the Ardennes, Charleroi and Mons in the period between 7 August and 13 September, the French suffered about 300,000 casualties, of which 75,000 were fatal. On 22 August, 27,000 were killed, making it a day to rival the first day of the Somme for bloodshed. Yet there was a British war correspondent with the French named Gerald Fitzgerald Campbell of *The Times*, who failed to mention these appalling casualty lists, even in private letters to his editor. This terrible loss, representing twenty-five per cent of combatants and the largest suffered on any front during the whole conflict, went unreported. It was becoming clear at this early stage that the press were prepared to voluntarily suppress unpalatable facts in the cause of raising morale and to protect Britain's resolution to see the fight through to the bitter end. The details of this massive defeat were not revealed until after the war and *The Times* defended itself and its reporter: *'Such silence was prudent...had it been known in England that France had lost more than a quarter of a million men from her regular army in the first month of fighting, British determination must have been gravely weakened.'*[5]

Another *Times* journalist, Edgar Amphlett, a parliamentary correspondent, had been sent to pick up whatever news he could. He found himself in Boulogne after the British Army abandoned the town during the retreat from Mons. Amphlett, who had been a fencing champion in both the London and Stockholm Olympic Games, then travelled to Arras when it came under heavy bombardment from the advancing Germans. When things got too hot, he joined the stream of refugees as they fled the town. He was well into his forties when he volunteered for the Army. Eventually, he was accepted and commissioned as Staff Captain and served in France as a Railway Transport Officer.

On 5 September, the cover of the *London Opinion*, one of the most influential magazines of its day, carried the famous recruiting poster depicting Lord Kitchener above the words, YOUR COUNTRY NEEDS YOU. It was one of the most successful posters in history as millions of men volunteered for the new battalions that had to be formed. Already there was tacit agreement with the government and military that the newspapers would play down disastrous defeats and focus on anything that would not deter the thousands of volunteers from enlisting.

Henry Nevinson expressed his frustration in *The Nation* of 12 September:

'I have served as a correspondent for nearly twenty years in many countries and under all sorts of conditions. I think I know all the tricks of the trade, and I have seen many of them practised. But I cannot

foresee how any correspondent could give away his country or to do the smallest public injury under these regulations, even if he wanted to...

*   'We have all engaged servants, bought horses, and weighed out kit. Everything is ready, and yet we are kept chafing here, week after week, while a war for the destiny of the world is being fought within a day's journey, and others of our colleagues are allowed to go dashing about France in motors almost up to the very front. I do not make light of their splendid courage and resource. I can only envy their opportunities.'*

Philip Gibbs, correspondent for the *Daily Chronicle* and who became one of the most celebrated of the Great War reporters, was in Paris when war was declared. He wrote about these hectic and confused first weeks:

*   'Yet we went on, mixed up always in refugee rushes, in masses of troops moving forward to the front or backwards in retreat, getting brief glimpses of the real happenings behind the screen of secrecy, meeting men who could tell us the hidden truth, and more than once escaping, by the nick of time only, from a death-trap into which we had tumbled unwittingly, not knowing the whereabouts of the enemy, nor his way of advance.'*

Gibbs teamed up with William Massey of the *Daily Telegraph* and Henry Major Tomlinson of the *Daily News*, and they became known as The Three Musketeers. Massey later went to Palestine and was General Allenby's official correspondent. Tomlinson later became disillusioned with the conduct of the war and in 1917 returned to England to become literary editor of *The Nation*.

They visited Amiens and the surrounding area and received the familiar tales of confusion, forced marches – always south, heat, hunger and heavy losses with the Germans dogging their footsteps. With luck, they avoided being challenged and ordered away by the British military.

A chance meeting with a pre-war acquaintance, Lady Dorothy Fielding, enabled Philip Gibbs to join a volunteer medical group led by a Dr Munro. At Furnes the staff of an English hospital had just arrived and were setting up. Soon ambulances were arriving with wounded Belgian soldiers and Gibbs became a member of staff. They were behind a part of the front-line held by the Belgian Army at the town of Dixmude on the Yser river, north of the town of Ypres. Gibbs wrote:

> *'I made many journeys with the flying column under the leadership of Dr Munro. We went to Dixmude, sixteen kilometres away from Furnes. There were many wounded there, we were told. As we drove nearer to it, over a flat landscape through which went the Yser canal, we saw a line of villages and small towns. From each one of them rose separate columns of smoke, meeting in a pall overhead, and through the smoke came stabbing flashes of fire as German shells burst with thudding shocks of sound. This was the frontline of battle... Outside the town we had been brought to a halt by a frightful barrier of dead horses and dead bodies. A German shell had burst into an ammunition convoy and blown it to bits. One Belgian soldier had been cut in half by a scythe of flying steel. Our tyres were splashed by pools of blood. Dixmude itself was being destroyed as we entered. Shells were smashing into its streets, and the cobble pavements were whipped by shrapnel bullets. A shop collapsed like a house of cards as we went down one of the narrow streets...*
>
> *'Presently when there was work to do, getting up the wounded and packing them into the ambulances – it took fifteen to twenty minutes in the open square, with shells bursting close and that shrapnel whipping the cobblestones – I lost consciousness of myself...I did not expect to get out of this place alive. I felt numb and cold. I am sure that I was very frightened, but my hand was steady when I lit a cigarette. Here comes death, I thought.'*

Gibbs was accompanied by the *Daily Telegraph* correspondent, Ellis Ashmead-Bartlett, referred to with some accuracy by Frederick Villiers as 'The Toss'. They were probably among the few war reporters to have experienced artillery fire and to have some sense of what the men in the trenches endured on a daily basis.

The battle that raged along the line defended by the Belgian army between 18–30 October has been largely ignored by historians. The Germans were determined to reach Nieuwpoort on the coast and outflank the Allies. The Belgians' stout defence also bought time for the British and French at Ypres. Charles Repington acknowledged in *The Times* of 9 December:

'It was the remnant of an army, war-worn and weak in numbers. For two months and a half the Belgians at Liège, Namur, Louvain, Halen, Aerschot, Aalines, Termonde and Antwerp had confronted the Germans almost alone, and it was only the shattered, but still unconquered, remains of the field army which drew up behind the Yser after the retreat from the Scheldt. In this fine defence, which did honour to all the troops and commanders engaged in it, the Belgians performed a signal service to the Allied cause. Finally Dixmude fell and the Germans crossed the Yser River.

The pressure on the Belgians was so great that they took the unpalatable decision to inundate the 35-kilometre area between Dixmude and Nieuwpoort. On the nights of 26–29 October, the sluices at Nieuwpoort were opened during high tides until an impassable flooded area a mile wide protected the British left flank from enemy attack and effectively ended the 'Race to the Sea'. From now on the combatants settled into a static trench warfare that stretched from the coast to the border of Switzerland.

Another journalist who covered the Belgian defence at Dixmude was Basil Clarke of the *Daily Mail*. He had been sent by his paper at the last minute and arrived wearing a bowler hat and a Burberry coat. Keeping a low profile in Dunkirk, he managed to evade arrest the longest of the British reporters. Along with most of the inhabitants he fully expected the Germans to breakthrough and occupy the town: *'the silken slimness of the margin by which the struggling Allies avoided disaster'*.

The conclusion of the Battle of the Yser forced the Germans to try and break through at Ypres, the last major obstacle to the German advance on the Channel ports. Defended by the remnants of the BEF, it occupied a salient which bulged forward with a 16-mile perimeter into the German line. In what became known as the First Battle of Ypres was a series of battles that took place around the perimeter from 16 October to 14 November. In the end it was regarded as a British victory, albeit pyrrhic, for it saw the destruction of the highly trained British regular army and the loss of some of the Ypres perimeter.

Although he was unable to witness any of the fighting, Clarke did manage to enter the town to see the destruction made by the German bombardment, which destroyed its cathedral and the ancient Cloth Hall. Accompanied by a Belgian official, he toured the ruins and, so as not to alert the British military to his presence, couched his observations as through the eyes of a local witness.

Because of his precarious position as an 'outlaw', most of his reporting was stories of human interest and very little about what was going on at the front. In early January 1915, he was summoned to the Commissaire of Police in Dunkirk, who had been instructed by the War Office in London to arrest and expel him and another reporter named Christopher Lumby of *The Times*. The Commissaire said he intended to carry this out in eight hours' time and would that be enough time for the two reporters to leave the country, so, with great cordiality, Clarke and Lumby departed Dunkirk and the two last British reporters made their way back to England.

The American war reporter Richard Harding Davies wrote in *Scribner's Magazine* in January 1915 about the perils of meeting the military:

> *'We left Paris with the idea of watching from a point south of Soissons the battle then in progress on the Aisne. Our going to Rheims was an after-thought. Ashmead-Bartlett, of the London* Daily Telegraph, *Captain Granville Fortescue of the Hearst newspapers, Gerald Morgan of the same syndicate and I shared the automobile...he (Morgan) arranged our route that would keep us away from Villers-Cotterêts...The officers of the English General Staff had made it their headquarters, and had they been afflicted with leprosy, smallpox and bubonic plague, we could not have feared them more. Against war correspondents they had declared war to the death. Unless the setting sun did not show a line of correspondents in chains, they considered that day wasted.'*

Other war reporters had already left the Western Front weeks before. Frustrated that his reports were either ignored or watered down, Henry Nevinson representing the *Daily Chronicle*, decided to abandon writing for the time being. He joined the Quaker volunteers and drove an ambulance in the Ypres sector. He had been in Berlin when war was declared and returned to London before he could be interned.

Any alarm bells rung by Moore, Hamilton Fyfe, Basil Clarke, Philip Gibbs et al were soon stilled when, on 7 September, Colonel Ernest Swinton was appointed by the army as the official 'Eyewitness', which all papers were obliged to use. It was soon business as usual as the public were fed naked propaganda in the guise of real news: German atrocity stories, intrepid and steady Tommy/Jock/Mick/Taffy cheerfully holding back the fiendish Hun and extolling the collective wisdom of the Allied generals.

An ageing Frederic Villiers received permission from Marshal Joffre to visit the French Front, only to have this vetoed by the British. Like most of his colleagues, he spent weeks of frustration trying to get access to real news. Eventually he and Gordon Smith of the *Daily Herald* took to tramping around the French countryside on foot and bike armed with the cover story that they were looking for lost relatives and friends. They mostly covered the Champagne sector and did see fighting around Rheims. Their brief arrest as spies in Epernay and the frustrations of gathering hard news made them abandon their wanderings.

Instead, Villiers decided to embark on a long world lecture tour. Even during this trip he still tried to get permission to visit the war fronts that had sprung around the globe. He was unsuccessful in East Africa and Mesopotamia but did manage to see some fighting on the North West Frontier of India.

Egged on by Germany and her Muslim ally, Turkey, the Afghan Mohmand tribe threatened invasion and to incite the discontented elements in the Punjab. It was a war that rumbled off and on for a couple of years until the Anglo-Indian forces finally subdued the belligerent tribesmen. Villiers visited a sector where a continuous 25-mile stretch of barbed wire had been laid. What made it an effective barrier was a single strand of high voltage cable that ran through the entire length and accounted for several Afghan deaths.

The British also employed three Rolls Royce armoured cars. Villiers managed to travel in one of these and saw a crowd of attackers retreat at its approach. The Afghans particularly feared the aircraft, which they named 'White Eagles', and generally resented the new technology employed against them. Gone forever were the days of *jezails* versus Lee-Metfords.

Villiers continued his world tour, even lunching with Charlie Chaplin in Hollywood. The rigours of his profession and this last lecture tour caught up with him and he fell ill. Returning to England, he set about writing his life story which, like his friendly rival Melton Prior before him, he completed just before he died, in 1921. He truly was the last of the old-style 'specials'.

With the onset of winter, the two sides huddled in their trenches and dug-outs and waited for spring before resuming hostilities. True there were artillery and mortar exchanges as well as sniping, but it was mainly a period of uncomfortable peace. On Christmas Day a most remarkable thing happened: the guns ceased firing and men from both sides cautiously left the shelter of their trenches and walked towards each other in no man's land to exchange Christmas greetings. This was captured by the camera and on 5 January 1915, the *Daily Mirror* printed the resulting photos on its front page.

Philip Gibbs wrote many years later:

'The German soldiers called the war, the "Great Swindle". They had more sense of comradeship with our own men, who were killing them and whom they killed, than with their war lords and generals. In the first Christmas of the war they came out into No Man's Land, and said, "This killing of each other is senseless. Let's stop it. Let's all go home". It might have stopped war for ever in Europe and created a new comradeship across frontiers.'

One wonders if this spontaneous Christmas truce prompted the propagandists to go to even greater lengths to instil an ever increasing hatred of the enemy. Sadly, this spontaneous display of goodwill was not allowed to happen again during the long and terrible years that followed.

Notes

1 *The First World War 1914-1918* – personal experiences of Col. C. à Court Repington.
2 *The War Memoirs of David Lloyd George* Pub. 1933-38.
3 Smith-Dorrien was severely criticised and removed from his command. He was exiled to Africa as commander of the British African Forces.
4 *The Pageant of the Years* by Philip Gibbs.
5 *The History of The Times Vol.4.*

Chapter 3

Cat and Mouse

Philip Gibbs wrote about the huge difficulties in getting reports back to Fleet Street. Travelling down to Boulogne and Calais, he had to rely on the goodwill of strangers to carry his reports back for him. Several times, he somewhat cheekily approached one of the King's Messengers, usually an elderly senior officer, with a letter addressed 'To the Editor of the *Daily Chronicle*, care of the War Office'.

A few times Gibbs chanced the Channel crossing to see his editor with the possibility that he would not be allowed to return. Gibbs recalled a conversation with F.E. Smith at the Foreign Office:

> *'There was at this time, a conflict of opinion between the War Office and the Foreign Office regarding news from the Front. The War Office wanted to black out all but the official communiqués, and some innocuous articles by an official eyewitness...(F.E. Smith) congratulated me on the stuff I was writing. "We want more of it," he said. "I shan't cut out a word you've written. Those fellows at the War Office want a nice private war of their own, while our people are clamouring for news."'* [1]

A friend in the War Office warned Gibbs that Kitchener had given orders for his arrest next time he appeared in France. Gibbs thought he had found a way round this when he accepted an offer to be special representative with the Red Cross in France and Belgium. Armed with impressive credentials, Gibbs took the boat to Le Havre only to find three officers from Scotland Yard waiting for him who placed him under arrest. The commander of the base at Le Havre, General Bruce Williams, already had several other reporters under lock and key and expressed a desire to put them all, including Gibbs, up against a wall and shoot them. Instead Gibbs was put under house arrest in a hotel. He did manage to persuade one of the police officers to get a message back to England and, through the Foreign Office, was allowed to return home.

The official Press Bureau requested the newspaper editors not to indicate in any way where reports had been censored. It was felt that blank spaces or smudged-out columns could give the enemy hints as to the information that was being censored. It would also unsettle the British readers to think that they were not being told the whole truth.

With all the 'outlawed' war reporters safely away from the front line, there was a mid-winter period of reflection. The strict censorship, coupled with the bland reports from Colonel Swinton's 'Eyewitness', or as he was frequently called, 'Eyewash', and Sir John French's reports, was fuelling a strong argument to lift the ban on allowing war reporters access to the front line. The public certainly wanted more openness and the government was coming around to the idea that controlled reporting could be beneficial in the recruiting of volunteers.

Sir Edward Cook wrote:

> 'With regard to unofficial news, it is in many ways unfortunate that authorised correspondents were not sent to the Front at the first, and the irritation of the Press was the greater because it had been understood that they should be allowed to go and appointments had been made.'

In other words, reporters had already been prepared by their editors to go the front...

> 'But the extreme importance of secrecy in the opening moves, the indiscretion of some freelancers, and the opinion of our Allies must be remembered. It will be well to reprint here an announcement made in our Press on 2nd December 1914:
>
> 'The Government has instructed the Director of the Press Bureau to make the following announcement to the Press and public in regard to Special Newspaper Correspondents at the seat of war:
>
> '1. The decision to exclude the correspondents of newspapers from the lines of the Allied Armies in France and Belgium was originally taken in accordance with the decision of the French Government to exclude correspondents from their own lines.

'2. This rule has very recently relaxed as the result of an arrangement between the Governments of France and Great Britain with the concurrence of General Joffre, the Commander in Chief.

'3. The consequence of this relaxation: a party of selected journalists has been allowed to visit the lines of the French Army. The selection was made by the French Government as the date was fixed by them at too short notice to enable the British Government to take part in the selection.

'4. Arrangements are being made, with General Joffre's consent, for another party of British correspondents to visit the lines of the Allied Armies. The members of the last named party will be selected by arrangement with the British Government; due notice will be issued of the further steps which will be taken to secure that, so far as the necessary limited numbers of the party will permit, the selection shall be of impartial and representative character." [2]

The virtual loss of the remainder of the BEF at the First Battle of Ypres between 18 October and 11 November, put pressure on Kitchener's new untrained battalions to be rushed to the front as replacements. Left behind would be thousands of relatives and friends who would clamour for information they could only get through the newspapers. Well written patriotic articles extolling the heroism of the British soldier and the tactical wisdom of their leaders would be a boon to the propaganda effort.

The French and Belgian armies had been more welcoming to the war reporters than the British, who took the lead from Lord Kitchener's view that they were all 'drunken swabs' and could not be trusted. There were two war reporters who had managed to slip the net and cover the French Army's activities. Based in Nancy in the east of the country was *The Times* correspondent, Gerald Campbell, who, together with a young French assistant journalist named Fleury Lamure, made themselves acceptable to the local French general and were able to supply reports of fighting along the Verdun to the Vosges area. His editor, Geoffrey Robinson (he changed his name to Dawson in 1917), regularly wrote to Campbell praising him for the best reports from the French front. Eventually the Parisian authorities became aware of his presence and in January 1915 he was ordered out of the military zone.

The second correspondent was Maxwell Henry Hayes Macartney, who managed to report on the Battle of the Aisne. In *The Times* dated 13 November 1914, he wrote about the destruction of Soissons:

'All this beautiful valley of the Aisne, as one can imagine, has been banged and battered about in the most terrible way. Village after village has been knocked into the proverbial cocked hat. The damage done at Soissons is exceptionally severe. Of the 15,000 inhabitants or so who normally form the population only about 1,500 remain. The façade and towers of the Cathedral, one of the largest and handsomest Gothic churches in northern France is still intact...the Germans are threatening to destroy the building on the same ground as they justify their attack on Reims Cathedral. The pretext is a lie. The French have not established observation posts on the towers of Soissons Cathedral.'

In the event, the Cathedral was shelled and heavily damaged.

Like Campbell, Macartney received fulsome praise from Geoffrey Robinson who advised him: *'to settle in quietly with some French general and not to run the risk of being regarded with suspicion'*. Macartney did cover the Battle of Loos in 1915, but requested to be released from his employment so he could enlist. He ended the war attached to the Independent Air Force, which was the RAF's strategic bombing force.

A letter from a former American President to the British Foreign Secretary added further weight to make Britain see that she was losing the propaganda war. In a letter dated 22 January 1915, Theodore Roosevelt wrote to Sir Edward Grey:

'There have been fluctuations in American opinion about the war. The actions of the German Zeppelins have revived the feeling in favour of the Allies.[3] But I believe that for a couple of months preceding this action there had been a distinct lessening of the feeling for the Allies and a growth of pro-German feeling. I do not think that this was the case among the people who are best informed, but I do think that it was the case among the mass of not very well informed people, who have little to go upon except what they read in the newspapers or see at cinematograph shows. There were several causes for this change.

'There has been a striking contrast between the lavish attentions showered on American war correspondents by the German military authorities and the blank refusal to have anything whatever to do with them by the British and French Governments. The only real war news written by Americans who are known to and trusted by the American

people comes from the German side; as a result of this, the sympathisers with the cause of the Allies can hear nothing whatever about the trials and achievements of the British and French armies... It may be that your people do not believe that American public opinion is of sufficient value to be taken into account, but, if you think that it should be taken into account, then it is worth your while considering whether much of your censorship work and much of your refusal to allow correspondents at the front has been damaging to your cause from the standpoint of the effect on public opinion without any corresponding military gains.

'I realise perfectly that it would be criminal to permit correspondents to act as they acted as late as our own Spanish War, but, as a layman, I feel sure that there has been a good deal of work of the kind I have spoken in the way of censorship and refusing correspondents permission to go to the front which has not been of the slightest military service to you and which has had a very real effect in preventing any rallying of public opinion to you...'

After a Cabinet meeting on the subject, the government decided to change its policy and allow selected journalists to report the war. After some pressure on the military high command and a list of regulations to control war correspondents, four journalists were selected to visit the Western Front in early March. Philip Gibbs, his past transgressions forgiven, represented the *Daily Telegraph* and *Daily Chronicle*, Valentine Williams acted for the *Daily Mail* and *Daily Mirror*, Henry Nevinson for *The Times* and the *Daily News and Leader*, and Ernest Townley for the *Daily Express* and the *Morning Post*.

According to the proprietor of the *Daily Telegraph*, Lord Burnham: *'the men who at first went abroad for the Press were treated as if they were criminals let loose...'* As late as June 1915, he saw: *'many Press correspondents playing cricket in the grounds of the château at St Omer (GHQ) which they were not allowed to leave'.*

The four correspondents arrived at the British General Headquarters at St Omer just as the British assault on Neuve Chapelle was launched. Any prospect that they would be able to observe and report the fighting was soon dashed. The excuse given was that their presence near the front might delay reinforcements, which none of the journalists believed for a minute.

The battle of Neuve Chapelle, fought between 10–13 March 1915, was the first British-initiative offensive of the war. Following pressure from the French, who had doubts about British commitment to the war, General Haig planned to attack the line which was comparatively lightly held by the Germans. Meticulously planned, the intention was to punch a gap in the enemy defences, capture the high ground at Aubers Ridge, release the cavalry and attempt to take Lille. Despite poor weather conditions the infantry, including Indians of the Meerut Division, quickly advanced. They successfully overran the German trenches and entered the village. With the Germans on the point of being overwhelmed, the attack halted for five hours in confusion, while each corps waited for the other to act. In the meantime, the Germans had rushed reinforcements into the area and began to counter-attack. The result was stalemate and the opportunity had passed. Haig ordered another wasteful attack and at the end of the battle, the British had gained just over a mile of ground with the terrible casualty toll of 11,200 men, including 4,200 Indians.

Reports of the battle, however, did appear in the papers the following day written in the usual cheerful and space-filling style of 'Eyewitness', who reported:

'At 7.30am, on 10th the battle began with a bombardment by a large number of guns and howitzers. Our men in the trenches describe this fire as being the most tremendous both in point of noise and in actual effect they have ever seen or heard. The shrieking of the shells in the air, their explosions and the continuous thunder of the batteries all merged into one great volume of sound. The discharge of the guns were [sic] so rapid that they sounded like the fire of gigantic machine guns.

'During the 35 minutes it continued, our men could walk about in perfect safety. Then the signal for the attack was given, and in less than half an hour almost the whole of the elaborate series of German trenches in and about Neuve Chapelle were in our hands. Except at one point there was hardly any resistance for the trenches, which in places were literally blotted out, were filled with dead and dying partially buried in earth and debris, and the majority of survivors were in no mood for further fighting.

'The enemy for the time being was beaten and on the run. It was the consciousness of this which filled the hospitals and ambulances with the cheeriest crowd of wounded ever seen.'

The disappointment of being denied the chance to observe a British attack was felt by all of the reporters, none more so than Henry Nevinson, the most experienced of them all. He had reported the Greek-Turkish War of 1897, the Spanish-American War 1898 and the South African War, during which he was besieged at Ladysmith. He was what could be described as a scholar reporter, with a determination to stand up for the under-dog, be they Irish Nationalists or Women Suffragettes. He wrote of his visit...

> 'unhappily, the brief visit of our small party of correspondents to the British Expeditionary Force is now coming to an end...One would like, as in the old days of war corresponding, to live with the army rather than pay a call or visit as a guest... Owing to various 'operations' in different parts of the line we have never been admitted close to the front. Our officers were obliged even to alter the proposed programme which would have shown us something, at all events, of the fighting line and something at least of the enemy. Well, I don't want to play the old war-horse and neigh lamentations over days that do not return; but there was a time when it was the obvious duty and privilege of the correspondent to ride to the sound of the battle, and in those days he was not hurried off at once in the opposite direction as soon as the guns began. But one would have thought some compromise between the old way and the new could be devised with a certain amount of profit to our Army and country alike.'

What the correspondents were treated to was a detailed tour of the GHQ and how it functioned. Ignorant of the Neuve Chapelle battle raging just 20 miles away, Philip Gibbs wrote a fulsome report on 11 March, under the headline: HOW THE STRIKING POWER OF THE ARMIES IS ORGANISED. CONTRASTS OF PEACE & WAR NEAR THE FRONT. In it he contrasts his experiences as an 'outlaw' the previous autumn with the 'privilege' of wearing a little tin badge of identification around his neck and to carry documents to show he was an accredited correspondent.

Valentine Williams was the son of the chief editor of Reuters and had journalism in his blood. He, too, wrote enthusiastically about his visit to GHQ:

> 'Since my arrival here on Monday I have had the opportunity of going through the whole organisation of the British Army in the field, which

is centred at Headquarters. Of the details of this organisation I shall write later. I am convinced that nothing we may be destined to see in the spectacular line can surpass in sheer impressiveness the miracle of organisation which has gradually built up in the somnolent atmosphere of this quiet corner of France.'

All the journalists wore their everyday civilian clothes and this aroused the suspicion of the French police as they drove through a small town. Phoning on ahead, the police alerted the next village and as the car turned a corner, they were confronted by a line of British infantrymen blocking their way, rifles at the ready. It took ten minutes to convince the soldiers that they were not German spies but gentlemen of the press. It may have been this experience that persuaded all future visiting war correspondents to be fitted with a khaki uniform.

Before they returned to London, the four reporters were granted a brief audience with Field Marshal Sir John French. Philip Gibbs was not greatly impressed, describing him as: *'a stocky, heavy-jowled man...As a cavalry leader he was probably first-class, but he was not a heaven-born Commander-in-Chief, especially when the war became fixed in trench lines.'*

Field-Marshal French, however, did have an admirer amongst the war reporting fraternity – Colonel Repington of *The Times*. Lieutenant-Colonel Charles à Court Repington had enjoyed a distinguished military career, during which he ran a branch of the British Secret Service. He was a handsome and charming philanderer, conducting a long affair with Lady Garstin, the wife of a British embassy official in Cairo. When this became public, he gave his written promise to end the affair. During the divorce proceedings, it was revealed that Repington had ignored warning about his behaviour and he was forced to resign his commission.[4] He soon became the military correspondent of *The Times* and relied on his contacts with senior officers and both Great War prime ministers, Asquith and Lloyd George, for his information. Through these contacts and the informed gossip he heard during society dinners and country house weekends, he was a remarkably well-informed man and wrote just about the clearest interpretation of the progress of the war. Encouraged by his boss, Northcliffe, Repington used the information he picked up to highlight the deficiencies in the conduct of the war. One of his contacts was Lord Kitchener, whom he had known for many years. Repington was used to popping along to the War Office and having discussions with Kitchener. Then one day, Kitchener referred any future discussions to his deputy. Repington was greatly affronted by this snub and from then on Kitchener became a target for all that was going wrong with the war.

Repington then turned to another contact as a means of bypassing Kitchener: General Sir John French. He frequently visited GHQ and was there on a private visit at the time of the Neuve Chapelle battle. French used his friendship with Repington to reveal that the failure at Neuve Chapelle and the subsequent assaults on Aubers Ridge and Fromelles were largely due to a lack of HE (high explosive) shells. In addition, the British artillery equipment and ammunition were in poor condition, the first through over-use, the second through faulty manufacture. Although Repington went to great pains to state that he did not receive any suggestion of shortages from his friend, his subsequent telegram was tacitly approved by Sir John. On 12 May, he sent off the telegram to *The Times* containing the words that would lead to the fall of the government: *'that the want of an unlimited supply of high explosive shells was a fatal bar to our success'.*

Repington was further dismayed as he witnessed the disastrous assault at Fromelles and recorded his distress in his diary:

> *'We obtained insignificant results at the cost of heavy loss. I visited the 2nd Battalion of my old regiment* [The Rifle Brigade]*, and saw its commanding officer, Colonel R.B. Stephens, immediately after the action at Fromelles. He gave me a paper showing that the battalion had gone into action with 29 officers and 1,090 other ranks, and had come out, 24 hours later, with only one officer, who had been in the Cambridge Eleven the previous year, and 245 other ranks unwounded. I was enraged by this loss which was attributed by the troops solely to the failure of the guns, due in its turn for want of shells.'*

The issue over the lack of HE shells was the one that *The Times*, and Lord Northcliffe, could use against the government and Lord Kitchener. Northcliffe wrote in the *Daily Mail* on 21 May 1915:

> *'Lord Kitchener has starved the army in France of high-explosive shells. The admitted fact is that Lord Kitchener ordered the wrong kind of shell – the same kind of shell which he used largely against the Boers in 1900. He persisted in sending shrapnel – a useless weapon in trench warfare. He was warned repeatedly that the kind of*

shell required was a violently explosive bomb which would dynamite its way through the German trenches and entanglements and enable our brave men to advance in safety. This kind of shell our poor soldiers have had has caused the deaths of thousands of them.'

Lord Northcliffe's outspoken condemnation of a national hero had an adverse effect. Overnight the *Daily Mail*'s circulation dropped from 1,386,000 to 238,000. A placard was hung across the newspaper's nameplate with the words 'The Allies of the Huns'. Members of the London Stock Exchange passed a motion against 'the venomous attacks' of the Harmsworth Press, and afterwards ceremoniously burnt copies of the *Mail*.

Repington was in no doubt as to who was blame for the lamentable breakdown in supply:

'I had been able, during my frequent visits to France to ascertain how lamentably short we were of high explosive shells for our field artillery in particular, and it was with this gun and this projectile, at this period of the war, that we prepared for the infantry assault. We were also short of heavy guns of all calibres, in which the enemy enormously outnumbered us, and of shells for those which we possessed; we were short of trench mortars, of Maxims [machine-guns], of rifle and hand grenades, and, in fact, of almost all the necessary instruments and materials for trench warfare; and the trouble was that Lord K did not comprehend the importance of artillery in the war, took no effective measures to increase our supplies of it, and concealed the truth of the situation from his colleagues in the Cabinet...'

Repington added that: *'There were no regular Press correspondents with our Army at this time.'* He also told the old Victorian hero, Lord Roberts: *'Censorship is being used as a cloak to cover all political, naval and military mistakes'*.

Kitchener's response to General Sir Archibald Murray's earlier assessment that the proportion of HE shells should be radically increased was met with abuse. Murray was informed that he was not fit to serve as a General Staff Officer and the British Army ought to be able to take positions without artillery. Repington noted that Kitchener: *'even instanced the Atbara as a precedent, proving himself to be totally unacquainted with the lessons of the campaign.'*[5]

When it was reported, Repington's article did have great repercussions but not entirely as was intended. It led to the Liberal Party being forced into a coalition government. Lloyd George was moved from the Chancellorship and put in charge of munitions, formally under the jurisdiction of the War Office. French, whose wasteful tactics were criticised, held out until the end of 1915 before being replaced by Douglas Haig, but Kitchener survived. Furious with Repington, Kitchener had him banned from visiting GHQ in France, but once the dust had settled the following year. *The Times* man was once more a frequent visitor. Another significant result from the 'shell crisis' was that the authorities finally acknowledged that the controlled presence of war correspondents at the front could be to their advantage.

Notes

1 *The Pageant of the Years* by Philip Gibbs.

2 *Press in War Time* by Sir Edward Cook. Pub. 1920.

3 The first Zeppelin raid against Britain was on the night of 19–20 January 1915 when bombs were dropped on the East Anglian towns of Great Yarmouth, Sheringham and King's Lynn, killing four and injuring 16.

4 Repington's wife refused him a divorce. Nevertheless, Mary Garstin supported him through all their vicissitudes. She took his name, lived with him as his wife, bore him a daughter and forgave his many indiscretions.

5 The Battle of the Atbara in the Sudan was fought on 8 April 1898 against the artillery-less, spear-waving hordes of the Mahdi.

Chapter 4

Khaki War Reporters

In May 1915, attired in the uniforms of officers, without badges or rank insignia but sporting the green armbands of Military Intelligence, the first five officially credited war reporters visited the Western Front. They were Herbert Russell, Perry Robinson, Percival Phillips, John Buchan and Philip Gibbs.

Gibbs was born in London in 1877 and received a home education. From an early age he was determined to become a writer, like his two brothers and later his son. Gibbs was an intense man and an experienced investigative journalist. He had been shot at during the so-called 'Battle of Sidney Street' and, in 1909, he had exposed the American, Dr Frederick A. Cook, as a fraud for claiming to be the first man to reach the North Pole ahead of Commander Peary. Resisting pressure from the Norwegian authorities and fellow journalists, Gibbs stuck to his story as the truth was learned. His first taste of war was in the 1912 Balkans conflict as the artist/reporter for the *Daily Graphic*. His adventures the previous autumn had been forgiven by the authorities and he was chosen to represent the *Daily Chronicle* and the *Daily Telegraph*. Although the composition of the accredited reporters changed many times over the next three years, Gibbs, along with Percival Phillips, was a permanent presence.

American-born, Percival Phillips was the same age as Gibbs. As a fledgling journalist, he had covered the Greek-Turkish War of 1898 and the Spanish-American War of 1898. In 1901, he moved to England and joined the new *Daily Express*. He reported the Russo-Japanese War of 1904 from both sides. Like Gibbs, he also covered the Balkan campaign of 1912. In his new official capacity, he reported for the *Daily Express* and the *Morning Post*.

Henry Perry Robinson, born in 1859, was the oldest of the reporters. At the outbreak of the war, he was sent to Belgium and narrowly missed being captured. As the Germans approached Antwerp in October, he managed to escape from the city and make his way to Holland. In the summer of 1915, he was sent to report on the fighting in Serbia. In April 1916, he was chosen to represent *The Times* and *Daily News* and replaced John Buchan. Robinson was cantankerous and dogmatic and the least popular member of this small group. He also bore a striking resemblance to Rudyard Kipling.

Herbert Russell, formerly of the *Daily Express*, moved to Reuters and represented the News Agencies. He did go to Gallipoli but returned to France which he covered until the end of the war. Tragically, his son Lieutenant Sydney Russell was killed in action in July 1918. Still deeply depressed, Russell committed suicide on 23 March 1944 by gas poisoning.

The fifth member was also its most celebrated. John Buchan was a popular novelist who had published his most famous book, *The Thirty-Nine Steps*, the previous year. With its plot of German spies being thwarted by the heroic John Hannay, it became an immediate best seller. Buchan replaced Henry Nevinson, who accompanied the Army on its ill-starred Dardanelles campaign. Buchan had also been recruited by Charles Masterman, the head of the War Propaganda Bureau, to write an ongoing history of the war in magazine form. Given the heavy propaganda bias and the material he had to work with, Buchan's *History of the War* proved historically inaccurate and unfashionably jingoistic. Buchan's reporting role was with *The Times* and the *Daily News*, but his writing commitments increasingly kept him away from France. Despite this, he did cover the battles of Loos and the Somme.

Valentine Williams was the youngest of the reporters who stood in when one of the regulars was ill or was writing a book about the war. He was born on 1883, the son of the chief editor of Reuters News Agency. After joining his father, he left in 1909 and worked for the *Daily Mail*, also covering the Balkan War. He disagreed with *'the unenlightened and unimaginative censorship'* and in late 1915 left to volunteer for the Army. He was commissioned as a Second Lieutenant in the Irish Guards and, in 1916, was seriously wounded. He also received the Military Cross for gallantry.

Another journalist who stepped in when one of the original five was absent was Francis Prevost Battersby. He had been commissioned in the Royal Irish Rifles and was severely wounded in the Boer War. Invalided from the Army, he joined the *Morning Post* and covered the Somaliland campaign of 1903. He was a prolific and popular poet and novelist. In 1916, the nose-cap of an exploding shell caught him in the stomach and curtailed his war reporting career.

William Beach Thomas, an academic who taught at Bradfield and Dulwich, began contributing to *The Globe* and was soon persuaded by Alfred Harmsworth to join the *Daily Mail*. He was a countryman at heart, a keen hunting man and writer of books on the subject. For years he wrote a regular column of country life and in 1908, a selection of these articles appeared in the book *From a Hertfordshire Cottage*. With this bucolic background, it seemed a very odd choice to appoint Beach Thomas as an accredited war correspondent. One must wonder if Evelyn Waugh was familiar with this when he wrote *Scoop*, his 1938 humorous take on Fleet Street. In it, Lord Copper's (Lord Northcliffe?) national newspaper, the *Daily Beast*, sends its gentle contributor of nature notes, William Boot, off to a war zone, with hilarious results.[1]

Beach Thomas joined the accredited reporters early in 1916 and remained with them until the Armistice. Gibbs fondly recalled Beach Thomas as…

'a very tall man whose puttees were always coming down, and who walked with a quick short step, was very knowledgeable about birds, and flowers, and trees, and all growing things, and the way of nature day by day in English fields…It would come out even in the description of a battle scene when he would add a little colour to his picture by the vivid yellow of some weed which grew in the fields of Flanders or the Somme, or he would mention that he heard some bird singing above the roar of guns. This was very disconcerting to our Tommies who read the Daily Mail *and Beach Thomas's description of battles in which they were fighting.*

Henry Major Tomlinson, one of Gibbs's 'Three Musketeers', was another unlikely war correspondent who acted as a reserve. He was very deaf, which gave him an advantage on a battlefield as he could not hear all the unpleasant noises. As he and the other reporters entered Bapaume on the day of its capture, he heard the high-pitched whistle of an incoming shell. Tomlinson put his hand to his ear and turned to the ornithology expert, Beach Thomas, and asked: *'What bird is that?'*[2] At the end of 1917, he had become disillusioned with the war and quit to become literary editor of *The Nation*.

Accompanying the reporters were the censors. Early on there was a succession of three ex-Indian Civil Servants but the one who was to remain with them for the rest of the war was Charles Edward Montague, former leader writer for the *Manchester Guardian*. Despite being 47 years of age, prematurely white-haired and married with seven children, Montague felt he should try and enlist. Dyeing his hair black, he was finally accepted into the 23rd (Service) Battalion, Royal Fusiliers, known as the Sportsman's Battalion, as it largely comprised of men who had made their name in sports and the media. He served in the trenches as a sergeant and was mentioned three times in despatches. In early 1916, he was pulled out of the ranks, given a commission and appointed censor, along with a young officer, Captain Cadge. Gibbs greatly admired him but thought he was slightly unhinged. Montague seemed to thrive on being under fire and Gibbs recalled them watching the British soldiers attacking the enemy trenches:

'We were close enough to see Germans running out of their dugouts and being shot as they emerged. Bunches of them were caught in the open by our shells, which plugged into the midst of them, blowing them to bits; and every time this happened, Montague, sitting on a pile of sandbags above the captured trench, laughed in a goblin way... I do not write this as a criticism of Montague who was a better and wiser man than I have ever been, but as a glimpse of some oddity in him, some conflict within him, almost a touch of dual personality.'

Montague did not have a particular regard for the correspondents and critically wrote:

'They would visit the front now and then, as many staff officers did, but it could only be as afternoon callers from one of the many mansions of GHQ, that have security and comfort. When autumn twilight came down on the haggard trench world, of which they caught a quiet noon-day glimpse, they would be speeding west in Vauxhall cars to lighted chateaux...The average war correspondent – there were golden exceptions – insensibly acquired a cheerfulness in the face of vicarious torment and danger. In his work it came out at times in a certain jauntiness of tone that roused the fighting troops to fury against the writer. Through his despatches there ran a brisk implication that the regimental officers and men enjoyed nothing better than "going over the top"; that a battle was just a rough jovial picnic, that a fight never went on long enough for the men, that their only fear was lest the war should end this side of the Rhine. This, the men reflected, in helpless anger, was what people at home were

offered as faithful accounts of what their friends in the field were thinking and suffering.'

Charles Montague spent the remainder of the war as a censor and writing propaganda. He also accompanied distinguished visitors, politicians and writers, on a tour of the trenches. George Bernard Shaw remembered that after being lavishly entertained at GHQ, he was taken to the front line:

'The standing joke about Montague was his craze for being under fire, and his tendency to lead the distinguished visitors, who did not necessarily share his taste into warm corners...Both of us felt that, being there, we were wasting our time when we were not within range of the guns. We had come to the theatre to see the play, not to enjoy the intervals between the acts like fashionable people at the opera.'

After the war, Montague gave vent to his feeling about the war and its terrible effects in his angry books *Rough Justice* and *Disenchantment*.

Montague was a little harsh about some of the correspondents who genuinely wanted to be able to witness a battle on the front line. Philip Gibbs, Percival Phillips and even William Beach Thomas had risked arrest the previous year in order to reach the battle areas. Now, accepting that they had to follow strict guidelines laid down by the military, they settled down into a routine. The way the system worked was that, following a briefing by the press officer, each reporter would be taken to an allotted section to watch either a bombardment or to walk over newly captured ground. They would then tour rear areas and see the walking wounded and captured enemy soldiers and see the bustle of traffic going to and from the front lines. They would then move further back to get an update of news from the area headquarters before returning to GHQ. Here they would all get together and exchange information before retiring to their rooms and writing up their reports before dinner. Having been passed by the censor, these would be sent to the War Office where they would be distributed to the various newspapers, who were not allowed to alter or cut anything their correspondents wrote.

By giving the illusion that they were being allowed to report the truth, the press were doing little more than adding colour to official releases. They had come to accept the establishment view that the public should not be unduly alarmed by the slaughter nor upset by the dreadful conditions to which their loved-ones were condemned. They wrote thrillingly of steadily advancing men, the continuously thundering roar of the guns and the huge numbers of prisoners of war making their way into captivity. After truth, the second casualty of this new trust was Colonel Swinton's 'Eyewitness' who was now redundant.

Much later, Gibbs wrote that:

'There was an idea, still lingering, that we war correspondents of the First World War were "spoon fed", and just wrote what we were told. That was partly due to an arrangement we made amongst ourselves. We decided to pool all our information, in order to give the fullest record of any action, reserving only to ourselves our personal impressions and experiences.

'The limitations of censorship were, of course, irritating. We could not give the figures of our losses – the immense sum of our casualties, as on the first day of the Somme battle. That was inevitable because that was what the enemy would have liked to know. But the worst handicap we had was the prohibition of naming individual units who had done the fighting.'

Gibbs spoke for all correspondents when he admitted:

'We identified ourselves absolutely with the armies in the field, and we wiped out of our minds all thought of personal "scoops", and all temptation to write one word which would make the task of officers and men more difficult or dangerous. There was no need of censorship of despatches. We were our own censors.'[3]

For such a fearless writer, he was soon seduced by the military trappings and, apart from some general complaints about not seeing actual fighting, he compromised.

This attitude was reinforced by Hamilton Fyfe, who had been banned from France in 1914, but was allowed to return in 1917. He wrote about the enormous change he found:

'My next assignment was to the British Front in France. What a contrast I found there – in the comfortable chateau allotted to the correspondents, in the officers placed at their service, in the powerful

cars at their disposal – to the conditions prevailing in the early months of the war! Then, we were hunted, threatened, abused. Now everything possible was done to make our work interesting and easy – easy, that is, so far as permits and information and transport were concerned. No scrounging for food: we had a lavishly provided mess. No sleeping in hay or on bare floors of empty houses: our bedrooms were furnished with taste as well as every convenience, except fitted basins and baths. But then, we each had a servant, who brought in a tin tub and filled it after he had brought early morning tea.

'I felt a little bit ashamed to be housed in what, after my experiences, I could not call luxury. It had an unfortunate result too, in cutting us off from the life of the troops. I made an application soon after I arrived to be allowed to stay in the trenches with a friend commanding a battalion of the Rifle Brigade. No correspondent, I learned, had done this. They knew only from hearsay how life in the front line went on.'

In May, there was another attempt to take Aubers Ridge, which resulted in an unmitigated disaster, with no ground won and no tactical advantage gained. John Buchan, who had observed the insufficient British bombardment, added his voice to those attacking Kitchener's administration:

'All the strategy and tactics of the war depend today upon one burning fact. The enemy has got an amazingly powerful machine and unless we can provide ourselves with a machine of equal vigour he will nullify the superior fighting qualities of our men. That machine consists of a great number of heavy guns and machine-guns, and an apparently unlimited supply of high explosive.'

As the war ground relentlessly on, so the relationship between newsmen and their hosts, the military, grew warmer. Even the ironic directive to: *'Say what you like, but don't mention any people or places or facts'* was eventually accepted as the norm. Also, they did not seem to mind unduly when it became common knowledge that the Army's Press Officer had orders to waste the time of war correspondents brought to General Headquarters.

There was no great action on the Western Front during the summer months of 1915. Instead, Britain was concentrating on building up its strength with new divisions and, as Gibbs wrote: *'hardening them in the forward trenches with rats and lice and filth and fire'.* The artillery was still short of ammunition but the use of specialist Royal Engineer tunnelling companies laying tons of explosives under the German lines, and the use of chlorine gas, were thought enough to compensate for lack of firepower.

The coming battle was forced on Sir John French by the French C-in-C, Marshal Joseph Joffre, whose plan was an Anglo-French attack along the Artois-Champagne front. Both French and Douglas Haig (GOC British First Army) regarded the ground chosen for the coming battle as unsuitable. Centred on the large mining village of Loos, the six-mile front the British were to attack was over flat terrain dominated by the huge slag heaps and pit-head winding towers. These were used by the Germans, who could look down on the advancing British, and wreak havoc with their well-placed machine-guns.

The Battle of Loos began on 25 September with the release of chlorine gas, which was totally reliant on wind direction. The Germans had used gas in their attack on the northern section of the Ypres salient on 22 April to devastating effect. Two divisions of French colonials retreated in the face of this deadly green cloud and opened a gap of some four miles. Thanks to the resistance of the Canadian battalions, the German advance was halted until more British and Canadian reinforcements arrived. Although the use of chemical weapons had been banned by the 1907 Hague Convention, and signed by both Germany and Britain, Haig had no compunction in using it at Loos in a spirit of retaliation. He wrote to Field Marshal Sir William Robertson, Chief of Staff GHQ: *'In my opinion, under no circumstances, should our forthcoming attack be launched without the aid of gas.'*

After the preliminary artillery barrage with its limited number of shells, the chlorine gas was released at dawn on the morning of 25th. Then, some 75,000 British soldiers scrambled out of their trenches and began to cross the open fields towards the well-entrenched enemy.

For the first time, British war correspondents were taken by their censors to witness a full-scale battle. In fact they were about two miles behind the front line at the village of Noeux-les-Mines and, from their vantage point on top of a black slag heap, peered through their binoculars into the gloom. Gibbs wrote:

'No man saw the attack unless he took part in it, and then only his own immediate environment. The battalions disappeared into a fog of smoke from shells and bombs of every kind. They fought behind a

veil from which came only the noise of battle and later the first stream of wounded.'

Even if the reporters had wanted to truthfully describe a battle, they would have found it almost impossible so to do. They would have been reminded of Churchill's words that the war was going to be fought in a fog. Although present, they had little or no idea just how much of a disaster was the Battle of Loos.

First the gas, that had been released to blow over the German trenches, filled the British front line in the still air. Those troops that had not been asphyxiated fought hard to dislodge the Germans from their front line only to be held up through lack of reinforcements. Belatedly, when the Germans had recovered, newly arrived and untried territorials were thrown into the attack and slaughtered.

The reporters had little to go on except that the British had paid a heavy price for what they optimistically hoped was a victory. They based the 'heavy price' on the high numbers of wounded they could see being ferried to the hospitals. It would be several days before the shocking truth of the battle would be learned.

In place of describing a battle they could not see, they wrote of the attack along the entire 500-mile front from Ypres to the French right flank. Valentine Williams wrote:

'The tension of the past few weeks was broken yesterday by the thunder of the guns which rolled almost incessantly throughout the day right along the Allies from the North Sea to the Vosges...It is too soon to write in any detail about operations, as fighting is still in progress. The attack at Loos completely surprised the Germans, according to the prisoners taken there, with many of whom I spoke this afternoon. They describe our bombardment as "unspeakable", and say that the first thing they knew about the assault was the appearance of lines of British troops streaming away over their trenches to the right and the next moment, the inrush of a horde of khaki-clad figures upon their trenches from three sides...'

John Buchan, accompanied by Philip Gibbs, did advance through the communication trenches and observed the ground over which the British advanced and saw *'a scene of devastation and death'*. This was a description that was self-censored and appeared in memoirs after the war. In all the reports, there was no mention of the use of poisonous gas, which suggested that they were unaware of its use. Buchan was criticised by his editor, Geoffrey Robinson, who wrote to another *Times* reporter at Loos, Maxwell Macartney. In it he implied that Buchan had been somewhat lax in his reporting and that Macartney's reports were just the ticket He was advised to remain in the area as the British had made some progress and there was, for a while, the chance to break through the German line. Unfortunately, the reserves that could be used were still 40 miles away. By the time they arrived and were thrown into the attack forty-eight hours later, the Germans had been reinforced and inflicted heavy casualties on the exhausted newcomers.

William Beach Thomas visited the battlefield close to the captured formidable Hohenzollern Redoubt and, in his inimitable style of seeing beauty in the grimmest circumstances, he wrote of an aerial dog-fight:

> *'No picture could be have been more idyllic. There was great aerial activity. The machines looked like silvered butterflies chasing one another on a summer morning. Even the sound of the machine-guns followed by the patter of bullets here and there, dwarfed by the great space of intervening air, to the tap of a nesting woodpecker. Even when a plane was hit – and I saw one hit – it slipped to earth like a homing seabird, giving no sense of catastrophe.'*

He continued in this vein when describing distant shelling: *'the shrapnel made soft pillows for a cupid's bust'*. Quite what the men in the trenches made of this was probably unrepeatable.

Without much to go on, Percival Phillips wrote about these men of Kitchener's volunteers:

> *'The New Army proved itself a worthy successor to the Army of tradition. As fine exploits will be recorded of the wresting of this strip of mining country from the invaders as those performed at Ypres and Festubert and other historic spots within the unbroken British line.*
>
> *'Battalions of the New Army gained their first experience of heavy fighting while capturing a position as strong as many stormed by the veterans of a year ago. The price was heavy, but they paid it without faltering. We may be proud of them.'*

The price was indeed heavy: just under 11,000 inexperienced men advanced and within just over three hours they had lost 385 officers and 7,861 men. Overall, the British casualties amounted to 59,247.

Another casualty of the battle of Loos was the BEF's Commander-in-Chief, Sir John French. He had long been criticised since the retreat from Mons and the disaster at Loos finally cost him his command. He blamed Haig for the failure of Loos, but it was a failure he shared. In December, he was forced to resign and take up the post of Commander-in-Chief, Home Forces. To soften the blow, he was eventually appointed 1st Earl of Ypres. Despite the heavy criticism in the newspapers and from many leading figures, the public still supported Lord Kitchener, whose position at the War Office remained strong, despite having to surrender the supply of weaponry, which was controlled by David Lloyd George's new Ministry for Munitions.

Those reporters who stayed on after the dimly perceived battle were rewarded three weeks later by a local action just to the north of the Hohenzollern Redoubt. With the advantage of a crystal clear afternoon, Maxwell Macartney was able to describe an attack covered by poisonous gas in his report dated 18 October:

'Yesterday we attacked on a comparatively narrow front running roughly from a point about one-third of a mile south-west of Hulluch up to the Hohenzollern Redoubt. The attack – in which gas was employed – was essentially local, and as far as I could judge, our operations were self-contained and were not supported in force by movements on the part of our allies...

'Into the midst of this still and ugly countryside, hell was suddenly turned loose. The efforts of a few ranging shots had been transmitted by the airplanes that flew backwards and forwards over our heads or by the observation balloons that hung motionless far to our rear, and then a flash, the fire of our concentrated guns was poured in upon that narrow section of German lines. Away on my extreme left, an especially dense cloud of smoke, pure white on top, and strangely tinted with red and green below showed where we had loosed our gas-attack in the direction of the Hohenzollern Redoubt, and where we were endeavouring to retaliate upon the Germans for their use of this poisonous weapon. A cloud, perhaps a mile broad and varying considerably in height at different places, ...drifted steadily towards the enemy's lines and muffled them in a thick embrace. But this cloud

*soon became almost indistinguishable from the other pillars of smoke
that leapt up from the ground and blended in one vast canopy in the
air...Again at other times all the enemy's positions were blotted out
by the swirling jumble of smoke and flame and up-churned trenches
and buildings and when again Hulluch showed through the cloud,
even its ugly towers took on some of the misty graciousness of a
Turner water-colour.'*

Rather predictably, the attack petered out with the German lines intact and
a few more New Army volunteers added to the casualty list.

About this time, King George V made the first of his several visits to the
Western Front to inspect his Army and meet her commanders. Philip Gibbs
was on hand to witness the near-fatal accident to the king:

*'I was within yards of the King when he had his accident by his horse
falling under him. It was outside Béthune where he was reviewing the
Royal Flying Corps, drawn up in three bodies along the road. It was
a soggy day and the ground was greasy. The King's horse had been
rehearsed to stand steady under odd noises, but when, at the call of
an officer, the RFC raised their caps and cheered tremendously the
horse was scared and reared three times. The King kept his seat
perfectly, but the third time the frightened horse slipped on the greasy
ground and rolled right over on him.*

*'The generals were frightened. They dismounted and ran to the
King's assistance but he lay there still for a few moments, until they
lifted him up and carried him to his big motor car. A senior officer
shouted at me: "Tell the men along the road not to cheer". The men
further down the road had no notion that anything had happened to
the King, and when his car passed them they cheered wildly before I
could pass on the order. Inside the car lay the gravely injured man
with his eyes shut, looking very ill.'*

The king was rushed to a hospital train at Aire, where it was found that he
had sustained a fractured pelvis. There, on 1 November 1915, despite his
pain, he insisted on bestowing the Victoria Cross on Sergeant Oliver Brooks
of the Coldstream Guards for outstanding gallantry at Loos. In what has
become known as the 'Bedside VC', Brooks knelt beside the king's bedside
while his monarch pinned the VC to his tunic.

In time, as the list of casualties was read by the public, the feeling grew that they were not being accurately informed by the newspapers. Soldiers on home leave had long given up telling civilians what conditions were like in the trenches as these had not been reported in the papers and, therefore, could not be true. Fighting men, officers and other ranks alike, grew to despise war reporters for not telling the truth about the war. There is a school of thought that says that if the newspapers had printed the facts then the war would have been over much earlier. For this to have happened it would have been necessary for some of the reporters to actually experience fighting conditions to offset the ingrained patriotism that coloured their writing, and for their employers to have been willing to risk prosecution.

Notes

1 Evelyn Waugh may also have used a young Bill Deedes as his model for William Boot.
2 *The Pageant of the Years* by Philip Gibbs.
3 *Adventures in Journalism* by Philip Gibbs.

Chapter 5

Propaganda

B ritain's negative feeling towards Germany began to gain momentum after the Franco-Prussian War in 1870–71. Although Britain remained aloof, the general support was for the Prussians. After all, France was perceived as the old enemy and also there was a recent royal connection with the Prussians. This changed soon after the war when the Unification of Germany presented the British with a threat greater than France. When Wilhelm II succeeded his father, Friedrich III, who had ruled for just ninety-nine days before dying of cancer, he set about expanding and modernising his army and navy. The bellicose attitude of the new monarch alarmed the British, who began their own rearmament programme. Fears of war inspired a spate of invasion novels to be written about the possibility that Britain might be Germany's next victim.

Anti-German feeling deepened when Kaiser Wilhelm II openly supported the Boers in the Anglo-Boer War. From about this time, relations between Britain and France underwent a great change and were formalised with the signing of the Entente Cordiale. In the following decade, articles and books were written that heightened German phobia so that when war was declared, it was easier for the propagandists to build on this hatred. The increasing anti-German hysteria finally persuaded the British monarch in 1917 to change his name from Saxe-Coburg-Gotha to Windsor and for his cousin to reverse the spelling of his name from Battenburg to Mountbatten.

Britain had no organised propaganda machinery at the beginning of the war and the responsibility for propaganda was divided between several agencies, which led to a lack of co-ordination. The agency that had the most influence was set up at Wellington House, and was initially called the War Propaganda Bureau. It was headed by Charles Masterman, a former journalist who became a successful Liberal MP serving in Lord Asquith's government.

Propaganda came in two forms, black and white. Black propaganda was negative with the purpose of spreading ideas, information and rumours that would damage the image of Germany, particularly with the neutral countries that the Allies were trying to win over to their side. One country above all was heavily targeted for its industrial clout and huge manpower – the United States.

Falsehood is a recognised and extremely useful weapon in warfare, and every country uses it quite deliberately to deceive its own people, to attract neutrals, and to mislead the enemy. The first and most obvious source for spreading false rumours was Germany's invasion of Belgium. Throughout the beginning of the war there was little doubt that the Belgians were brutally treated by the German invaders. In the towns of Liège, Andenne, Leuvan and Dinant there is evidence of violence against civilians. In Dinant alone 647 civilians, including women and children, were killed. In Leuvan, the University's library of 300,000 medieval books and manuscripts was deliberately set on fire, 248 people were killed and the entire population of 10,000 expelled. There were cases of rape, looting and murder. The destruction of whole communities forced one and a half million people (20 per cent of the entire population) to become refugees, mostly to France.

There was certainly enough evidence to launch a factual propaganda attack against Germany but the temptation to exaggerate and falsify was too great. The British, largely through Brigadier-General John Charteris, Head of British Military Intelligence, saw to the spread of gruesome tales of captured British and Canadian soldiers being crucified by the Germans. Using a plausible background of Canadian soldiers wounded at Ypres, they were said to have witnessed a comrade pinned to a wall by bayonets thrust through his hands and feet, with another bayonet driven through his throat. He was then finished off by a hail of bullets. Just to add credibility to this tale, the Canadians said that men of the Dublin Fusiliers had also been witnesses.

Terrible tales of women stripped naked, impaled with bayonets and with breasts sliced off, and children with severed hands, all increased the public's loathing of the Germans. They were also now referred to as 'Huns' after Attila's barbaric hordes who had swept all before them. All these outrages were published under the heading of 'The Rape of Belgium', and were read in all the neutral countries. In Britain, they were used to engender a great hatred of Germany aimed at boosting recruitment of volunteers anxious to wreak revenge. As General Charteris cynically remarked: *'to make armies go on killing one another it is necessary to invent lies about the enemy.'*

Many of these stories were accompanied by graphic cartoons, mostly from the pen of the Dutch artist, Louis Raemaekers. His cartoons depicted the Kaiser as an ally of Satan and the Germans as slavering pigs or red-eyed apes. Following the execution of the British nurse, Edith Cavell, he produced *Thrown to the Swine: The Martyred Nurse*, showing pigs in pickelhaubes rooting around the corpse of Nurse Cavell. Raemaekers so incensed the German Government that they offered a reward for the cartoonist, dead or alive. The bounty on his head encouraged Raemaekers to leave Holland for England, where he was employed by *The Times*. In 1915, the War Propaganda Bureau published a pamphlet entitled 'Report on Alleged German Outrages', which gave credence to the reports that the German Army was systematically torturing Belgian civilians and used Louis Raemaekers' drawings to emphasise the point.

The propaganda poster was another effective means of getting the message across to the public. Two of the best known posters that assaulted the emotions urged men to volunteer through shaming them. 'Daddy, what did YOU do in the Great War?' by Savile Lumley appealed to family pride as young children ask their father about his military prowess. The second was by E.V. Kealy entitled, 'Women of Britain say – GO!', depicting a mother, daughter and son embracing as they watch a file of soldiers marching bravely off to war. This was brought out in 1915 by the Parliamentary Committee. Most British First World War posters were patriotic and could be classified as white propaganda.

In stark contrast, many of the posters that were displayed in Australia and the United States were the stuff of nightmares. The Australian artist Norman Lindsay produced some bloodcurdling graphics, including one without words but a large question mark beside a pickelhaube-wearing German ogre with blood-drenched hands greedily grasping the bloodied world. Probably the best-known of the black propaganda posters was by the American artist H.R. Hopps. He depicted a half-naked girl being carried away by a gorilla wearing a German helmet and brandishing a bloodied club engraved with 'Kultur'. The beast is stepping ashore in America with a ruined Europe in the background. The message, in red, screams, 'Destroy this Mad Brute. ENLIST'.

Another false story but loosely based on fact was that the Germans boiled down human corpses in order to extract from them lubricating oils and other useful substances. A pamphlet entitled, 'The 'Corpse Conversion' Factory:

A peep behind the German line', was published in 1917 and distributed to neutral and allied countries. The story of this secret 'corpse factory' was received with revulsion throughout the world and helped swing some of the neutrals to back the Allies. Years after the end of the war, General Charteris admitted that he invented the story. It had been based on a real factory, a *Kadaververwertungsanstalt*, which made glue from the carcasses of dead horses, of which there were plenty.

The Germans did not help their cause when they sank the Cunard liner RMS *Lusitania* off Ireland on 7 May 1915. The ship sank in 20 minutes killing 1,198 passengers including many prominent Americans. Any propaganda leverage the Germans hoped to gain from this attack backfired when a commemorative medal was struck by Karl Goetz to satirise Cunard's determination to continue business as usual in wartime. He blamed the British Government for ignoring the warnings of Germany's American embassy about sailing in British waters. The reverse of the medal shows a skeleton selling Cunard tickets with a motto that translated meant, 'Business Above All'.

The propaganda department at the British Foreign Office decided to exploit the anti-German sentiments raised by the sinking and struck their own replica of the medal. This was boxed with a propaganda leaflet and 250,000 were sold, with the proceeds going to charity. Too late, Goetz realised his medal had been the cause of increasing anti-German feeling and that Britain had pulled off a propaganda coup.

At the same time as stirring up hatred for the Germans through black propaganda, Charles Masterman and the War Propaganda Bureau also employed the white equivalent. On 2 September 1914, Masterman invited 25 leading authors to Wellington House to discuss ways of best promoting British interests during the war. Amongst those who attended were Arthur Conan Doyle, Arnold Bennett, John Masefield, G.K. Chesterton, John Galsworthy, Thomas Hardy, Rudyard Kipling and H.G. Wells. Several who attended agreed to write pamphlets and books in support of the war effort.

Amongst the writers who accepted the invitation was John Buchan who embraced the need to engender patriotic fervour and was among the most industrious of writers in getting that message across to the public. Besides writing pamphlets, he embarked on writing a monthly history of the war, which he eventually published through his own company. After working as an accredited journalist for *The Times* he was recruited by the Army to draft communiqués for Sir Douglas Haig and other staff officers at GHQ. Because of his close relationship with the military leaders, he was entirely uncritical of the way the war was being conducted. When it was published, Buchan's *History of the War* gave the public a completely false impression of what was going on at the Western Front. He had planned this history as early as October 1914 but did not follow his own advice:

> '*I do think we shall not get absolutely accurate details of most of the fighting till after the war, and therefore a history on the scale of* The Times *and the* Daily Mail *is impossible; but I am satisfied that three months after the fighting we shall know enough to write an accurate history on the scale which I propose – viz monthly parts.*'[1]

In his pamphlet, Buchan described the battle of the Somme as so successful that it marked '*the end of trench fighting and the beginning of the campaign in the open*'. His report is filled with exaggerations that falsify the entire military situation on the Western Front; soldiers and commanding generals are painted in the most glowing colours despite evidence to the contrary.

In February 1917, the War Propaganda Bureau had expanded to become the more obscurely named Department of Information with the newly promoted Lieutenant Colonel John Buchan in charge. In the years that followed the end of the war, Buchan wrote successful novels and biographies, became a director of Reuters before being elected as a Conservative MP. Unlike several of his fellow journalists, he never wrote a word to apologise for the wild inaccuracies of his reporting of the war.

In effect, Charles Masterman had been demoted and was now responsible to Buchan. His department, still at Wellington House, dealt with printed materials, photographs and paintings. In May 1916, he commissioned the Scottish artist, Muirhead Bone, as the first official British war artist. Given the honorary rank of Second Lieutenant, he arrived during the Battle of the Somme. He completed 150 drawings, mostly scenes of devastated villages and woods, before returning to England in October 1916.

Philip Gibbs wrote about Bone when they entered the village of Contalmaison:

> '*I went into the village when it was still burning, and when the enemy was all around. My companion was Muirhead Bone who had been sent out as a war artist with the rank of lieutenant. This was his first experience of standing in the flaming heart of war and it was heroic*

of him to bring out his sketch book and make rapid notes of the scene around him. Once when a shell burst near him, his pencil went clean through his paper, but he carried on while our men were taking cover behind bits of wall, and the wounded being carried off.'

Later, talented modern artists like Paul Nash and Christopher Nevinson were recruited to help put across to the public a more erudite message about Britain's commitment to the war.

War artists, whose works appeared in the popular magazines, were almost entirely gung-ho in their approach. The most popular was the precociously talented war artist, Richard Caton Woodville, whose accomplished painting usually featured cavalry or infantry charges but reflected little of the feel of a First World War battle.

It was to Charles Masterman's great credit that he gave a number of modern artists the opportunity to visit the Western Front and interpret what they had witnessed on canvas. One of them was Christopher Nevinson, the son of the accredited war reporter, Henry Nevinson. A pupil of the Slade School of Art, he became part of the Futurist Movement, whose style was avant garde. At the outbreak of the war, he joined the Friends' Ambulance Unit with his father and was deeply disturbed by his work tending the French wounded. For a while, he served as a volunteer ambulance driver until, in 1916, ill health forced his return to England.

He then set about using his experiences to produce a series of powerful paintings including *La Mitrailleuse* (Machine-gunner), which depicts the subject as part of a machine and which he described as: *'warfare on an industrial scale fought by men deprived of their individuality'*. Nevinson did revisit France in 1917 as an official war artist and produced paintings of desolation, with water-filled craters, or the famous *Road from Arras to Bapaume*, with its endless road undulating towards the horizon through featureless fields, broken trees under grey skies – a comment perhaps on the endless war.[2] His strong and harsh style made an impact with the small but influential circle of admirers.

One of the limits put on the artists was that they should not show dead bodies, particularly British. Nevinson, however, did produce a painting entitled *Paths of Glory*, that depicted two fallen British soldiers in a field of mud and barbed wire, which was banned from being displayed. He had shown his earlier war painting at the Leicester Gallery in London in September 1916, and, whereas his style of painting had met with adverse criticism before the war, his new way at looking at the war struck a chord with critics and public alike. As a result, Masterman recruited him as an official war artist.

Paul Nash served at the front as a second lieutenant in the Hampshire Regiment until a broken rib luckily brought him out of the trenches just before the Passchendaele battle in 1917. Before the war, he was a rural landscape artist who painted rather romantic, if brooding, scenes. Nevinson advised him to approach Masterman, who added him to the list of official artists.

His war paintings were almost always without human figures, depicting the terrible destruction of the landscape by the warring armies. One of his most famous works is the ironically entitled *We are Making a New World*.

Reacting to the severe censorship which restricted the subject matter, Nash wrote to his wife. In one of the most descriptive accounts of conditions on the Western Front he vented his hopeless anger:

'I have seen the most frightful nightmare of a country more conceived by Dante or Poe than by nature, unspeakable, utterly indescribable. In the fifteen drawings I have made I may give you some vague idea of its horror, but only being in it and of it can ever make you sensible of its dreadful nature and of what our men in France have to face. We all have a vague notion of the terrors of a battle, and can conjure up with the aid of some of the more inspired war correspondents and the pictures in the Daily Mirror *some vision of a battlefield, but no pen or drawing can convey this country – the normal setting of its battles taking place day and night, month after month. No glimmer of God's hand is seen anywhere. Sunset and sunrise are blasphemous; they are mockeries to man, only the black rain out of the bruised and swollen clouds all through the bitter black of night is fit atmosphere for such a land...*

'The rain drives on, the stinking mud becomes more evilly yellow, the shell holes fill up with green-white water, the roads and tracks are covered in inches of slime, the black dying trees ooze and sweat and the shells never cease. They alone plunge overhead, tearing away rotting trees stumps, breaking the plank roads, striking down horses and mules, annihilating, maiming, maddening, they plunge into the grave which is this land; one huge grave, and cast up on it the poor dead. It is unspeakable, godless, hopeless.

'I am no longer an artist interested and curious. I am a messenger who will bring back word from the men who are fighting to those who want the war to go on forever. Feeble, inarticulate, will be my message, but it will have a bitter truth, and may it burn their lousy souls. '3

Nash, along with Nevinson, had probably experienced more horror at first hand than any of the other Official War Artists and their work at this period is regarded as their best. They were, however, no more successful in being allowed to portray the realities of war during the conflict than their journalistic counterparts. Restrictions were imposed upon them so they could not depict death or anything too harrowing.

By the end of the war, the body of work produced by these new artists was truly significant, for which Charles Masterman must be applauded. His final years were not happy. He refused to support Lloyd George's coalition government and lost his seat in the 1918 election. In 1923, he was re-elected only to lose again in 1924. Increasingly he took to drink and, in 1927, died in a nursing home.

Finally, the war reporters themselves, whether they liked it or not, contributed to the white propaganda. Their reports increasingly reflected their submission to the military, with whom they felt completely at ease. The relationship between the press and the military grew ever closer so that by 1917, General Haig had a totally relaxed attitude about newsmen. He had developed a rapport with the most powerful of the press barons, Lord Northcliffe, and could be confident that he would enjoy full support from the newspapers.

There was also another pitfall the reporters were told to avoid: concealing anything that reflected credit on the enemy. A correspondent who mentioned some chivalrous act by a German that helped an Englishman during battle would receive a rebuke from his editor, telling him not to mention good Germans. Philip Gibbs later wrote: *'At the close of the day, the Germans acted with chivalry which I was not allowed to tell at the time. '4*

Charles Repington recorded a conversation he had had with a seemingly intelligent member of the public:

'He told me that the Serbians were going to beat the Germans, that there was nothing in front of our Army in France and that we would be in Constantinople in ten days' time. These are the kind of beliefs

into which the country has been chloroformed by the censorship...
The ignorance of the British public concerning the war, owing to
censorship, is unbelievable.'

With the correspondents exercising self-restraint, the censors keeping their ever-watchful eye and the newspaper proprietors on the side of the generals, the public were fed a diet of pro-military propaganda. By identifying so closely with the military, the war reporters had been, to all intents and purposes, formed into another regiment, which could have easily taken the title of the 'Royal Corps of Propagandists'.

Notes

1 John Buchan in letter to George Brown 16 October 1914.
2 *Art from the First World War* Pub. Imperial War Museum.
3 *Outline: An autobiography and other writings* by Paul Nash.
4 *Realities of War* by Philip Gibbs.

Chapter 6

Ellis Ashmead-Bartlett and the Gallipoli Disaster

A s the Allies were enduring the stalemate of a wet and chilly winter in their trenches in northern France, another front was about to be opened in the Eastern Mediterranean. On 2 November 1914, Turkey decided to join the war and sided with Germany and Austria-Hungary. In an effort to both draw the Central Powers' attention away from Europe and enable the Allies to establish contact with their Russian allies, it was decided to adopt Winston Churchill's audacious stratagem. As First Sea Lord of the Admiralty, he proposed to send a large number of obsolete battleships, which could not operate against the German High Seas Fleet, in an attack up the Dardanelles leading to the capture of Constantinople. It was hoped that this would bring Greece and Bulgaria on to the Allies' side and relieve the pressure on Russia in the Caucasus.

It was felt that the demoralised Turks, having suffered yet more humiliation at the hands of Serbia and Bulgaria in the 1912–13 war, would offer little resistance. She was also heavily committed to repelling the Russians in the freezing mountains of the Caucasus. Furthermore, Turkey was also distracted in her deadly determination to exterminate all Armenians living in the country.[1] It was to be yet another example of the British military fatally underestimating the resilience of their opponents.

On 18 March 1915, the numerically impressive fleet launched its attack. The Anglo-French fleet of eighteen pre-Dreadnaught battleships, supported by cruisers and destroyers, sailed into the Dardanelles and targeted the Narrows, where the straits are only a mile wide, before opening into the Sea of Marmara. Although they succeeded in silencing the guns in the forts, the minefield had not been effectively swept. First the French battleship

Bouvet struck a mine, causing her to capsize with the loss of over 600 crew. Then HMS *Irresistible* and *Inflexible* were badly damaged. HMS *Ocean* went to the rescue of *Irresistible* but was also badly holed and both ships eventually sank. Two more French battleships were also damaged before the fleet commander, Vice-Admiral Sir John de Robeck, ordered a withdrawal.

On 12 March, Lord Kitchener summoned 62-year-old General Sir Ian Hamilton to the War Office and appointed him Commander-in-Chief of the Army that was to invade Turkey.[2] Although he was well liked for his charm and known for his physical bravery, Hamilton lacked ruthlessness. Like many of his contemporaries, he was also intimidated by the formidable Kitchener.

The plan was for the Anglo-French army to land at Gallipoli, the long peninsula which lay on the western side of the Dardanelles. With naval support, they would march up the Gallipoli peninsula to Constantinople. Hamilton's appointment was not popular amongst many of the high-ranking officers, who did not think he was the right commander for the job. Events were to prove them right.

The campaign was doomed from the start. There was an almost total lack of intelligence about the terrain, no accurate maps and only guesswork regarding enemy troop dispositions and numbers. The conduct of the expedition was placed in the hands of incompetent and redundant generals commanding inadequate numbers of men and bedevilled by a shortage of supplies and munitions. With next to no intelligence to guide him, Hamilton set off for the Mediterranean equipped with little more than his enthusiasm.

On 25 April the Anglo-French forces landed on seven separate beaches heralding nearly eight months of misery and bloodshed which accomplished nothing. Some 60,000 Allied soldiers lost their lives with many more wounded or made sick from disease.

Swelling the ranks of the men preparing for the invasion were two accredited war reporters. The newspapers had made an arrangement similar to that operating on the Western Front. The provincial papers were represented by Reuters' man Lester Lawrence. Besides being inexperienced, Lawrence was further handicapped by being very short-sighted and dependent on others for information. As an eye-witness he was somewhat of a non-starter.

The *Daily Telegraph* correspondent, Ellis Ashmead-Bartlett, was made the sole source for news gathering by the London Newspaper Proprietors'

Association. Arguably, of all the Great War reporters, Ellis Ashmead-Bartlett made the greatest impact.

Initially accredited to the navy, the two reporters left London by train on 25 March and arrived in Malta on 1 April. They met with Admiral Limpus, who had previously trained the Turkish Navy, and was to be the first of many officers who were sceptical about the prospects of the expedition. He felt that the abortive attack on 18 March had given the Turks plenty of warning that they were about to be invaded via Gallipoli.

Arriving at Mudros Harbour on the island of Lemnos, which was the main base for the invasion, the two reporters split up. Ashmead-Bartlett enjoyed the hospitality he received from the officers on HMS *London* and, as an Admiralty accredited correspondent, he was duty bound to sail with the navy when they bombarded the Turkish positions. It was a chore he hated and his description of the experience is vivid:

> *'I am sure, however, we hit nothing, except mother earth, and there was the usual fearful waste of ammunition, and consequent discomfort caused to everyone on board, when 12-inch and 6-inch guns are let off. The short 12-inch carried by these ships knocks hell out of you. I have tried every spot on deck to escape the concussion, running round like a scared rabbit whenever I see these monsters being trained on their invisible target. For hours afterwards my head aches as if to burst, and the wardroom looks as if a free fight had taken place in it, all the furniture being overturned, and the cabins full of dust and debris. I wish I could get on a ship without guns.'*

Ashmead-Bartlett had a short but interesting life. He was the eldest son of the American-born Conservative MP, Sir Ellis Ashmead-Bartlett, who served as Lord of the Admiralty between 1885 and 1892. At the age of 16, Ellis accompanied his father with the Turkish army in the war with Greece in 1897, and both were arrested in Crete. He was commissioned and served as a subaltern with the Bedfordshire Regiment in the Boer War. This lasted only a few months as he became so ill that he was sent home and spent seven months in hospital. This undisclosed malaise dogged him for the rest of his life.

He then continued his legal studies but quit to become a war reporter. His first assignment, and one that established him as an excellent reporter, was his account of the siege and capitulation of Port Arthur in the Russo-

Japanese War of 1904. He spent the next decade developing his political career, socialising in London and Paris, with the occasional spot of war reporting for Reuters in Morocco, first with the French and then with the Spanish as they carved up that part of Africa. He fought and lost two elections as a Conservative candidate, both in safe Liberal seats. He returned to war reporting for the *Daily Telegraph* in the Balkan Wars of 1912-13 and found himself in Bucharest when Britain declared war.

Returning home to volunteer for his old regiment, he was turned down on medical grounds. Instead, he went to Belgium to report before the strict censorship finally brought him back to London, where he got wind of the Royal Navy's activities in the Dardanelles. Using his father's previous position as First Sea Lord in Gladstone's government, he wrote to the current First Sea Lord, Winston Churchill on 11 March 1915 requesting permission to: *'accompany the forces to Constantinople'*. Thirteen days after his letter to Churchill, he received notice that his application had been approved.

During the build-up to the invasion of Gallipoli, Ashmead-Bartlett noted the average British soldier, who, with the exception of the Guards, was inclined to be small, pallid and under-nourished looking. He compared them to the newly arrived men from Australian and New Zealand, known collectively as the Anzacs, who:

> *'created an excellent impression with their fine physique and general bearing. A truly magnificent body of men; but their ideas of discipline are very different from those of our regular army. The men seem to discipline themselves, and the officers have very little authority over them through holding a military rank – personality plays a much more important role.'*

So began Ashmead-Bartlett's mutual admiration with the Anzacs.

Even before he had set foot on the Gallipoli Peninsula, Ashmead-Bartlett had gained a reputation for criticising the conduct of the campaign and Hamilton in particular. Convinced that the expedition was doomed to failure, he had a particularly irritating manner and imposed his views on anyone he could collar.

The invasion was now an open secret and the Turkish defenders had a pretty good idea when it would be launched. Finally, on the afternoon of 24 April, troops began to board the assembled armada. The 11th Australian Infantry had rehearsed the coming landing from the *London*, and now all

500 men came aboard and were given special treatment. Ashmead-Bartlett wrote:

> *'At seven o'clock dinner was served in the wardroom, where the Australian officers were entertained as our guests. Everyone feigned an unnatural cheerfulness, the wine passed round, not a word was said of what the morrow might bring forth, yet over the party there seemed to hover the dread angel of death. After this tragic repast we surrendered our cabins to our Dominion friends and snatched some sleep in the wardroom chairs.'*

At 2.30am, the big ships stopped two and half miles from shore. Four thousand Australian troops climbed down into the boats and the twelve steam pinnaces[3] set off for the shore towing four boats each. Ashmead-Bartlett wrote:

> *'Every eye and glass was fixed on the grim line of hills in our front, so shapeless, yet so menacing in the gloom, the mysteries of which the boats, looking so fragile and helpless, were about to solve...At 4.33am, there came a very sharp burst of rifle fire from the beach, and we knew that our men were at last at grips with the enemy.'*

Unknown to the witnesses on board the ships, the Australians had been landed at the wrong beach. Instead of the expected low sandbanks, the soldiers now faced steep cliffs and a narrow beach. Based on the reports of the returning sailors on the pinnaces, Ashmead-Bartlett began writing his report on the landing at Gaba Tepe, soon to become more famously known as Anzac Cove. Even though he was not on the spot until 15 hours later, it was a report that would immortalise him and the Anzacs:

> *'The Australians, who were about to go into action for the first time in trying circumstances, were cheerful, quiet, and confident. There was no sign of nerves nor of excitement.*
>
> *'As the moon waned, the boats were swung out, the Australians received their last instructions, and men who six months ago had been living peaceful civilian lives had begun to disembark on a strange and unknown shore in a strange land to attack an enemy of a different race...the boats had almost reached the beach, when a party of Turks,*

entrenched ashore, opened a terrible fusillade with rifles and a Maxim. Fortunately, the majority of bullets went high.

'The Australians rose to the occasion. Not waiting for orders, or for the boats to reach the shore, they sprang into the sea and, forming a sort of rough line, rushed at the enemy's trenches.

'Their magazines were not charged, so they just went in with cold steel. It was over in a minute. The Turks in the first trench were either bayoneted or they ran away, and their Maxim was captured.

'Then the Australians found themselves facing an almost perpendicular cliff of loose sandstone, covered with thick shrubbery. Somewhere, half-way up, the enemy had a second trench, strongly held, from which they poured a terrible fire on the troops below and the boats pulling back to the destroyers for the second landing party.

'Here was a tough proposition to tackle in the darkness, but those colonials, practical above all else, went about it in a practical way... They stopped for a few minutes to pull themselves together, got rid of their packs, and charged their magazines. Then this race of athletes proceeded to scale the cliffs without responding to the enemy's fire. They lost some men, but did not worry.

'In less than a quarter of an hour the Turks were out of their second position, either bayoneted or fleeing...But then the Australasians, whose blood was up, instead of entrenching, rushed northwards and eastwards, searching for fresh enemies to bayonet. It was a difficult country in which to entrench. Therefore, they preferred to advance.

'The Turks only had a weak force actually holding the beach. They relied on the difficult ground and the snipers to delay the advance until their reinforcements came up.

'Some of the Australasians who pushed inland were counter-attacked, and almost outflanked by the oncoming reserves. They had to fall back after having suffered heavy losses.

'These counter-attacks were continued by the Turks throughout the afternoon, but the Australasians did not yield a foot on the main ridge...Some idea of the difficulty may be gathered when it is remembered that every round of ammunition and all water and stores had to be landed on a narrow beach and carried up pathless hills and valleys several hundred feet high to the firing line.

'The whole mass of our troops was concentrated in a very small *area, and was unable to reply when exposed to a relentless and incessant shrapnel fire which swept every yard of ground. Fortunately much of the enemy's fire was badly aimed, and their shells burst too high.*

'A serious problem was getting the wounded from the shore. All those unable to hobble had to be carried from the hills on stretchers and then their wounds hastily dressed and the men carried to the boats. The boat parties worked unceasingly through the entire night... The courage displayed by these wounded Australians will never be forgotten. Hastily placed in trawlers, lighters and boats, they were towed to the ships, and in spite of their sufferings, cheered on reaching the ship from which they had set out in the morning.

'In fact, I have never seen anything like these wounded Australians in war before. Though many were shot to bits, without the hope of recovery, their cheers resounded throughout the night. You could see in the midst of suffering humanity arms waving in greeting to the crews of the warships. They were happy because they knew that they had been tried for the first time and had not been found wanting.

'For fifteen mortal hours our men occupied the heights under incessant shell fire, without the moral or material support of a single gun ashore, and were subjected the whole time to the violent counter-attack of a brave enemy, skilfully led, with snipers deliberately picking off every officer who endeavoured to give a command or lead his men...

'There has been no finer feat in this war than this sudden landing in the dark and storming the heights, above all holding on whilst the reinforcements were landing. These raw colonial troops in these desperate hours proved worthy to fight side by side with the heroes of Mons, the Aisne, Ypres and Neuve Chapelle.

'Early in the morning of April 26, the Turks repeatedly tried to drive the colonials from their position. The colonials made local counter-attacks, and drove off the enemy at the point of the bayonet, which the Turks never face.'

This report first appeared in the Australian newspapers on 8 May. Charles Edwin Woodrow Bean (known to the troops as 'Anzac Charley') had been selected by ballot as Australian official war correspondent, narrowly beating Keith Murdoch, father of Rupert. He had arrived on the beach at 10am and would have witnessed much of what the absent Ashmead-Bartlett wrote. Unfortunately, the staff at GHQ had not yet recognised Bean as an official correspondent and so his report was not published in Australia until 13 May.

Bean was a very diligent and pedantic man who made an ideal historian for the Anzacs, but was a dull reporter. In fact, several of the larger Australian newspapers stopped carrying Bean's copy due to its unappealing style. Bean acknowledged this and generously agreed: *'His* [Ashmead-Bartlett's] *written despatches are full of life and colour, hit hard, and give a brilliant idea which is remarkably true. He exaggerates a bit to make his points...and yet he's a lover of the truth.*

Bean wrote in his diary about Ashmead Bartlett's desire to embellish the Anzac's achievement:

'The success of an army like ours chiefly depends on what proportion of these strong independent-minded men there is in it. And in the Australia force the proportion is unquestionably undoubtedly high – may account to 50 per cent or more. I have seen them going up against a rain of fire and the weaker ones retiring through them at the very same time – the two streams going in opposite directions and not taking the faintest notice of one another.

'Well, this is the true side of war – but I wonder if anyone would believe me outside the army. I've never written higher praise of Australians than is on this page, but the probability is that if I were to put it into print tomorrow, the tender Australian public, which only tolerates flattery, and that in its cheapest form, would howl me out of existence. One has some satisfaction in sticking to the truth in spite of prejudice against it – the satisfaction of putting up some sort of fight. But I have the suspicion that I've spoilt my chances forever of being some day tolerably well off.'

The Australian historian, A.W. Bazley, wrote: *'Bartlett's dispatch was a brilliant one, despite a number of inaccuracies, and its publication in Australia led, I believe, to an immediate increase in the number of volunteers offering for the AIF.'*

When Ashmead-Bartlett did finally manage to get a lift on one of the pinnaces, he arrived at 9.30pm to: *'one of a scene of indescribable confusion. The beach was piled with ammunition and stores, hastily dumped from the lighters, among which lay the dead and wounded, and men so absolutely exhausted that they had fallen asleep in spite of the deafening noise of the battle.'*

He recognised General Birdwood, the Australian commander, and approached his group. Although Ashmead-Bartlett was in uniform, he was wearing an old green hat, which was enough to have him temporarily arrested as a spy. Fortunately his identity was confirmed by one of the crew of the pinnace and he was released.

As night fell it was touch and go whether the Turks would drive the Australians from their tenuous position just above the narrow beach and preparations were made to evacuate them at daybreak. In the event, they managed to hold out and consolidate their position. This confirmed Ashmead-Bartlett's growing admiration for the Anzacs.

Ashmead-Bartlett managed to get a ring-side seat for the much heralded assault on the Turkish held hill, Achi Baba and the village of Krinthia. The result of this clumsy frontal attack was 6,000 casualties and the possession of a few hundred yards of non-strategic ground. The reporter was getting angrier and more frustrated by the day. Unable to pass any comment in his censored reports, he had to confine himself to giving just a descriptive account of the attack. Ashmead-Bartlett was further disenchanted with General Hamilton's tactics and misplaced optimism. When the reporter pointed out before the battle that very large reinforcements would be needed, Captain Maxwell the Chief Field Censor, replied that he had asked for two more divisions but added: *'We must not worry the old man* [Kitchener] *too much. He is very pleased with us now and in time we shall get all we want out of him.'* Another example of the spectre of Lord Kitchener looming over the conduct of the campaign.

Another war correspondent who witnessed another landing was George Renwick of the *Daily Chronicle*:

'The most terrible of all the landings was that at V Beach, which is situated immediately to the west of Seddul Bahr. Between the village and No.1 Fort the ground, sloping down to the water, forms an amphitheatre with a radius of three or four hundred yards. The beach is only about ten yards wide and the ground behind rises to a height of about a hundred feet, sloping upwards in terraces…The great difficulty which presented itself at this point was that of getting men ashore under a fire which was certain to be extremely heavy, and to get them ashore quickly. It is not surprising that within sight

of the region where the wooden horse of Troy was employed, ancient history should suggest a means for landing the invading force that would be safer than the method employed elsewhere would have been. The counterpart of the Trojan Horse was the steamship River Clyde, *which could hold two thousand men. Big doors were cut in the side of the vessel, and from them were fixed gangways by which the men could reach the lighters forming a bridge to the shore after the vessel had run aground.*

'*The enemy's positions were first of all searched with heavy gun-fire from HMS* Albion. *When the bombardment was over, three companies of the Dublin Fusiliers were in their boats ready to be towed ashore. The boats were closely followed by the* River Clyde *which had on board the remainder of the Dublin Fusiliers, the Munster Rifles, half a battalion of the Hampshire Regiment, the West Riding Field Company and various details...The men in the boats rushed gallantly forward, but only very few of them reached the escarpment. The boats were quickly destroyed by the Turks' fire and the crews killed to a man.*

'*Now came the problem of getting the men ashore from the* River Clyde. *Against its iron sides thousands of bullets were rattling and under that heavy fire the lighters from the end of the gangway to the shore had to be placed in position. Not only did the heavy fire make the work highly difficult and dangerous, but there was also a strong current to contend with. Men who had been through the whole horrors of the Gallipoli campaign have told me that there was nothing quite so eerie and terror-inspiring as the time of waiting near one of the doors of the* River Clyde, *while bullets by the thousand were flattening themselves against the ship, waiting for the order to rush down the gangway swept by the enemy's fire.'*

Gaining a toe-hold on the beach, the task of getting more men ashore began again as darkness fell. After more desperate fighting, V Beach was eventually taken with an enormous loss of life.

At the end of May, the navy were alarmed at the increased activity of German submarines which had been sent to the Eastern Mediterranean. On 25 May, Ashmead-Bartlett witnessed the sinking of the battleship *Triumph* by the German submarine, *U-21*.[4] Two days later, he actually experienced first-hand a sinking vessel beneath his feet. He was staying aboard the old battleship, *Majestic*, a ship more renowned for her comfort than fighting capabilities, when she was hit by a torpedo from the same submarine despite being screened by other vessels.

Anchored off Cape Helles, Ashmead-Bartlett recalled the feeling of inevitability amongst the officers that they would be shortly torpedoed:

> *'We, on board, had no illusions as to our eventual fate, and in spite of these precautions felt no sense of security. Personally, I felt convinced the end was near. Tonight we agreed to have a kind of farewell dinner in the wardroom, in order to drink the few remaining bottles of champagne, as it would have been a tragedy had they gone down with the ship. The port was also saved in considerable quantities from a watery grave. There was one officer belonging to the* Majestic *on Lancashire Landing (W Beach) with a beach party, and he felt so certain about our fate, that he went round to his soldier friends and said, "Mind you are up early tomorrow morning, and you will see a sight you have never seen before – a battleship sunk by a submarine."'*

Ashmead-Bartlett also took the precaution of having his mattress brought up on deck so he would not be trapped in his cabin. Whether or not it was the effects of the amount of alcohol he consumed, he fell into a deep sleep only to be woken by a crew member calling: *'There's a torpedo coming'.* Then there was a dull heavy explosion on the port side. He wrote:

> *'The hit must have been very low down, as there was no shock from it felt on deck. The old* Majestic *immediately gave a jerk towards port, and remained with a heavy list; then there was the sound as if the contents of every pantry in the world had fallen at the same moment, a clattering such as I had never heard, as everything loose in her tumbled about. I could tell at once that she had been mortally wounded somewhere in her vitals, and felt instinctively she would not long stay afloat.'*

Ashmead-Bartlett managed to drop into the sea and reach an already overcrowded boat. Within minutes the stricken ship had turned turtle and sunk with the loss of fifty lives.

Unable to accept any more losses, the Navy withdrew its remaining battleships to the comparative safety of Mudros. Also, Hamilton and his staff were advised to establish their GHQ on Imbros instead of their headquarters staff ship, *Arcadian.*

Although he was rescued, Ashmead-Bartlett had lost all his kit. Getting a berth on a Malta-bound vessel, he decided to continue his journey and return to England to re-equip. On leaving Malta, he learned that Hamilton had cabled the Governor, Lord Methuen: *'Do not let Ashmead-Bartlett say a word about the Expedition, as he is a Jeremiah.'*

While he was in London, he dined with the Churchills and found Winston very depressed about Gallipoli and being replaced as Lord of the Admiralty. He met Sir Edward Carson who said it was important that he met certain ministers to explain the situation at Gallipoli. For a week, he had meetings with Prime Minister Asquith, Bonar Law, Arthur Balfour, who had replaced Churchill at the Admiralty, and even Lady Hamilton, wife of Sir Ian. He was asked by Asquith to write a memorandum which was discussed at the Cabinet meeting the following day. Ashmead-Bartlett attended Downing Street, but not the meeting, and was questioned afterwards by a couple of the ministers, including Lord Kitchener. He recalled: *'I found nothing in his attitude to inspire either fear or awe, rather a good-natured benevolence...'*

The reporter had a meeting with the Newspaper Proprietors' Association during which he had poured out his misgivings about the campaign. Northcliffe urged him to continue probing and exposing the shortcomings of the men in command. With the 'shell scandal' still rumbling on, Northcliffe wanted to discredit Kitchener further with the Gallipoli fiasco and in Ashmead-Bartlett he had a perfect ally.

With Ashmead-Bartlett absent, General Hamilton seized the opportunity to temporarily fill the vacancy with a writer of his choice. The man he chose was the Scottish author and playwright, Compton Mackenzie, who was a Royal Marine subaltern serving on the Staff.

Reluctantly, Mackenzie had to accept and reported to the Press Censor, who was the former *Daily Telegraph* war reporter, William Maxwell, now a captain in the Intelligence Corps. Mackenzie found Maxwell to be a self-important little man bearing a great resemblance to Tweedledum and who resented an amateur being foisted on the Fourth Estate. Maxwell, who had helped in the formation of the *Ladysmith Lyre* during the Boer War siege, now edited a daily sheet called *The Peninsula Press*, which Mackenzie disparagingly referred to as *The Dardanelles Driveller.*

Ashmead-Bartlett returned on 24 June and was annoyed to find that he could no longer enjoy naval hospitality and the comfortable life-style of the wardroom, but had to be based near GHQ on Imbros. He was joined at this time by another accredited correspondent, the 60-year-old veteran Henry Nevinson, who represented the *Manchester Guardian.*

With Nevinson's arrival, General Hamilton found he had an admirer. Their association had started in the Boer War and, being the same age, they were easy in each other's company. Hamilton even took Nevinson on a personally conducted tour which brought them within shooting range of the Turks. The general was barely fazed as he continued explaining his tactics.

All correspondents were now billeted in the same camp as the officers of the Manchester Regiment. Ashmead-Bartlett caused more resentment by bagging the prime position and having an elaborately furnished tent erected. Amongst the surrounding squalor, Ashmead-Bartlett maintained his taste for the fine things in life, including bringing a cook from Paris. He would often be seen dressed in a robe of yellow silk shot with crimson, reclining outside his tent and sipping champagne.

The Australian correspondent, C.E.W. Bean, asked Maxwell why all the correspondents had been rounded up and sited in one camp. He was told the reason was that they wanted to keep an eye on Ashmead-Bartlett.

Another anecdote, told by Compton Mackenzie in his book *Gallipoli Memories* to illustrate Ashmead-Bartlett's unpopularity, occurred when they were both walking to Divisional Headquarters. The journalist, who hated walking, decided to return to the beach leaving Mackenzie to go on alone. When he reached the camp he was alarmed to find it deserted. As he wondered what to do, a head popped out from a hole at his feet and exclaimed: *'Oh, it's you, Mackenzie. We thought it was Ashmead-Bartlett, and we didn't want to invite him to lunch.'* He then called out that the coast was clear and the rest of the Staff emerged from their hiding places.

Returning to the peninsula, Ashmead-Bartlett made many visits to Anzac Cove and met the new official correspondent for New Zealand, Malcolm Ross, whose own son, Noel, had been wounded in an earlier action and was now hospitalised in Egypt.

Ashmead-Bartlett witnessed the muddled landing at Suvla Bay on 7 August. Hamilton had asked for more troops and was supplied with 20,000 fresh soldiers. Sadly, he was saddled with: *'the most abject collection of generals ever congregated in one spot.*[5] The landings should have led to victory as the area was lightly defended thanks to the destination being kept a secret. He was accompanied by Henry Nevinson, and together they landed and witnessed the total confusion and aimlessness of the troops. Nevinson had walked right round the far side of the Salt Lake. His report was most discouraging:

> 'Our infantry are demoralised, weary, and absolutely refuse to advance. The muddle is beyond anything I have ever seen. Never since Nicholson's Nek and Lombard's Kopje [Boer War] have I seen British infantry behaving so badly.'

Ashmead-Bartlett felt that there was much to excuse them as…

> 'they could not stand the pangs of thirst any longer, burnt black, begrimed with dirt, with their tongues blackened, shrivelled, and lolling out of their mouths, their clothes in shreds, and many only in their shirt sleeves. Some, when they reached the sea, rushed into it, even swallowing the salt water… Confusion reigned supreme. No-one seemed to know where the headquarters of the different brigades and divisions were to be found. The troops were hunting for water, the staffs were hunting for their troops and the Turkish snipers were hunting their prey.'

The next day, he and Nevinson set off for Chocolate Hill and came to the attention of the Turkish gunners. Two shells burst close to them, one overhead and the other five yards away covering them with mud. As more followed, Ashmead-Bartlett dived into some reeds and sank up to his knees in mud, while more shells exploded around him. Fortunately, all the damage sustained was to their dignity.

A few days later, they again came under intense fire on Chocolate Hill. Nevinson received a wound during the bombardment when a burst from a Turkish shell caused a splinter to gash his head. Fortunately the thickness of his sun helmet lessened the impact but he was badly shaken. Ashmead-Bartlett was in a trench when a shell exploded just behind him, burying him in earth and rock. A soldier saw his plight and dug him out.

On another occasion, Ashmead-Bartlett, Nevinson and Lawrence were staying in the Suvla camp when they received a message to return at once to GHQ. As they made their way to the beach, another high explosive shell landed close by throwing Ashmead-Bartlett to the ground. He was beginning to think that the Turks were targeting him.

With the failure of the Suvla Bay landing, it was obvious that the army was in no state for more fighting. With winter on the horizon, the troops could look forward to months of misery confined to their cheerless trenches. Certainly, Ashmead-Bartlett thought the campaign was over for the time being and was anxious to return home. He got his wish but not in the way he expected.

In early September, an Australian correspondent, en-route to London, arrived to see first-hand the condition of the Anzac contingent. This was Keith Murdoch and his suspicions about the conduct of the campaign were soon realised. Within a short time, both he and Ashmead-Bartlett agreed that they should forcefully acquaint the British Government with the shambolic state of the campaign. With the knowledge that he was bypassing the censor, Ashmead-Bartlett wrote an outspoken letter and gave it to Murdoch to personally deliver to Whitehall. In the event of it being discovered, Ashmead-Bartlett coached Murdoch on all essential points.

In the letter dated 8 September, he wrote:

> *'Dear Mr Asquith...I consider it absolutely necessary that you should know the true state of affairs out here. Our last great effort to achieve some success against the Turks was the most ghastly and costly fiasco in our history since the battle of Bannockburn.'*

He then went on to list the failure of leadership, the selection of impossible points to attack and the throwing away of so many lives for nothing. It is now clear that Nevinson got wind of their intentions and, in a spirit of loyalty to Hamilton, wrote a letter exposing the plot. A cable was sent and Murdoch was intercepted by the military police at Marseilles where the letter was confiscated. Undeterred, Murdoch reached London and related the facts to the Australian High Commissioner. Ashmead-Bartlett was recalled to London and was able to add his strident voice to those calling for the evacuation of Gallipoli. His place was taken by Ward Price of the *Daily Mail*, who was chosen to represent the Newspaper Proprietors' Association.

C.E.W. Bean, commenting on Ashmead-Bartlett's letter, said he: *'...put the state of things in rather a crude light. It was a brilliantly written letter... rather overstating the case as Bartlett always does, but a great deal of it was unanswerable and badly needs understanding.'*

Although the newspapers knew of Ashmead-Bartlett's report, none was prepared to publish for fear on contravening the censor. One paper, however, broke ranks. This was the struggling *Sunday Times*, which got around the problem by presenting the report in the form of an interview, which did not breach censorship regulations. This was published on Sunday 17 October and caused a sensation. By Monday, all the papers produced extracts and Keith Murdoch called Ashmead-Bartlett to say he had cabled in full to the Australian press. Within a short time, Prime Minister Asquith, with the backing of those opposed to the Gallipoli landings, had ordered Kitchener to sack Hamilton and arrange a withdrawal from Turkey. On 14 October, Sir Ian Hamilton was recalled and by 23 November the government decided to evacuate Gallipoli by early December.

Weather that had been predicted as glorious turned out to be no more accurate than any of the military predictions. Blizzards and thunderstorms added to the soldiers' misery while they awaited the evacuation. Many suffered from frostbite and some drowned in the flooded trenches. Finally, over a month after the planned withdrawal, the last troops departed on 8 January 1916.

After this intense spate of lobbying, Ashmead-Bartlett contracted jaundice and spent a month in hospital. He was no longer a war correspondent – the military made sure of that. Another door opened for him and he was contracted to deliver 25 lectures in England and 75 in Australia and New Zealand. When he arrived in Sydney on 11 February 1916, he was greeted at the dockside by a large number of returned soldiers. Still the British War Office would not let go and he was visited by the local military censor and told he could not deliver the lecture until it had been screened. Ashmead-Bartlett handed over the carbon copies of all his articles and telegrams he had written from the Dardanelles – about fifty thousand words. Confronted with so much reading matter, the censor read 12 pages, gave up and passed the rest.

Although his ostentatious life-style gave the impression that he was something of a *dilettante*, Ashmead-Bartlett was, in fact, a very good, clever and energetic reporter. Nevinson and Bean were regarded as more accurate writers, but they lacked the sparkle of Ashmead-Bartlett's style despite the latter's lapses into exaggeration. What he wrote was largely accurate and unpalatable to the authorities. Although he was heartily disliked for his snobbery and arrogance, he nevertheless single-handedly exposed the incompetence and waste of life in this futile campaign. Significantly, he was one of the few accredited war reporters not to be honoured with a knighthood after the war.

During the following decade, he served as Conservative MP for North Hammersmith between 1924 and 1926, until bankruptcy forced his resignation. He returned to foreign reporting for the *Daily Telegraph*, visiting China, Russia, Palestine and India. He became ill while covering the Spanish Revolution and died in Lisbon on 4 May 1931, aged 50.

Notes

1 The first genocide in modern times was the extermination of the minority Armenian population of Turkey. The total number of people killed has been estimated at between 1 and 1.5 million.

2 Ian Hamilton had twice been considered but turned down for the Victoria Cross. The first time was during the defeat at Majuba in 1881 when he was told he was too young and would get another chance later in his career. The second was during the Battle of Elandslaagte during the Boer War on the grounds that he was too senior in rank.

3 Pinnace – small vessel used as a tender for larger ship.

4 U-21 was one of the most famous and successful submarines in the Imperial German Navy. She sank the cruiser HMS *Pathfinder* in September 1914, the first ship to be sunk by a submarine-launched self-propelled torpedo. In 1915, she sailed to Gallipoli, being the first submarine to be refuelled at sea. By the end of the war, she had sunk a total of 40 Allied ships.

5 *Damn the Dardanelles – The Agony of Gallipoli* by John Laffin.

Chapter 7

Shooting the Action

For newspaper correspondents, reporting the war had been an uneven struggle and the press were resigned to conforming to the military's strict rules. For another type of reporter, the photographer, the situation was even worse. On pain of execution, no civilian photographers were allowed near the front. The only official photographs permitted were those taken by a couple of Royal Engineer officers from the Photography Section.

Although it was frowned upon, some serving soldiers had carried cameras since first arriving in France. One regiment actually had its own photographer, Sergeant Christopher Pilkington of the Artists' Rifles. He was a former professional photographer who was attached to the 2nd Battalion, Scots Guards and he recorded their activities from training through to the First Battle of Ypres. Officers wishing to keep a personal record of their service favoured carrying the new Kodak Vest Pocket Autographic Camera, which could be folded flat and easily secreted in the large tunic pockets. The majority of these amateur photographs were taken during the period of 1915 to March 1916, after which the ban on personal photography was strictly enforced.

Most of these soldier/photographer images are amateurish, rather grainy and mostly anonymous. One exception was Lieutenant (later Major-General Sir) Edward Spears, a cavalry officer on the Staff who acted as the liaison officer with the French Army. He did take photographs of the French in action and a particularly memorable one of British soldiers advancing through the smoke and gloom at Loos. Following the lead of the Newspaper Proprietors' Association, the photographic agencies formed themselves into a similar organisation, the Proprietors' Association of Press Photographic Agencies, more conveniently abbreviated to PAPPA.[1] They negotiated with the government and reached a similar agreement to that made with the NPA, which allowed a rota system with a few accredited photographers.

Charles Masterman, who ran the War Propaganda Bureau at Wellington House, saw the great potential in have accredited photographers on the battlefield who could temper the grim surroundings with encouraging images of stalwart Tommies and lines of German prisoners.[2] Photographs were already being used in the *Daily Mirror* and popular magazines like *The Illustrated War News* and *War Illustrated* to show the positive and patriotic side of soldiering.

The first accredited photographer was Ernest Brooks, previously with the *Daily Mirror*. Born in 1878, he grew up near Windsor, where his father worked on the Royal Estate. As a child, he frequently encountered members of the Royal Family and after he left school at the age of ten, he went to work on the estate. One of his duties was to look after a mule given to Queen Victoria by Lord Kitchener.

When he was old enough, he joined the Army as a boy soldier in the 3rd Dragoon Guards. His first encounter with photography was when he left the army and took a position with Lady Vivian, the widow of Hussey, 3rd Baron Vivian. Her twin daughters each had a camera and Brooks was given the task of developing the plates.[3] This prompted him to buy a camera of his own and he began to take pictures of prominent people which he sold to various publications.

Encouraged to be making money, he returned to Windsor to work as a freelance news photographer. Using his contacts at the royal household, he was able to arrange access to the Royal Family. Within a short time, he was appointed their official photographer. In 1911, he accompanied King George V to India for the Delhi Durbar and, on his return, set up a studio close to Buckingham Palace.

On 25 January 1915, Brooks enlisted in the Royal Naval Volunteer Reserve. When the Gallipoli landings were being prepared, Brooks, as a professional photographer already in uniform, was appointed as official naval photographer.

He came upon Ellis Ashmead-Bartlett, who had just returned to Gallipoli after the sinking of the *Majestic*. While Ashmead-Bartlett was in London, he paid a visit to his literary agent, Hughes Massie, who suggested that he should take back a cinematograph to the Dardanelles:

'The idea fascinates me, but what about the authorities and my own ignorance of its use. The following day I went to see Alfred Butt, who has agreed to do the financing of the cinema, and I started taking

lessons this afternoon.[4] *It is an automatic machine which winds up, and you just turn it on when you have something to take. I was supplied with ten thousand feet of film, which is an immense load to lug around. However, for better for worse I shall try.'*[5]

Ashmead-Bartlett did use the camera at Anzac Cove, Cape Helles and Suvla Bay, but it was not until he ran into Ernest Brooks on 4 August that he realised he had been operating it incorrectly. Nonetheless, this 20 minutes of imperfectly filmed footage was preserved and has been digitally restored by the Australian War Memorial and Peter Jackson's Weta Digital company. It is the only newsreel film to have been taken during the Gallipoli campaign.

Ernest Brooks took over the chore of operating the Aeroscope after Ashmead-Bartlett survived a scare at Suvla:

'I left the battlefield at 8pm, stripped bare, with nothing left but my trousers and shirt. It came about in this way. About 5.50 the Turkish artillery fire on Chocolate Hill having diminished, I endeavoured to set up my cinema above the parapet of the partly destroyed trench to get some pictures of the wonderful panorama of the shellfire and burning scrub. The gunners were on me like a flash. I could not believe that they would have picked up a target so quickly. One shell whizzed past my head and stuck in the back of the trench without exploding. Then came another. I saw a bright flash and found myself in total darkness. I struggled to get clear but realised that I was buried. Shortly afterwards a spot of light appeared and I became conscious that I was being dug out. My benefactor turned out to be a soldier who had seen my mishap and who immediately ran to my assistance. I found the fuse of a high explosive shell lying on my legs but I had not received a scratch. My belongings did not fare so well. Owing to the heat, I had taken off my coat and placed it beside me with my small camera, walking stick, field glasses and waterbottle. They were blown to smithereens and, in any case, disappeared for ever. The infernal old cinema, of which I was heartily tired, the cause of all my troubles had, of course, survived and I was reluctantly compelled to drag it back to camp.'

Brooks and Ashmead-Bartlett experienced another peril with the Aeroscope:

'I left for Suvla Bay armed with my cinema, accompanied by Brooks, the official photographer who has returned from England...We went beyond Chocolate Hill into the front trenches, where the Turkish lines were about fifty yards away. We were out after pictures, and nearly caused a battle. Finding a trench occupied by an Irish battalion, Brooks asked them to assume positions just as if they were resisting an attack. But the men would look round at the camera. Brooks said: "That is not realistic enough." "Oh", exclaimed an Irishman, "I'll make it realistic." Whereupon he started to shoot at the Turks, followed by all his comrades. The day being perfectly quiet, the latter imagined we were about to attack, and replied furiously. A sustained duel then began and in all the excitement the Irishmen forgot all about us. Soon the Turkish artillery joined in, and it looked as if we had started a battle all along the line. They telephoned down from brigade headquarters to find out what was happening, whereupon one of the NCOs replied: "Oh nothing, sir; it is only the cinema". But I thought the matter had gone far enough, so we crept away to avoid the wrath of the divisional headquarters.'

March 1916 was notable for the issue of the first British steel helmet. It was also the appointment of the first official photographer. Ernest Brooks was transferred from the Admiralty to the War Office, given the honorary rank of second lieutenant and appointed the official photographer on the Western Front. He was soon followed by John Warwick Brooke, a former photographer with the Topical Press Agency. The favoured camera for use on the Western Front was the folding-plate Goerze-Anschultz, which was both robust and compact.

Warwick Brooke was born in London in 1886 but soon moved to Bristol to live with his grandparents. He joined the Royal Navy from school and had a somewhat chequered service career. He appears to have been a qualified signalman but blotted his copybook by going absent without leave several times, culminating in serving seventy days hard labour. When was able to leave the navy, he joined the Topical Press Agency off Fleet Street. He also joined the 2nd Regiment, King Edward's Horse, Special Reserve, at the Duke of York's barracks, Chelsea.

When war was declared, the regiment was mobilised, by which time

Brooke was a sergeant. They were sent to France on 5 May 1915 and joined the 4th Cavalry Brigade. On 14 January 1916, The *London Gazette* announced the awarding of the Distinguished Conduct Medal to:

> '606 Sergeant J.W. Brooke, King Edward's Horse. For conspicuous bravery and resource. Our communications were repeatedly cut by heavy shell fire, and most of the linesmen were killed or wounded. Sergeant Brooke continued to repair the wires regardless of personal danger, and it was owing to his courageous action that communication was maintained at a most crucial time.'

On 2 July 1916, Brooke was invalided out of the army, then given an honorary commission of lieutenant, in order to take up his new appointment as an accredited war photographer.[6]

Basil Clarke, the *Daily Mail* reporter who managed to evade the authorities for so long in 1914, knew Brooke and later wrote this about him:

> 'Lieutenant [Ernest] *Brooks's colleague on the British front in France is Lieutenant Brooke. The names are often confused, and it is one of the little jokes in the war zone to name each of the two official photographers "Brooks – or – Brooke".*
>
> *Brooke is quite a different type of man from Brooks. There is less of the bubbling merriment of boyhood about him, less wealth of joke and cheery anecdote, but he is a clever photographer and a sterling man. At the outbreak of the war, Lieutenant Brooke gave up his work as a Press photographer and joined King Edward's Horse as a trooper. He won quick promotion, and was decorated with the Military Cross (sic) for conspicuous gallantry in the field. Brooke was invalided out before he accepted an offer to take up photographic work again as official Army photographer. His work now is no less risky than before.'*

The photographers, unlike their writing comrades, were allowed to photograph what they liked. Censorship of their work only affected what photos could be published, not taken, thereby leaving them to generally choose their subject matter. The discarded unsuitable images were not deleted or destroyed, but put into storage. Later, these images were deposited and kept for posterity in the archives of the world's major war museums.

The date of Warwick Brooke's appointment, 2 July, is significant. This was the second day of the Battle of the Somme and it was immediately realised that Ernest Brooks could not record the whole of the British attack and needed another photographer. The demand on both men was heavy for they had to take as many and varied photographs as possible; a difficult task for just two men covering an army of two million and they were helped by men from the Photographic Section of the Royal Engineers.

Max Aitken, later Lord Beaverbrook, was determined that Canada's contribution to the war should be publicised and set up the Canadian War Records Office in London. He further used his considerable political influence to have Canada's own accredited photographer to record the Canadian Army on the Western Front.

April 1916 was when Canada's first photographer, Captain Harry Knobel, was appointed but his health failed after just two months. He was replaced in August by William Ivor Castle (formerly of the *Daily Mirror*). Castle lasted a year and was reprimanded for doctoring his images. While official faking of photos was relatively rare, orchestrated images were harder to avoid. The practical difficulties that photographers faced occupying a frontline trench full of men about to launch an attack across no man's land were immense. The way to overcome this was to film reconstructions in England, as in the case of the famous 1916 film, *The Battle of the Somme*. Very rarely were photographers on hand to record the real thing. The most serious faked photos of troops going 'over the top' were the work of Ivor Castle. Amongst other fakes was one of an aerial dog-fight where models were employed. A convincing famous battle scene was the surrender of German troops to the Canadians, merging two images into one. In November 1916, Castle sold a faked image of a knocked-out tank doctored to look as if it was in action for which he was paid £1,000 by the *Daily Mail*.

In June 1917, Castle was replaced by William Rider-Rider as Canada's accredited photographer. Born in London in 1889, he had worked at the *Daily Mirror* since 1910 and when attempting to volunteer for war service, he was rejected because of poor eyesight. He was recommended by Max Aitken and transferred to the Canadian Army as an accredited photographer in the French sector. Promoted to lieutenant, he then moved to the Canadian sector at Vimy Ridge and went on to cover the attack on Hill 60, the horrors of Passchendaele and the battles of 1918.

Australia was not far behind Canada in appointing its own official photographer. Taking a different approach to that of the Canadians, it was left to C.E.W. Bean, who assumed the mantle of media director, to employ Herbert Baldwin, a diminutive British photographer with the Central Press Agency, as the first accredited Australian photographer. He had considerable experience having covered the Balkan War 1912–13 and Mesopotamia in 1916. He and Bean visited the Somme battlefield on 23 November and that evening Bean wrote in his diary: *'He is not perfectly educated but a good chap with an opinion I have already learned to respect…a modest little chap, like many of them are not, in his line.'*

Bean and Baldwin worked together for the next eight months recording and documenting Australia's involvement in the war. Ever the historian, Bean considered Baldwin as a recorder of his observations and not as a war photographer. On 24 April, Baldwin was asked by General Sir William Birdwood, commander of the Australian forces to photograph the Canal du Nord:

> *'The day was hot and Baldwin, an English press photographer, ready for any adventure, but physically small and delicate, drank some of the canal water, which is believed to have been polluted by the Germans. A few days later he became seriously ill, and though he returned to the front for the battle of Messines, he was soon forced to give up his work and died a few years later.'*[7]

It has been suggested that Baldwin was already sick from his experiences in Mesopotamia but his condition worsened on the Western Front. Baldwin was present at the battle of Messines, his final consignment. During his eight months in France, he was plagued by chronic, often debilitating, anxiety made unbearable by the deafening barrage at Messines. He suffered from almost continuous diarrhoea, dramatic weight loss and high blood pressure. Sadly, he did not survive long after the war ended.

C.E.W. Bean replaced Baldwin with two photographers: Frank Hurley and Hubert Watkins. He was about to find out just how different one of them was to the pliant Baldwin.

Sydney-born, James Francis 'Frank' Hurley came with an impressive photographic pedigree. He was employed as official photographer on both the Mawson Australasian Antarctic Expedition between 1911–1914 and the Shackleton Imperial Trans-Antarctic Expedition of 1914–1916. With the latter, he is famously remembered for his 1915 photo of HMS *Endurance* trapped in Antarctic pack ice. The photographs had already made a big impression when they were shown at the Grafton Galleries in London in 1916.

From the start, Hubert Watkins was left to do the 'record photography' while Hurley concentrated on assembling a powerful collection of photographs, lantern slides and cine film suitable for mounting in a show that might compete with Max Aitken's Canadian Western Front Exhibition which was staged in the Grafton Galleries. There was great inter-colonial rivalry and Hurley saw his rival as Ivor Castle, who used a similar approach to photography. Hurley declared: *'Canada had made a great advertisement of their pictures and I must beat them.'*

His efforts to photograph a battle proved disappointing. In an essay on War Photography, he wrote:

'None but those who have endeavoured can realise the insurmountable difficulties of portraying a modern battle by camera. To include the event on a single negative, I have tried, but the results are hopeless... On developing my plate there is disappointment...All I find is a record of a few figures advancing from the trenches...and background of haze...Now if negatives are taken of all the separate incidents in the action and combined, some idea may be gained of what modern battle looks like.'

He often came under fire in order to get the result he wanted. He recalled:

'In spite of heavy shelling by Bosche, we made an endeavour to secure a number of shell burst pictures. Many of the shells broke only a few score paces away, so we had to throw ourselves into shell holes to avoid splinters...I took two pictures by hiding in a dugout and then rushing out and snapping.'

Resorting to using the photomontage combination technique to produce authentic looking battle scenes, he was soon in conflict with the dogmatic Bean who said it was a falsification of reality. Finally, in June 1917, Hurley was reassigned to cover the Palestine campaign and beyond Bean's reach. Here he was able to stage re-enactments against the more romantic background of the Holy Land. In 1918, he displayed his photographs at the Grafton Galleries, including a huge photographic image of the Battle of Zonnebeke, which measured 20ft by 15.6ft, and was a combination of twelve negatives.

Hubert Watkins continued to cover the war in France until the Armistice. On his way back to Australia, he broke his journey to visit and photograph, in colour and black and white, the battlefield on Gallipoli.

By 1918, there was not much for photographers of the stature of Ernest Brooks and Warwick Brooke to occupy themselves, so they spent most of the final year on the Italian campaign or working on naval subjects. Their places were taken by Tom Atkins and Armando Consolé. At this stage of the war, every available man not already in the trenches was likely to be in very poor physical condition, and so it was for Atkins and Consolé. Both suffered from bad health and for poor Consolé he did not last long when he lost a leg in a shell burst. Another photographer, who was a bit more robust, was David McLellan, another product of the *Daily Mirror*. He was appointed in December 1917, having been transferred from the Royal Flying Corps. His most famous photo was taken right at the end of the war and shows hundreds of men of 137 Brigade, 46th Division on the bank of the St Quentin Canal.

War photography came of age during the Great War and many of the images still have the capacity to move the beholder.

Notes

1 PAPPA was made up of Central News, Alfieri's, Central Press Photos, London News Agency, Sport and General Press Agency, Central Press Photos, News Illustrated, Topical and Barrett's.

2 The War Propaganda Bureau was better known by the name of its HQ, Wellington House.

3 One of the twins, Dorothy, married Douglas Haig.

4 Sir Alfred Butt was a London impresario.

5 The camera was the Aeroscope manufactured by Cherry Kearton Ltd. It was used extensively by the RFC for military purposes. The camera carried 400 feet of 35mm film and was used by many combat cameramen and several died filming from the front line. It was dubbed the 'camera of death'.

6 Curiously, the British gave their photographers the honorary rank of lieutenant, while the Colonial received the honorary rank of captain.

7 *Official History of Australia in the War of 1914-1918.*

Chapter 8

1916 – Build Up to The Somme

The war in France stagnated after the Battle of Loos and there were no more large scale attacks during the winter. The newspapers, unable to make much out of the miserable daily routine of the soldiers in the trenches, temporarily looked to other fronts for news. For the soldiers, death and destruction were still a daily reality and there was resentment that they were being forgotten by the media. William Beach Thomas, who arrived in France at the beginning of 1916, did write about their plight:

> '*Nothing imaginable is worse than the atmosphere of trench warfare. Men crouched in mud and are bashed out of existence by bits of metal thrown from miles away. The chemicals that explode destroy hearing, displace the heart and set the nerves in a quiver which may last lifelong.*'[1]

The Military Service Bill of January 1916, provided conscription for single men aged 18–41, and extended to married men in May. The war was now touching every fit male.

The realities of war could not always be reported. Censors deleted over-graphic descriptions of trench warfare and fudged casualty figures by concentrating on acts of heroism. Mass investitures were held at Buckingham Palace, where King George V dispensed gallantry medals. He was insistent that he personally decorate all Victoria Cross recipients even, as on one occasion, from his sick bed.[2]

During the dreary winter months, Philip Gibbs wrote about visiting the Sikhs and Gurkhas in their waterlogged trenches. He was of the opinion that they should never have been sent to such an inhospitable environment. On one occasion, the commanding officer of a Gurkha regiment thought it would be a morale boosting idea for Gibbs to review his men. Gibbs wrote:

'when I reminded him that I was only a war correspondent, without military rank, he said that his men would take me for a prince and would be well pleased.'[3]

The war reporters finally got to meet the replacement Commander-in Chief, Field Marshal Sir Douglas Haig, at the new GHQ at Montreil, near Le Touquet. The interview was not a great success, with Haig showing ill-disguised contempt for the gentlemen of the press. He could not see why facilities should be extended to them to record the progress of the war. Amongst the dismissive comments he made was: *'You want to get hold of little stories of heroism and so forth, to write them up in a bright way to make good reading for Mary Ann in the kitchen, and the man in the street.'*

Philip Gibbs could not let that pass and said that they were not writing just for: *'Mary Ann, but for the whole nation and that he could not conduct the war in secret, as though the people at home, whose sons and husbands were fighting and dying, had no concern in the matter.'* Gibbs spoke persuasively and with passion enough for Haig to change his attitude and allow the war reporters their demands for greater access. But this promise of a relaxation of the censorship took many months to filter down though the military system.

Haig remained an aloof and distant commander and one who did not inspire his men. In fact he was rarely, if ever, seen by the thousands of men who served under him. Occasionally, he rode out with an escort of lancers looking handsome but emotionless. As Gibbs later wrote of him:

'No man felt like dying for him, as the Old Guard did for Napoleon, or our men did for Wellington. To them he was a ghost beyond their reach or interest, and there was no thrill among them at the sight of him.'

Gibbs wrote in *Realities of War*, about the bitterness that regimental officers felt about the Staff at GHQ:

'GHQ lived, said our guest, in a world of its own, rose-coloured, remote from the ugly things of war. They had heard of the trenches, yes, but as the West End hears of the East End – a nasty place where common people lived. Occasionally they visited the trenches as society people go slumming, and came back proud of having seen a shell burst, having braved the lice and the dirt.'

As the long winter passed into 1916, morale in Britain and in the trenches declined alarmingly. A major war-ending offensive was needed, not only to lift spirits of the British public, but also to relieve pressure on the French Army, who were locked in an attritional battle at Verdun.[4] General Joffre pressed the British Government to stage a major diversionary offensive to serve as a drain on German manpower. Originally planned for 1 August, it was brought forward to 1 July at the insistence of the French. The British had little alternative but to comply with her ally's wish.

In early spring, William Beach Thomas had been taken to observe the action at St Eloi, to the south of Ypres. This was a particularly confusing encounter fought amongst the numerous water-filled mine craters which ended with many casualties and no gains. Once again Beach Thomas lapsed into 'nature-notes' mode when he described the scene from a distant mound:

'All I saw during this night and morning was of surpassing charm. A sensitive woman would have enjoyed every moment. Nature and art were combined in investing the spectacle with splendour.

'The sun rose, blood-red.

'The shrapnel hung like clouds painted by old masters to hold medieval angels.

'The horizon glittered with firefly sparks.

'In spite of the tumult the first songs of spring were twittered in the hedgerow. Good news reached us. All was well with the world.'

In fairness, he did contrast this bucolic scene with the hellish struggle going on below in the morass of St Eloi's craters.

Between early May and July, the first six divisions of Kitchener's New Army left England for France. These were the first of the civilians who had responded to Kitchener's call for volunteers and had endured months of muddle and hard training until they resembled disciplined soldiers. When they arrived in France, they would have been encouraged at the preparations that were being made for the anticipated 'big push'. The reporters observed the build-up to the offensive. Gibbs wrote:

'In the Spring of 1916 we could already see portents of things to come – battles on a larger scale than anything that had yet happened. The new battalions were pouring out with the fine flowers of our youth, full of high hopes for the "Great Push". New batteries

THE BOILING POINT.

Balkan Troubles – cartoon from *Punch*.

Granville Fortescue – the first reporter to alert the world of the German invasion of Belgium.

Albert Rhys Williams – 'Shot as a Spy' joke photo published as the real thing.

Colonel (later Major-General Sir) Edward Swinton – the military's 'Eyewitness'. He was credited with the development of the tank and the term 'no-man's land'.

Henry Hamilton Fyfe – one of the first to report the British retreat from Mons which led to his expulsion from France.

F.E. Smith (later Lord Birkenhead) – the first censor.

Philip Gibbs of the *Daily Chronicle*.

The famous recruiting poster that first appeared as a cover on the *London Opinion* magazine.

William Beach Thomas of the *Daily Mail*. From Country Matters to War Reporting.

Basil Clark of the *Daily Mail* – last of
the 'outlaws' to leave the Western Front.

Charles à Court Repington – *The Times'* military
correspondent and diarist.

Henry Wood Nevinson of
the *Daily Chronicle* – man
of peace who loved war.

Frederic Villiers – still covering wars in his seventies.

Ellis Ashmead-Bartlett – the London
Newspaper Proprietors' Association's
representative reporter in Gallipoli.

Cover of *Daily Mirror* – the spontaneous Christmas Truce 1914.

Lester Lawrence –
the myopic Reuters
reporter.

C.E.W. Bean and
Ashmead-Bartlett in
Gallipoli.

The end of Ashmead-Bartlett's billet – the
sinking of HMS *Majestic* on 27 May 1915.

Keith Murdoch – Ashmead-Bartlett's ally.

Compton Mackenzie – reluctant censor

Valentine Williams of the *Daily Mail* – won the Military Cross with the Irish Guards.

Sir Alfred Harmsworth, Lord Northcliffe circa 1917.

American-born Percival Phillips of the *Daily Express* – changed his nationality to receive a knighthood.

Henry Perry Robinson – the irascible *Times* reporter who bore an uncanny resemblance to Rudyard Kipling.

John Buchan – supreme propagandist.

William Beach Thomas (2nd right) and Henry Perry Robinson (right), with a British and two Belgian officers, examine dud shell in what looks like a flower bed.

The Censors – C.E. Montague and Captain Cadge.

C.R.W. Nevinson – whose Futurist-style suited the brutality of the war.

Louis Raemaekers – master of the black propaganda cartoon.

Paths of Glory – the banned painting by C.R.W. Nevinson

Charles Masterman – Head of Propaganda.

Paul Nash – painter of war-ravaged landscapes.

Ernest Brooks (left), photographer, with Geoffrey Malins, cinematographer.

John Brooke's famous image of a stretcher team struggling in the swamp of Passchendaele. Note the two extra men used to pull the bearers out of the mud.

Frank Hurley's doctored photo using three separate photographs of the 1917 Battle of Zonnebeke which incurred official displeasure.

Frank Hurley – official Australian
photographer

Ivor Castle – Canada's official photographer until
dismissed for doctoring his images.

Charles Bean and photographer Hubert Watkins.

Stanley Washburn with Polish refugees.

Arthur Ransome in official Russian war reporter's uniform.

Alice Schalek – Austrian correspondent with front line troops.

Photo taken in London in 1919 of T.E. Lawrence and Lowell Thomas.

Harry Chase – top American cinematographer.

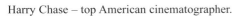

Floyd Gibson wounded under fire.

David McLellan's oustanding image of Brigadier General John Campbell VC addressing the 137 Brigade at the entrance to the Riqueval Tunnel on the St Quentin Canal, 2 October 1918.

Hohenzollern Bridge, Cologne 1919.

of field guns were camouflaged behind the lines. Heavy guns – nine-point-twos and fifteen inches – poked their snouts out of barns, or were hidden like black monsters behind trees and hedges. Ammunition dumps were piled up along roads from the coast. Casualty clearing stations were prepared and enlarged at Poperinghe, and other places away back to Etaples – a grim reminder that there would be a tide of blood in those coming battles. But the "Great Push" was still some months ahead and the routine of trench warfare went on.'

As well as the fresh troops of the New Army, there were men back from the Gallipoli campaign: Territorials, Canadians, Anzacs and the remnants of the old Regular Army. They were all welded into the new Fourth Army under the command of General Sir Henry Rawlinson, whose task was to produce a plan of attack.

The area chosen for the big push was near the River Somme, for no reason other than it was where the British line joined the French. When it came, the British would launch their attack along a 20-mile front from Curlu in the south to Gommecourt in the north. Here, the countryside was green and rolling and had not yet been laid waste like the flat land of Flanders to the north.

It was not just the British who were making preparations. The German High Command had warned its senior officers that one of the consequences of the Verdun assault would be relief attacks against their positions elsewhere along the front. Wherever these attacks occurred, the defenders could not expect reinforcements. In anticipation of heavy bombardments, the Germans started to construct extensive fortifications and deep shelters interconnected by tunnels. The wire in front of their positions was progressively added to until, as one officer observed, it was so thick that nothing could be seen through it.

While most concentrated on the land battle to come, another huge clash was taking place in the North Sea off the Danish coast of Jutland. On 31 May 1916, in what was an accidental meeting of the British Grand Fleet and the German High Seas Fleet, the latter inflicted greater material damage, managing to extricate itself and seek refuge in its home port. The British casualty toll was high: 6,094 sailors lost their lives as opposed to 2,551 Germans. The popular expectation of an outright victory had been dashed and there was disappointment throughout the Grand Fleet. On the other hand, the sailors of the *Kaiserliche Marine* were showered with honours and awards and there was an outpouring of triumphalism.

Unfortunately, the Admiralty handled the Press badly by releasing a statement that was both too little and ambiguous. Sir Edward Cook wrote:

> *'The Press was left to make what it could of the first news from the Battle of Jutland and it must be admitted that a mess was made of it. The Admiralty put out through the Press Bureau the bald facts and did not help the editors to interpret them. The result was not happy. Comments appeared like "the Germans had been credited with partial success", "the battle was an unfortunate incident – nothing more", "it is a check – not to the enemy but to our country". Another paper wrote: "This grave disaster and unlooked-for reverse" and "we must admit defeat. In the face of yesterday's news, the demand for the return of Lord Fisher to effective control of the Navy must again become insistent".[5]*
>
> *'Belatedly, the Navy reacted that it was the greatest victory since Trafalgar and criticised the Press for fixing upon the losses and ignoring the fact that the German fleet, aided by poor visibility, returned to port never again to confront the Royal Navy.'*

The material successes of the *Kaiserliche Marine* began to fade into insignificance in comparison with the crushing strategic success of the Royal Navy. The Germans never again emerged to threaten Britain's command of the sea. In time, posterity showed that the British won the Battle of Jutland.

Five days later, on 6 June, the nation was shocked to read of the death of one of its revered heroes, Lord Kitchener. Setting off on a diplomatic mission to Russia, his ship, the cruiser HMS *Hampshire*, struck a mine off Orkney. The weather was atrocious, blowing a force-9 gale, and there was little chance of picking up survivors. Kitchener was amongst the 643 drowned.

Not everyone mourned his passing. The editor of the *Manchester Guardian* remarked that 'as for the old man, he could not have done better than to have gone down, as he was a great impediment lately.' Lord Northcliffe agreed: *'the British Empire has just had the greatest stroke of luck in its history.'* Charles Repington was kinder, acknowledging his stature and popularity with the public, but noting that *'his old manner of working alone did not consort with the needs of this huge syndication – modern war. He made many mistakes. He was not a good Cabinet man. His methods did not suit democracy.'*

Meanwhile the build-up continued apace. Light railways were constructed to bring the railheads closer to the front line. Labour units were busily engaged in building and repairing roads, widening bridges and constructing camps for the half a million soldiers. Miners from the North-East and Cornwall began digging tunnels under no man's land to place tons of high explosives beneath the German trenches. Fortunately, this was a period when the Royal Flying Corps held mastery of the air and were able to keep the German spotter planes from observing this massive preparation. In contrast, the RFC photographed the German lines almost with impunity, which greatly aided the artillery.

General Rawlinson issued his final orders of 22 June. After a sustained premier bombardment, during which the German wire would be cut or flattened, the infantry assault would be launched. The artillery would then elevate their guns to bombard the enemy's second position. Both Haig and Rawlinson were convinced that the artillery would pave the way for the infantry's success. Rawlinson said: *'nothing could exist at the conclusion of the bombardment in the area covered by it.'*

Notes

1 *With the British of the Somme* by W.B. Thomas.
2 This was the famous bed-side VC awarded to Sergeant Oliver Brooks of 3rd Battalion, Coldstream Guards in the hospital train at Aire, France on 1 November 1915.
3 *The Pageant of the Years* by Philip Gibbs.
4 The Battle of Verdun started on 21 February 1916 and ended on 16 December 1916, making it the longest battle of the Great War.
5 Admiral of the Fleet Jackie Fisher had formerly been Lord of the Admiralty.

Chapter 9

1916 – The Somme

O
n 24 June, the first guns began firing in a bombardment that was to last until 1 July. It was the greatest bombardment in the history of the Royal Artillery in which over 1,700,000 shells were fired. The sound of such heavy and sustained fire reached southern England and even Hampstead Heath in London. Not only were the soldiers awaiting to attack in awe of it, so also were the war reporters. Henry Perry Robinson wrote:

'Never since the war had entered on its stationary phase in the existing positions had there been anything approaching the scope and intensity of the shelling and miscellaneous fighting which raged along a hundred miles front. It was only the overture; but it was stupendous and terrifying, even though what one saw or heard was only a small section of the dreadful whole.'[1]

Philip Gibbs wrote:

'The British attack began with the great bombardment several days before 1 July and was a revelation, to the German Command and to the soldiers who had to endure it, of the new and enormous power of our artillery.

'The number of batteries were unmasked for the first time, and the German gunners found that in "heavies" and in expenditure of high explosives, they were outclassed. They were startled, too, by the skill and accuracy of the British gunners whom they had scorned as "amateurs" and by the daring of our airmen who flew over their lines with the utmost audacity 'spotting' for the guns, and registering on batteries, communication trenches, cross-roads, railheads, and every

vital point of organisation in the German war-machine working opposite the British lines north and south of the Ancre.[2]

The sound and fury of the guns could not, however, mask the deficiencies of the mass bombardment. Each night, small groups of infantry went into no man's land to inspect the damage to the German wire. Some reported that it was badly damaged but most stated that it was unbroken. Despite these unpromising reports, there was no suggestion the attack should be postponed. Another problem was the number of dud shells that had just landed, unexploded, in the mud:

'Britain had been late in developing high explosive projectiles, and those in the hands of the British artillery in 1916 suffered from a variety of faults caused by poor materials, poor design, and rushed production...in the haste to overcome these a number of mistakes in design and manufacture were made which had serious consequences in the battles of 1916.'[3]

In the early morning of 1 July, Philip Gibbs stood with a mass of cavalry opposite the German-held village of Fricourt, and recalled:

'Haig as a cavalry man was obsessed with the idea that he would break the German line and send the cavalry through. It was a fantastic hope, ridiculed by the German High Command in their report of the Battles of the Somme, which afterwards we captured.

'In front of us was not a line but a fortress position, twenty miles deep, entrenched and fortified, defended by masses of machine-gun posts and thousands of guns in a wide arc. No chance for cavalry! But on that night they were massed behind the infantry. Among them were the Indian cavalry, whose dark faces were illuminated now and then for a moment, when someone struck a match to light a cigarette.

'Before dawn there was a great silence. We spoke to each other in whispers, if we spoke. Then suddenly our guns opened out in a barrage of fire of colossal intensity. Never before, and I think never since, even in the Second World War, had so many guns massed behind any battle front. It was a rolling thunder of shell fire, and the earth vomited flame, and the sky was alight with bursting shells. It

seemed as if nothing could live, not an ant, under that stupendous artillery storm.'

On 30 June, the war correspondents were paid an unprecedented visit at their billet in Amiens by General Charteris, the Chief Officer of Military Intelligence. He told them of the arrangements that had been made for them to view the coming battle and, significantly, the permission to use official wires during the first day. On the face of it, this seemed to be everything the newsmen could have wished.

After the rain of the previous week, 1 July dawned bright and cloudless. Assembling at their vantage point on a ridge near the town of Albert, the reporters saw the climax of the tremendous artillery barrage with the detonation of an enormous mine at La Boiselle under the German lines. They were too far away to hear the whistles blown by the officers as they climbed the ladders out of their trenches and led their men towards the enemy lines. Weighed down with over 60lbs of equipment, the soldiers had been told to walk across no man's land as they would meet little resistance. Soon they disappeared into the dust and smoke that covered the battlefield. As with the Battle of Loos, the correspondents had to make some assumptions as they could not actually see the fighting. Unlike Loos, however, they were fed a constant stream of official information, which they then relayed directly over the telegraph to London. The result was the public were told that the battle was going well and the German lines had been penetrated.

John Buchan described the battle:

'The British moved forward in line after line, dressed as if on parade; not a man wavered or broke ranks; but minute by minute the ordered lines melted away under the deluge of high explosives, shrapnel, rifle, and machine-gun fire. The splendid troops shed their blood like water for the liberty of the world.'

Philip Gibbs reported:

'Our bombardment had done great damage and had smashed down the enemy's wire and flattened his parapets. When our men left their assembly trenches and swept forward, cheering, they encountered no great resistance from German soldiers, who had been hiding in their dug-outs under our storm of shells.'

In fact only the last statement was accurate. Once the barrage was lifted, the Germans raced from the protection of their bunkers, set up their machine-guns and mowed down the lines of walking Tommies. Those who did reach the German wire would find it largely intact and, with nowhere to shelter, were cut down by the chattering machine-guns.

All this was invisible to the watching reporters, who were buoyed up by the encouraging news that was reaching them. Beach Thomas recalled the spirit of triumph of hope over reality: *'Staff Officers and observers behind were peering through the smoke and confusion for evidence of the progress of the day and almost all decided that things were going well.'*

The first report received was forwarded by the correspondents via official wire:

> *'British Offensive – At about 7.30 o'clock this morning a vigorous attack was launched by the British Army. The front extends over some 20 miles north of the Somme. The assault was preceded by a terrific bombardment, lasting about an hour and a half. It is too early to as yet give anything but the barest particulars, as the fighting is developing in intensity, but the British troops have already occupied the German front line. Many prisoners have already fallen into our hands, and as far as can be ascertained our casualties have not been heavy.'*

One of the regular accredited correspondents, Percival Phillips of the *Daily Express*, had been taken ill and returned home. His place was taken by John Duguid Irvine, a veteran political reporter who had never witnessed a battle. Using the official report, he seems to have got carried away by the excitement, embellishing it with:

> *'A perceptible slackening of our fire soon after seven was the first indication given to us that our gallant soldiers were about to leap from their trenches and advance against the enemy. Non-combatants, of course, were not permitted to witness this spectacle, but I am informed that the vigour and eagerness of the first assault were worthy of the best traditions of the British Army. I have myself heard within the past few days men declare that they were getting fed up with life in the trenches, and would welcome a fight at close quarters...*

'We had not long to wait for news, and it was wholly satisfactory and encouraging. The message received at ten o'clock ran something like this: "On a front twenty miles north and south of the Somme we and our French allies have advanced and taken German first line trenches. We are attacking vigorously Fricourt, La Boiselle and Mametz. German prisoners are surrendering freely, and a good many have already fallen into our hands."'

This was the up-beat tone conveyed by all the war correspondents to their editors. As they were positioned three miles back from the front line and could see very little through their binoculars, they were all, in effect, conveying what they were told by the military.

William Beach Thomas produced a touch of common sense in his flowery style when he wrote:

'Such a view of battle gives no hint of the fortune of the day; and men in high places were as ignorant as we. No true news was known by anyone for hours. One division could not tell its neighbour division where the men were or how far the trenches were won. Flashes of hope, half-lights of expectation, hints of calamity only penetrated the smoke and dust and bullets that smothered the trenches. The tension was unendurable. The telephones, the carrier pigeons, the guesses of direct observers, the records of the runners, the glimpses of the air-men, all combined could scarcely penetrate the fog of war. The wounded who struggled back from German trenches themselves knew very little.'

The reality of what was happening on the battlefield was somewhat different from what was fed to the correspondents. For instance, at Fricourt, the closest objective to the watching reporters, the men of the Yorkshire regiments in the 50th Brigade, 17th (Northern) Division, suffered hugely in the assault on the village. Whole lines of Green Howards fell in the first 50 yards and, within three minutes, they had 351 casualties. Two companies of men of the 10th West Yorkshire Regiment were cut down by a single burst of machine-gun fire. By the time Fricourt was captured, the West Yorks casualty toll was the highest suffered by a single battalion on that terrible first day: 22 officers, 750 other ranks, including 400 killed. Another grim statistic included the death of the youngest soldier, 16-year-old Albert Barker of 7th East Yorks.

Philip Gibbs summed up the first day:

'And so, after the first day of battle, we may say with thankfulness; all goes well. It is a good day for England and France. It is a day of promise in this war, in which the blood of brave men is poured out upon the sodden fields of Europe.'

While the war correspondents peered into the obscured field of battle from their hill behind the front line, two cameramen were recording the battle from the front line.

In March 1915, the British Kinematograph Manufacturers' Association obtained permission from the War Office to allow two cameramen to film on the Western Front. The chosen men were Geoffrey Malins and Edward Tong. Both were given the honorary rank of lieutenant and left for France in November 1915. Together, they made twenty-six short films of the British Army behind the lines. Unfortunately, Tong fell ill in early June 1916 and was repatriated to England, never to return.

Geoffrey Malins had started his career as a portrait photographer but, in 1910, joined the Clarendon Film Studios as a cameraman. With the outbreak of war, he became a freelance cameraman filming in Belgium and France. At the beginning of June 1916, the War Office and Propaganda Bureau decided that there should be a film made of the coming Somme 'big push', which was fully expected to be a British victory. A replacement for Tong was found in the shape of another experienced cameraman, John Benjamin McDowell, who joined Malins in the Somme sector on 23 June. Unlike Malins and Tong, he was not given an honorary commission.

The two cameramen set to work filming the preparations for the offensive. They used the suitcase-sized Pathé 35mm film movie cameras, which were screw-mounted on sturdy tripods. The inbuilt motors were unreliable, so the cameras were usually hand-cranked, which required hard concentration to avoid speeding up, especially under fire. The cameras were heavy and awkward to manipulate. Also the nitrate 35mm film was highly inflammable and dangerous to use in a confined space.

Commencing on 26 June, they filmed the preparatory artillery bombardment and the troops and equipment making their way to the front. The two men split the coverage, with Malins filming the northern sector around Beaumont Hamel and McDowell working in the south near Fricourt with the 7th Division. Before the battle, Malins filmed troops on the march waving cheerfully at the camera, horse-drawn vehicles of every kind and the heavy guns west of Gommecourt.

At the suggestion of General de Lisle, the commander of the 29th Division, Malins positioned himself at Jacob's Ladder near the White City trench system. This gave a good view of the attack on Beaumont Hamel. German shells were falling around the communication trench as he made his way forward to Jacob's Ladder. He then had to rise above the parapet to remove sandbags and set up his camera, which he then camouflaged with sacking. On 1 July, Malins filmed men of the Lancashire Fusiliers waiting to advance from a sunken road in no man's land, before returning to his camera set up at Jacob's Ladder. From here, he filmed the detonation of the huge Hawthorn Ridge mine which shook the area like an earthquake. He also shot a well-known scene of a soldier carrying a wounded comrade down a trench packed with soldiers. Later that day, a shell landed nearby and damaged the tripod which Malins repaired in time to film the sadly-depleted roll-calls in the evening.

By 9 July, Malins and McDowell had shot 8,000ft of footage. In spite of the difficulties and risks, enough action was taken to edit into a full-length feature film lasting 77 minutes. On 21 August, the first public screening of the completed film, entitled *The Battle of the Somme*, was shown simultaneously in thirty-four London cinemas. Soon it was playing to packed houses throughout Britain and the Empire. It made Malins the most famous cameraman of the First World War although, to his shame, he did not acknowledge McDowell's considerable contribution.

Malins continued filming in France but in 1917 he fell ill and returned to England. During his work near the front, he had received several wounds and been gassed. It is quite possible that he suffered from shell shock, for he briefly returned to France, but was again invalided out and discharged as unfit for service. McDowell continued filming until the end of the war and did receive his honorary commission in June 1918. At the end of the war, both men were awarded the Military Cross and the OBE.

By the end of the first day of the Somme battle, it was not clear whether the British had failed or had won. In some sectors gains had been made, while in others, particularly in the north around Gommecourt, the attacks had been repulsed, with heavy losses. Just how heavy these losses were was later revealed with the British suffering some 57,470 casualties, of which a third were killed, the highest number in any battle. The only noticeable success was south of the Somme where the French Army had taken all their objectives. In fact they gained another objective. General von Falkenhayn, the Chief-of–Staff of the German Field Army, recognised the huge effort being put into penetrating the line at the Somme and began moving men from Verdun, 125 miles south-east of the Somme front. By weakening the pressure at Verdun, he eventually conceded victory to the French.

Beach Thomas, writing the following year, still preferred the suppression of the huge losses when he wrote: *'it is a pity that wholly fantastic stories of British losses spread abroad, to be afterwards reported in German wireless messages to neutral countries…The courage, the calmness, the cheerfulness of the British soldier was the theme of France.'*

When most people refer to the Somme, they think of the first day with its truly grisly statistic. In fact the battle had just begun, with more hard-fought battles to be won until it ended on Sunday, 19 November.

The following day, as if shocked by the enormity of their losses, both sides took a pause to consolidate. Fighting still continued but on a smaller scale. The casualties, however, continued to mount. *The Times* published the lists of those killed: 3 July, 143 officers, 914 ORs; 24 July, 600 officers, 5,500 ORs; 21 and 31 August filled five full columns.

Despite the distressing list of casualties, the newspapers continued to put a spin on upbeat news. Taken at random, the headlines on page two of the *Daily Mirror* dated 7 September 1916 proclaim: OUR TROOPS WIN THE WHOLE OF LEUZE WOOD – FRESH RUSSIAN SUCCESS ON ROAD TO LEMBERG – GERMANS FAIL TO RECOVER LOST POSITION – AUSTRIAN LINE STORMED AND DESTROYED – BRITISH AIRMEN BLOW UP SUBMARINE – RUMANIANS REPULSE FOE – GUILLEMONT WON THROUGH HEAVIEST BOMBARDMENT IN HISTORY – HUNS ADMIT HEAVY LOSSES.

The next major assault was against Bazentin Ridge, which ran between Longueval to Bazentin-le-Petit village. On the night of 14 July, over 22,000 men of the 3rd, 7th, 9th and 21st divisions managed to creep forward in silence until they were close to the German line. After a barrage at 3.20am, the troops surged forward and took the Germans by surprise. Once again, the initiative was lost and the Germans were able to counter-attack, retaking many of their positions.

Philip Gibbs was on hand to deliver a report on an attack he was helpless to observe:

'The attack was to begin before dawn. Behind the lines, as I went up to the front in darkness, the little villages of France were asleep. And

*at 3.30 there was a sudden moment of hush. It was the lifting of the
guns and the time of attack. Over there in the darkness by Mametz
Wood and Montauban thousands of men, the men I had seen going
up, had risen to their feet and were going forward to the second
German line, or to the place where death was waiting for them,
before the light came...*

*'A new sound came into the general din of gunfire. It was a kind
of swishing noise, like that of flames in a strong wind. I knew what it
meant. "Enemy machine guns," said an artillery observer, who had
just come out of his hole in the ground. There must have been many
of them to make that noise.*

*'At about 4.30 I heard another furious outburst of machine-gun
fire in the direction of Longueval, and it seemed to spread westwards
along the Bazentin-le-Grand and Bazentin-le-Petit. I strained my eyes
to see any of our infantry, but dense clouds of smoke were rolling over
the ground past Contalmaison and between Mametz and Bazentin
Woods. It would seem we were putting up a smoke barrage there, and
later a great volume of smoke hid the ground by Montauban.'*

John Buchan, ever mistakenly up-beat, wrote:

*'The attack failed nowhere. In some parts it was slower than others,
where the enemy's defence had been comprehensively destroyed, but
by the afternoon all our tasks had been accomplished. The
audacious enterprise had been crowned with unparalleled success.
Germans may write on the badges that God is with them* [Gott Mit
Uns], *but our lads – they know.'*

Towards the end of the day's fighting, Haig got his wish to involve the
cavalry. In an effort to take High Wood, which had been abandoned and then
reoccupied by the Germans, the sabres of the 7th Dragoon Guards and the
lances of the Indian 20th Deccan Horse were rashly ordered to attack.
Gibbs's report appeared in the *Daily Chronicle*:

*'For a little while – yes, and even now – it seemed something rather
marvellous. We have broken through the enemy's second line:
through and beyond on a front of two and a half miles, and for the
first time since October 1914 cavalry has been in action...*

'It was about 6 o'clock in the evening that some British cavalry came into action. They were men of a small detachment of Dragoon Guards and also the Deccan Horse. They worked forward with the infantry on a stretch of country between Bazentin Wood and Delville Wood, rising up to High Wood, and then rode out alone in Reconnaissance, in true cavalry formation with commander in the rear.

'So they rode on into open country, skirting Delville Wood. Presently a machine gun opened fire upon them. It was in a cornfield, with German infantry, and the officer in command gave the word to his men to ride through the enemy. The Dragoons put their lances down and rode straight into the wheat. They killed several men, and then turned and rode back, and charged again, among scattered groups of German infantry. Some of them prepared to withstand the charge with fixed bayonets. Others were panic-stricken and ran forward crying "Pity! Pity!" and clung to the saddles and stirrup leathers of the Dragoon Guards. Though on a small scale, it was a cavalry action of the old style, the first on the Western Front since October of the first year of the war.'

Gibbs is mistaken in writing that the Dragoon Guards carried lances: it was the Deccan Horse who were the lancers:

'With 32 prisoners our men rode on slowly still reconnoitring the open country on the skirt of Delville Wood, until they came again under machine-gun fire and drew back. As they did so an aeroplane came overhead, skimming very low, at no more than 300 feet above ground. The cavalry turned in their saddles to stare at it for a moment or two, believing that it was a hostile machine. But no bullets came their way, and in another moment it swooped over the German infantry concealed in the wheat and fired at them with a machine gun. Four times it circled and stooped and fired, creating another panic among the enemy, and then it flew off, leaving the cavalry full of admiration for this daring feat.'

This brief action was down-played by the military and the reports may have been censored. What actually happened was that the cavalry came under fire from a machine gun in a field of wheat in front of High Wood. The Deccan Horse charged uphill, which slowed down the horses, and attacked the enemy position. They captured a few who surrendered but came under fire from machine guns firing down from High Wood. It was a fruitless waste of life which left 102 men killed along with 130 horses. It was thanks to the Royal Flying Corps pilot that the remainder managed to escape.

With the north of the British line still held at their starting point by the stubborn German resistance at Beaumont Hamel and Thiepval, the next major attack was again concentrated in the centre. On 15 September, a third attempt was made to break through the enemy's lines extending the gains made on 14 July. The objectives were to take the villages of Courcelette and Martinpuich standing either side of the Bapaume Road, clear High Wood and push on to Flers. The attack is significant in that it was the first time that tanks were to be used in battle. The tank was the brainchild of Lieutenant Colonel Ernest Dunlop Swinton, who had been appointed as 'Eyewitness' by the War Office until the newspaper correspondents were regarded as reliable enough to be trusted to toe the line. In a little over a year the first model Mark I tank was thought ready to be used in battle, despite unresolved teething problems.

Colonel Swinton was given responsibility for training the first tank units, drawing personnel from the Machine Gun Corps and drivers from the Army Service Corps. Officers were selected from volunteers. If first appearances promised a safe and fairly comfortable billet as a crewman, then they were in for an unpleasant awakening. The crew of officer, driver and four gunners were squeezed around an unsilenced and unshielded engine that filled the tank with fumes. The noise was deafening and instructions had to be made by hand. Vision was extremely limited and the temperature sometimes reached 128°F. Another downside was that, although armoured, the impact of small-arms fire on the hull caused small pieces of metal called 'splash' to fly around inside causing wounds and damaging machinery.

Once again, the Germans endured a heavy preliminary bombardment. The British artillery were now better equipped and had learned from previous bombardments to employ the creeping barrage, which gave the infantry a better chance to reach the German lines more or less safely. The tanks arrived at their assigned start positions, but already their unreliability was in evidence. Of the 49 ordered, only 32 were able to reach the start. As they were moved forward, a further seven failed to start. The remaining 25 trundled off to their appointed positions with the attacking divisions.

The first tank ever to see action advanced up the road from Delville Wood to Ginchy. Its formidable appearance and the fact that it had been kept secret, persuaded the Germans to throw up their hands in surrender. As one defender put it: 'the Devil is coming'. Unfortunately within a short time, the tank was struck with two shells and put out of action.

Percival Phillips wrote in the *Daily Express* on 18 September: '*Sinister, formidable and industrious, these novel machines pushed boldly into No Man's Land, astonishing our soldiers no less than they frightened the enemy.*'

At High Wood, the three tanks assigned to help the 47th (London Territorial) Division clear the wood were soon put out of action.[4] Elsewhere, the performance of the tanks was patchy. They did, however, create a psychological advantage over the Germans which the infantry was able to exploit. For the war correspondents, the tanks became a welcome subject to enliven their reports.

William Beach Thomas again waxed lyrical: '*The tanks moved into the wood like obscene monsters, but even they could not face the music or thread the maze.*'

Philip Gibbs wrote of the way this newcomer to warfare had lifted the attackers' morale:

> '*Many of them went over, too, in the greatest good humour, laughing as they ran. Like children whose fancy has been inflamed by some new toy, they were enormously cheered by a new weapon which was to be tried with them for the first time – "the heavily armoured car" mentioned already in the official bulletin.*
>
> '*The description is a dull one compared with all the rich and rare qualities which belong to these extraordinary vehicles. The secret of them was kept for months jealously and nobly. It was only a few days ago that it was whispered to me…*
>
> '*It appeared, also, that they were proof against rifle bullets, machine-gun bullets, bombs, shell-splinters. Just shrugged their shoulders and passed on. Nothing but a direct hit from a fair-sized shell could do them any harm…*
>
> '*I have seen them, and walked around them, and got inside their bodies, and looked at their mysterious organs, and watched their monstrous movements.*'

One can imagine the impact this had on the readers. It must have seemed as if the machines from H.G. Wells's 1898 book, *War of the Worlds*, had come to life. In fact, Beach Thomas did liken the tank to another fictional beast:

'"Autos blindés" is the French term. They looked like blind creatures emerging from the primeval slime. To watch one crawling round a battered wood in the half-light was to think of "the Jabberwocky with eyes of flame who came whiffling through the tulgey wood and burbled as it came".'

Beach Thomas's colourful writing was almost beyond parody, and one publication managed to capture his inimitable style; 12 February 1916 saw the debut of the trench newspaper, *The Wipers Times*, edited by Captain Fred Roberts and Lieutenant Jack Pearson of the 12th Battalion, Notts and Derby (Sherwood Foresters) Regiment. Using a 'liberated' print press, they began a weekly satirical paper, which used the cathartic power of comedy to cheer up the men in the trenches. They poked fun at pompous staff officers, offered tongue-in-cheek advice, produced limericks and advertised fantastic inventions like: *'the new Combination Respirator and Mouth Organ. The dulcet tones of the Mouth Organ will brighten even the worst Gas Attack.'* They wrote spoof Sherlock Holmes serials, made terrible puns and generally made life in the trenches a little more bearable.

One of the paper's targets was the *Daily Mail*'s man at the front, William Beach Thomas. The editors resorted to their usual way of parodying their targets by reversing the first letters of the victims name – thus Teech Bomas was born. The 1 December 1916 edition carried this report:

HOW THE TANKS WENT OVER
By Our Special Correspondent
Mr.Teech Bomas
'In the grey and purple light of a September morn they went over. Like great prehistoric monsters they leapt and skipped with joy when the signal came. It was my great good fortune to be a passenger in one of them. How can I clearly relate what happened? All is one chaotic mingling of joy and noise. No fear! How could one fear anything in the belly of a perambulating peripatetic progolodymythorus. Wonderful, epic, on we went, whilst twice a minute the 17in gun on the roof barked out its message of defiance. At last we were fairly amongst the Huns. They were round us in millions and in millions they died. Every wag of our creature's tail threw a bomb with deadly precision, and the mad, muddled murderers melted. How describe the joy with which our men joined the procession until at last we had a

train ten miles long. Our creature then became in festive mood and, jumping two villages, came to rest in a crump-hole. After surveying the surrounding country from there we started rounding up the prisoners. Then with a wag of our tail (which accounted for 20 Huns) and some flaps with our fins, on we went. With a triumphant snort we went through Bapaume pushing over the church in a playful moment and then steering a course for home, feeling that our perspiring panting proglodomyte had thoroughly enjoyed its run over the disgruntled, discomfited, disembowelled earth. And so to rest in its lair ready for the morrow and what that morrow might hold. I must get back to the battle.'[5]

In the edition of 15 August 1917, entitled 'WE ATTACK AT DAWN', Mr Teech Bomas wrote:

'All was still as the first flush of dawn lit the sky. Then suddenly the atmosphere was riven by the crescendo chorus which leapt to meet the light as a bridegroom to his bride. The delicate mauve and claret of the dawning day was displaced by a frothy and furious fandango of fire. The giant troglolythic ichnyosaurus crept fawning from their lairs, and gambolled their way to the line oblivious of anything that barred their passage. The disgruntled bosom of mother earth heaved with spasmodic writhings as the terrible tornado tore the trees. I was picking wallflowers in Glencorse Wood when all this happened...'

Things did not always run smoothly between reporter and editor. Henry Perry Robinson, prickly at the best of times, received a stiff letter from *The Times* editor, Geoffrey Dawson, in which he concluded:

'I write all this for fear you should have any lingering idea that we in the office did not appreciate your work. On the contrary we are all agreed that it has been quite first-rate. What is more, it is universally approved by the Army which is more than can be said for your more picturesque colleagues.

'But I must confess I am very nervous about your proposal to run over to England for a few days now. I wrote to you on this subject, I think, on Friday. If you are really in danger of breaking down we must of course do the best we can. But it does seem to me a thousand pities

that there should be a gap in our correspondence just now in the middle of this tremendous battle.'

In the event, Perry Robinson did stay on and was still reporting from France in 1918.

Despite the presence of the tanks, the hoped for breakthrough was not achieved. All the British public's expectation of a victory before Christmas came to nought and the mood of despondency returned. Philip Gibbs sensed that the newspaper reports had exaggerated the gains the battle achieved when he wrote: *'It is only the beginning. People at home must not think that the German army has lost its power of defence and that a great rout is at hand.'*

One corporal, Albert Rochester, who had been wounded on the Somme, tried to describe the plight of the average soldier in a letter to the *Daily Mail*. The letter was intercepted by the censor and he was one of a string soldiers to face a court-martial that took place in December 1916. He was particularly exasperated by the writings of William Beach Thomas, whom he described as sending:

'ridiculous reports regarding the love and fellowship existing between officers and men. In the infantry arm of the service, there are no less than 60,000 [or 3 complete divisions] of men employed as servants. Look next at the Infantry Brigade Headquarters staff – comprised of six officers. Those half dozen men retain around them fifteen to eighteen servants, grooms, mess waiters etc, Infantry brigade headquarters therefore swallow up another 5,000 men [5 battalions]...Each General, Colonel, Major, many Captains and Subalterns have their horse and groom...It is generally recognised that those animals...are to Officers in France, practically useless, excepting for a once-a-fortnight canter...Probably if a roll call was taken of the batmen, grooms, servants, waiters, commissioned and non-commissioned 'cushy' jobs, it would be found that quite half a million men were performing tasks not necessary to the winning of this war.'

Rochester, stripped of his corporal's stripes, was hauled before a court-martial charged with *'conduct to the prejudice of good order and military discipline'* and sentenced to 90 days Field Punishment Number One.[6]

For the Germans, the Somme had been a terrible battle. The battle had inflicted on the Germans a sense of helplessness which had sapped much of their strength. The constant bombardments had taken their toll and there was a drop in morale.

The fighting during the constant rain of October to its end in November was described as the muddy grave of the German Army. In the meantime, the war reporters returned to London for the winter to write their versions of the battle of the Somme.

Notes

1 *Turning Point – The Battle of the Somme* by Henry Perry Robinson.

2 *The Battle of the Somme* by Philip Gibbs.

3 *The Somme 1916 – Crucible of the British Army* by Michael Chapell.

4 The author's great-uncle was a bomber in the 20th London (Blackheath and Woolwich) Regiment, which finally cleared the Germans from High Wood.

5 *The Wipers Times*. Introduced by Christopher Westhorp.

6 Field Punishment Number One included menial labour plus an hour every morning and afternoon of rapid marching wearing a full load of equipment. One of the most distressing things he had to do was to dig three post holes in the snow for the execution of his cell-mates. *(To End All Wars: How the First World War Divided Britain* by Adam Hochschild).

Chapter 10

1917 – Arras and Messines Ridge

'They are drawing back their guns, but saving most of them. They are retreating, but will still stand again, and dig new trenches and defend other villages. There will be greater and fiercer and more desperate fighting before the end comes, and God alone knows when that will be.

Philip Gibbs was referring to the German strategic withdrawal from the Somme to prepared positions called the Hindenburg Line, stretching from Vimy in the north to Rheims in the south. As they retreated, they created a desert, destroying everything in their path; flattening villages, booby-trapping ruins and dugouts, poisoning wells and blowing craters on roads and crossroads. The British patrols detected the withdrawal in mid-February 1917 and a cautious pursuit began. Conceding as much as 40 miles at its widest, the Germans shortened their line by 25 miles and were thus able to reduce the number of divisions to defend it.

A rather deflated Gibbs wrote in the *Daily Chronicle* dated 5 March, 1917:

'Nothing so far in this German movement has been sensational except the fact itself. Fantastic stories about gas shells, battles, and great slaughter in the capture of the enemy's position are merely conjured up by people who know nothing of the truth.

'The truth is simple and stark. The enemy decided to withdraw, and made his plans with careful thought for detail in order to frustrate any preparations we might have made to deal him a knockout blow and in order to save his man-power, not only by escaping this great slaughter which was drawing near upon him as the weeks passed, but by shortening his line and so liberating a number of divisions for offensive

and defensive purposes. He timed this strategic withdrawal well. He made use of the hard frost for the movement of men and guns and materiel, and withdrew the last men from his strongholds on the old line just as the thaw set in, so that the ground lapsed into quagmire more fearful than before the days of the long frost, and pursuit for our men and our guns and our materiel was doubly difficult. He destroyed what he could not take away, and left very little behind. He fired many of the dug-outs, and left only a few snipers and a few machine-gunners in shell-holes and strong posts to hold up our patrols, while the next body of rear-guard outposts fell back behind the barbed wire in front of the series of diagonal trench lines which defend the way to Bapaume...he hopes to make things easy for himself and damnably difficult for us.'

Confronted with these well-sited and well-entrenched fortifications, the Allies faced the prospect of another year in which they were going to suffer ever greater losses. The politicians and the military leaders were of the same opinion that there could be no spectacular breakthrough and that there was no alternative than to grind out a victory by inflicting more casualties on the enemy than they could on the Allies.

The French still clung to the idea of achieving a decisive breakthrough and the French prime minister, Aristide Briand, promoted General Robert Nivelle as head of the French army over Generals Pétain and Foch. His plan was to launch an all-out attack along the Aisne in Champagne. As with the Somme battle, the French sought to have the British mount an assault at Arras, 45 miles to the north, and draw away German troops from the area chosen by Nivelle. The plan was for the British to begin their attack two days before the French commenced theirs.

The preliminary bombardment of Vimy Ridge, five miles north of Arras, began on 20 March and was followed by a bombardment on the rest of the 24-mile sector on 4 April. It was an enormous exercise in firepower, with 2,689,000 shells being fired – over a million more than had been used on the Somme. William Beach Thomas described in the *Daily Mail*'s 10 April edition:

'Near Arras our troops leapt to the attack in the midst of such artillery fire as the world has never seen. It was accompanied by an onslaught of strange engines of war, while overhead, as soon as the clouds allowed, our aeroplanes, moving at 130 miles an hour, rushed to tackle any German machines they could find.

'From this vantage point, the full panorama from Vimy to Tilloy was etched in flames. I write immediately after watching the first storming. It is too early to give more than partial news, but the famous divisions directly in front of me, both of which I had before seen throw themselves on an entrenched and buttressed enemy, went straight through to their goal.'

General Nivelle was reluctant for the British to attack Vimy Ridge, which he regarded as too difficult to take. After all, the French had tried earlier in the war and failed to take what was probably the most formidable defensive position on the whole front. The task of storming Vimy Ridge was given to the Canadian Corps under the command of Lieutenant General Sir Julian Byng. He meticulously trained his men so, even if they lost officers, they knew their intended tasks and could act independently. The troops were thoroughly briefed with models of the Ridge.

Since October the previous year, the Tunnel Companies of the Royal Engineers had dug about 20 kilometres of tunnels in the chalky ground. The tunnel system had grown extensive enough to conceal 24,000 men, which enabled the troops to reach their starting points without the risk of enemy shelling. Their own shelling had been very effective, and the German wire and trenches had been pulverised.

At 5.30am on 9 April 1917, the Canadians began to advance across 4,000 yards through a snow storm. The westerly wind blew the snow into the faces of the Germans, and the combination of poor visibility and the creeping barrage, which accompanied the attackers, caught the defenders unawares and many were captured. By 1300 hours, they had overrun four lines of German trenches and the Ridge had all but been taken. Just the highest point on the Ridge, Hill 145, held out until the following day when it was taken. The capture of Vimy Ridge was one of the war's most outstanding Allied victories. It had cost the Canadians 11,000 casualties, of whom 3,598 were killed, but they captured over 4,000 prisoners and much ordnance.

Philip Gibbs met some of the prisoners as they were led to the cages already prepared for them:

'They were glad to be captured and out of it, they were cheerful in spite of being numbed by cold and snow...they described the horrors of our bombardment. Some of them had been without food for four days, because our gunfire had boxed them in.'

Elsewhere the battle had gone as well but without the outstanding success on Vimy Ridge. It was mainly conducted by the Third Army under the command of General Edmund Allenby. The advances made on 9 April were not followed up on 10 April. The cavalry were still kept in reserve looking for any chance to break through the disorganised German defences. When VI Corps, positioned south of Arras, saw an opportunity, the only nearby cavalry was a troop of the Northamptonshire Yeomanry who were ordered to advance towards the village of Fampoux. In a quote from Jonathan Nicholl's book *Cheerful Sacrifice*, Sergeant Bertie Taylor recalled the charge:

> *'The shells were dropping fast and thick, then we came to some slit trenches and we just jumped these with our horses squealing – just like a hunt! Then we passed through our leading troops and I remember seeing a lot of Scottish soldiers lying there, machine gunned...Soon we got into Fampoux...we came under shell fire and one of our officers, Captain Jack Lowther – who had an enormous nose – had the end of it sliced off by a piece of shrapnel. Well, we laughed didn't we, but he got off his horse and picked up the end of his nose and wrapped it in his handkerchief.'*

On 11 April, the infantry of VI Corps attacked and took the village of Monchy. The commander of 8 Brigade ordered his cavalry, a squadron each of the Essex Yeomanry, the 10th Hussars and the 3rd Dragoon Guards, to circle round the village to support a further advance. It was a rare display of a brigade of cavalry galloping into battle and one Highland officer recalled:

> *'During a lull in the snowstorm an excited shout was raised that our cavalry were coming up! Sure enough, away behind us, moving quickly in extended order down the slope of Orange Hill was a line of mounted men covering the whole extent of the hillside as far as we could see. It was a thrilling moment for us infantrymen, who never dreamt that we would see a real cavalry charge, which evidently was intended.'*

Philip Gibbs was also on hand to witness this stirring but foolhardy charge:

> *'I stood under a hill called Monchy, not far beyond Arras, and saw something which few men have seen – a cavalry charge against a fortified position. It was not a pleasant sight and it is a black mark*

against Sir Douglas Haig who ordered it, and against the cavalry
generals who were glad to take this chance.

'It was magnificent, but it was not war – in a war of machine-guns,
aeroplanes and artillery. There were masses of horses and dismounted
men in the fields below the hill, and I stood among them astonished,
and wondering what was going to happen.'

The cavalry:

'rode up the hill in a flurry of snow and were seen by the German
gunners and slashed by shrapnel..the men suffered many casualties,
including their General – Bulkeley-Johnson...his body was being
brought back slowly, raised high above the heads of the stretcher
bearers, as though a Roman officer were being carried back dead on
his shield...'

Riding into the teeth of German machine guns, saddles were emptied and
horses killed or hideously wounded. Although casualties amongst riders
were comparatively light, their mounts suffered great losses. The surviving
cavalry fell back into Monchy village and helped defend its north side until
relieved by the infantry.[1] As Gibbs summed up: *'The charge was an heroic*
adventure but very foolish.'

In the attack on Bullecourt on 10–11 April, the supporting tanks were
delayed by the bad weather and an abortive attack by the West Yorkshire
Regiment, who had not received the order to delay the attack, had alerted
the Germans. When the attack finally went in, the wire was found to be intact
and where positions were taken, they were soon retaken by the Germans.

Charles Repington, having served his penance for disclosing the shell
scandal, was now back in France. He was conducted around the Arras
battlefield, including Vimy Ridge, from where he could look across the plain
to Douai and Lens. Even though high ground had been taken, it brought its
own problems as Repington in *The Times* reported:

'The great value of our recent advance here lies in the fact that we
have everywhere driven the enemy from high ground and robbed him
of observation. Having secured these high seats (Vimy, Monchy and
Croisailles) and enthroned ourselves, it is not necessarily easy to
continue the rapid advance. An attack down the forward slope of high

110

ground, exposed to the fire of lesser slopes beyond, is often extremely difficult and now on the general front...there must intervene a laborious period, with which we were familiar at the Somme, of systematic hammering and storming of individual positions, no one of which can be attacked until some covering one has been captured.'

Repington met and dined with most of the main players on the front including Haig, Allenby, Charteris, Trenchard and Byng, who treated *The Times* man as a confidante. The Allies continued to press their attacks east of Arras to keep the pressure on the Germans and help Nivelle's French Army in the Champagne sector. A series of fierce battles were fought between 23 April and 4 May but they could not repeat the spectacular success of the first two days of the Battle of Arras. Any success had to be offset by the high casualty list. The British lost about 150,000 men and had gained little ground since the first day.

Just as disappointing was the news from the French assault in Champagne, which had ended in a costly failure. General Nivelle was sacked and General Pétain was installed as the new commander-in-chief.

Coincidentally, Repington also had a meeting with Generals Nivelle and Pétain which he recorded in his diary:

'I was at a loss to know whether Pétain or Nivelle knew of Pétain's new appointment, but, in fact, as it turned out afterwards, Pétain and I knew, but Nivelle did not. There was, therefore, a certain comedy about the deference which Pétain and I showed to the supposed but already fallen Commander-in-Chief.'

Another casualty of command was General Edmund Allenby of the Third Army, whose casualty list (87,226) was deemed unacceptable. He was reassigned to command the Egyptian Expeditionary Force in Palestine, something he regarded as a *'badge of failure'* but which ultimately brought him great fame.

Kept from the newspapers were the reports that French soldiers had had enough of being sacrificed in pointless assaults and had refused to attack. The mutiny soon spread throughout the army. One division arrived on the battlefield drunk and without arms and there were many demonstrations and acts of insubordination. Some 27,000 soldiers deserted and all offensive measures suspended. When he viewed the conditions and grievances of the poor French soldiers, Pétain soon set about improving their lot and the mutiny was quelled. In the meantime, the burden once again fell on the British to sustain pressure on the Germans.

On 6 April, the Allies received the heartening news that the United States Congress had voted for a declaration of war on Germany. With the promised influx of manpower and industrial might, the flagging Allies could glimpse a distant victory.

In early 1916, the British had planned to mount the Flanders campaign aimed at clearing the Germans from the Belgian coast where they had their U-boat bases. The offensive would begin from the Ypres Salient, starting with the capture of the Messines Ridge in the south. This plan was postponed due to pressure from the French to mount an assault in the Somme sector. Now, with Nivelle's failed offensive, Haig decided to revive the Messines plan to help relieve pressure on the French army.

The Messines Ridge was a strategically important objective as, in such a flat land, its height of 264ft dominated the southern area of the Ypres Salient. The British had begun mining operations when the original attack was planned. Now, over a year later, they had dug twenty-two galleries at a depth of 80–120ft under the German lines and filled them with 447 tons of ammonal explosive.

Since early 1916, the British artillery had greatly improved, both in equipment and tactics. The use of a creeping barrage protected the advancing infantry, while standing barrages would bombard targets further back in the German rear. This was also a period when the Allies had retaken air supremacy after a bleak period when the *Luftstreitkräfte* ruled the skies.

The commander of the Second Army, Lieutenant-General Sir Herbert Plumer, a careful, prudent man, planned with great attention to detail. He took note of General Byng's preparation for the attack on Vimy Ridge by replicating German positions on a practice course at Steenvoorde. Covering more than an acre, the model of the ridge was highly detailed with contours, woods, farms and strongpoints. Here the infantry were versed in their individual objectives. Together with the artillery support and mines, the ordinary soldier felt confident that he was not just being hurled defencelessly against German firepower.

All along the 12-mile front, the bombardment began. On 6 May a preparatory barrage sought out German artillery positions. This intensified on 23 May and by 1 June it was one thunderous roar. The German defences were demolished and the front line troops were ordered to move forward into shell-holes during the day and return to shelters at night. The effect of the constant shelling and the knowledge that mines had been placed under their lines demoralised the Germans.

The war reporters were now housed in a chateau on the hill town of Cassel not far from Ypres. On the evening of 6 June, they were brought to Second Army's HQ and given an explanation of the attack on the following day. They were aware of the largest concentration of mines beneath the Messines Ridge, and were wryly amused by General Harrington's introduction: *'Gentlemen, I don't know whether we are going to make history tomorrow, but at any rate we shall change geography.'*[2]

In the small hours of 7 June, the reporters stood back from the front line opposite the demolished village of Wytschaete and witnessed an extraordinary display of pyrotechnics. The ever-lyrical William Beach Thomas wrote in the *Daily Mail*:

'I have seen several of the heaviest bombardments ever conceived by scientific imagination, none of them approached this in volume or variety or terror, and one moment in it will live forever in the mind of all who were within range of a spectacular miracle of the world. An hour before dawn, as we stood over the dim valley, where the black tree-tops looked like rocks in a calm sea, we saw what might have been doors thrown open in front of a number of colossal blast furnaces. They appeared in pairs, and in successive singles. With each blast the earth shook and shivered beneath our feet.'

Henry Perry Robinson vividly reported in *The Times* the following day:

'How many mines went up at once I do not exactly know, but it was nearly a score. Many of these mines were made over a year ago, and since then had lain under German feet undiscovered. In all, I believe over 600 tons of explosives were fired simultaneously. Can you imagine what over 600 tons of high explosives in 20 or so blasts along an arc of 10 miles looks like? I cannot describe it for you. Personally, I can only vouch for seeing nine of the great leaping streams of orange flame which shot upwards from that part of the front immediately before me, and each vast sheet of flame as it leaped roaring upwards threw up dense masses of dust and smoke, which stood like great pillars towering into the sky, all illuminated by the fires below.'

Philip Gibbs recalled that:

> *'Suddenly the earth quaked. A roaring noise rose up from it with tall pillars of earth and flame. Men who had been standing up fell flat. The earth tremor lasted for many seconds. Eleven mines had gone up under the German trenches and fortified positions. Enormous craters gaped open and in them were buried many German soldiers. It was infernal, as though hell had been opened up. Then our batteries began their drum fire and under cover of it our men moved forward. The living enemy was stupefied and stunned...*
>
> *'It was the most terribly beautiful thing, the most diabolical splendour, I have seen in war.'*

It was estimated that 10,000 Germans were killed when 19 of the 22 mines were detonated. The disorientated survivors were quickly overrun and made prisoners. In this well-planned assault, the British took all objectives in less than 12 hours. Philip Gibbs wrote:

> *'With our troops I stood on the ridge looking back to our own country. It was startling to see how much the enemy had had observation of us. It was impossible to believe that we had been able to live, to move, to send up transport, to put men into billets, to conceal our batteries for three years, in that ghastly region of the low-lying ground...'*

For the Germans, the battle has been described as: *'one of the worst German tragedies of the war'*. Ludendorff wrote that the British victory cost the German army dear and drained German reserves.

The offensive secured the southern end of the Ypres Salient and its success boded well for the main offensive at Ypres the following month.

Notes

1 The cavalry were really mounted infantrymen who, in theory, could gallop quickly to a position, dismount and engage the enemy with carbines and machine-guns.
2 *The Press and the General Staff* by N. Lytton.

Chapter 11

1917 – Passchendaele and Cambrai

After the euphoria of the victories at Vimy and Messines Ridges, Field Marshal Haig felt confident he could follow up with the expulsion of the Germans from the rest of the circling heights in front of Ypres. The British could then go on to capture the important rail heads at Tothut and Roeselare and deny the Germans their vital supply system. It would then be relatively easy to push the enemy from the coastal area above Nieuwpoort with a combined amphibious landing. The German U-boats were taking a huge toll on Allied shipping and their bases at Bruges and Ostend which were just 30 miles from Ypres, an objective that was feasible once the breakout from the salient had been achieved. The fact that the submarines operated mostly from Germany's home ports and that the peril would still exist did not deter him. This was Haig's thinking after the Messines battle, but he met with opposition from Prime Minister Lloyd George, Generals Foch and Pétain and, significantly, his own Intelligence staff. Astonishingly, Haig managed to get his way and so precipitated one of the most controversial and appalling battles of the war.

As so often, the High Command were lured into disaster by an initial success. Perhaps Haig's plan could have succeeded if the Messines victory had been immediately followed up. Instead, there was a six-week delay while artillery and men were moved into position. It was still summer and the weather had been fine. Meteorological records for the past eighty years showed that only three weeks of rain-free weather could be expected at that time of year. What Haig or his Fifth Army commander, General Hubert Gough, could not have predicted was the continuous rains that came early that year. Gough was the youngest army commander on the Western Front, which caused some jealousy among his contemporaries, and enjoyed a good relationship with Haig. He had, however, an abrasive personality and a bullying command style which made him an unpopular commander. His strategic style of an attack going too far in an attempt to gain as much ground as possible was at odds with the more measured and successful tactic of General Plumer's *'bite and hold'*. He later chose to ignore the advice of several of his corps and divisional commanders, who pointed out the appalling conditions, the exhaustion and disorganisation of the troops. General Rawlinson wrote in his diary that there was an intense feeling against Gough, who had made many enemies. He wrote of: *'the formation of a sect of officers called the GMG, which stood for "Gough must go".'*

The delay in the attack had allowed the Germans to make final adjustments to their new defensive strategy – defence in depth. Dispensing with the lines of trenches, the Germans ran their lines backwards in great depth. The front position consisted of three lines 200 yards apart, with breastworks rather than elaborate trenches and manned by a few infantry companies. Two thousand yards back was the second position, with concrete pill boxes to shelter the support battalions; then a third position a further mile back with reserves that could be rushed forward. The disconnected pillboxes and machine-gun nests were all mutually able to give supporting fire. It was a flexible form of defence and excellent for mounting counter-attacks against an exhausted foe.

Over 3,000 guns commenced a preliminary bombardment on 22 July. It was getting to be a habit to report that the bombardment was the heaviest so far mounted. The artillery fired some 4.5 million shells for the next ten days which proved a disaster for their own infantry. The barrage served to churn up the sodden land and further destroy drainage ditches causing the vast morass of craters to fill with water, thus creating a further barrier for the infantry in their advance on the German positions.

Torrential rain fell two days before the attack went in at 3.50am on 31 July. Philip Gibbs wrote:

'The line of attack was out of the ghost city of Ypres – now a vast heap of rubble, with a few rags and tatters of towers and churches – from the river Lys to Bosingnhu [Boesinghe]. It was the country beyond the Ypres Salient which we had held for three years. The enemy had all the rising ground, not very steep in this flat landscape but high enough to give him observation from Pilkem Ridge and St

Julian, and further on at Stirling Castle and the Frenzenberg Redoubt, west of Zonnebeke, and Inverness Copse and Glencorse Wood – terrible names in English history because so many of our best were killed in taking them. Little rivers – tributaries of the Lys – intersected this country until shell fire spread their waters and made new quagmires...

He later wrote:

'The order came to advance. There was no dramatic leap out of the trenches. The sandbags on the parapet were so slimy with rain and rotten with age that they fell apart when you tried to get a grip of them. You had to crawl through a slough of mud. Some of the older men, less athletic than the others, had to be heaved out bodily.

'From then on, the whole thing became a drawn-out nightmare. There were no tree stumps or ruined buildings ahead to help you keep direction. The shelling had destroyed everything. As far as you could see, it was like an ocean of thick brown porridge. The wire entanglements had sunk into the mud, and frequently, when you went in up to the knees, your legs would come out with strands of barbed wire clinging to them, and your hands torn and bleeding through the struggle to drag them off...

'All this area had been desperately fought over in the earlier battles of Ypres. Many of the dead had been buried where they fell and the shells were unearthing and tossing up the decayed bodies. You would see them flying through the air and disintegrating...

'On 1 August the heavy rainstorms began after our men had advanced to the Pilkem Ridge and the northern curve of the Ypres Salient, and it veiled the battlefields in a dense mist, keeping our airmen down and making artillery co-operation with the infantry very difficult. It continued like this for several days and this August was like the foulest weather of a Flemish winter...'

Percival Phillips described the first day in his report in the *Daily Express*:

'The weather changed for the worse last night, although fortunately too late to hamper the execution of our plans. The rain was heavy and constant throughout the night. It was still beating down steadily

when the day broke chill and cheerless, with a thick blanket of mist completely shutting off the battlefield. During the morning it slackened to a dismal drizzle, but by that time the roads, fields and footways were covered with semi-liquid mud, and the torn ground beyond Ypres had become in places a horrible quagmire.

'It was pretty bad in the opinion of the weary soldiers who came back with wounds, but it was certainly worse for the enemy holding fragments of broken lines still heavily hammered by the artillery and undoubtedly disheartened by the hardships of a wet night in the open after a day of defeat.'

Despite the atrocious conditions, the first day of the attack made considerable gains in parts of the salient. The most successful was the assault by XIV Corps and the French First Army on Pilkem Ridge on the left of the attack, which advanced 3,000 yards. Elsewhere, gains were made, but German counter-attacks drove the British back until mud and heavy fire brought it to a halt.

William Beach Thomas wrote of the second day in the *Daily Mail* on 2 August:

'Floods of rain and a blanket of mist have doused and cloaked the whole of the Flanders plain. The newest shell-holes, already half-filled with soakage, are now flooded to the brim. The rain has so fouled this low, stoneless ground, spoiled of all natural drainage by shell-fire, that we experienced the double value of early work, for today moving heavy material was extremely difficult and the men could scarcely walk in full equipment, much less dig. Every man was soaked through and was standing or sleeping in a marsh. It was a work of energy to keep a rifle in a state fit to use.

'The weather possibly arrested some counter-attacks. And certainly prevented all observation, but the enemy has the advantage of retiring on guns long since snug in their concrete beds, and profits by a certain amount of concrete dug-outs. No aircraft could leave its shed, no guns stir across country, and even the infantry were immobilised almost to the state of tree-stumps.

'The windless milky downpour, beginning soon after midnight, lasted throughout today, increasing in volume. The utter completeness of our yesterday's victory made the rain less momentous, for all had

been done that we wanted to do. We had not only won what we sought, we had also given ourselves time to make many trenches firm, and extend posts, and complete all junctions of troops during daylight in spite of heavy German shelling and counter-attacks. One unit on the flank of our principal advance made a great daylight raid subsidiary to the advance and captured 40 prisoners while on the left the Guards captured two garrisoned farms without the help of the artillery.'

It was clear that Haig's ambitious plan to sweep through the German lines and clear the enemy from Flanders had now degenerated into one of grinding attrition. Any further advance came to a halt on 3 August when the infantry took whatever cover they could in the many flooded shell-craters.

Philip Gibbs wrote about the third day:

'The weather is still frightful. It is difficult to believe that we are in August. Rather it is like the foulest weather of Flemish winter, and all the conditions which we knew through so many dreary months during three winters of war up here in the Ypres Salient are with us again. The fields are quagmires, and in shell-crater land, which is miles deep around Ypres, the pits have filled with water. The woods loom vaguely through a wet mist, and road traffic labours through rivers of slime. It is hard luck for our fighting men. But in spite of repeated efforts the enemy has not succeeded in his counter-attacks, after our line withdrew somewhat at the end of the first day south and south-east of St Julian.

'The general position remains the same. The weather remains the same, and the mud and discomfort of the men living under incessant rain and abominable shell-fire do not decrease; nevertheless, they have smashed up attack after attack, and their spirit is unbreakable. The enemy is suffering from the same evil conditions, and his only advantage is that perhaps he has better cover in which to assemble his men, and that, owing to his defeat, he is nearer to his base, so that they have not so far to tramp through the swamps in order to get up supplies of food for guns and men. As usual, we have behind us a wide stretch of shell-broken ground, which, in foul weather like this, becomes a slough.'

Gibbs later wrote:

'It is all rain and mud and blood and beastliness...Nevertheless, somehow or the other, our wonderful men...captured important ground, and crawled forward, and smashed their way through German pill-boxes and machine-gun posts and breastworks, under the flail of enemy shell fire. Wounded men struggled back yard by yard, plastered in mud, so that they looked like the dead who had crawled out of their graves, until the stretcher-bearers carried them back, sometimes falling with their burdens into bogs. They even took great numbers of prisoners, dazed by our barrage fire, cold to the bones, many of them with cramp in the stomach and very miserable. I talked to some of them and they were utterly downcast, saying that the German victories in Russia only lengthened the time of misery and that in the end Germany was bound to be beaten.'

The next move occurred on 10 August, when II Corps resumed the attack on Westhoek which included Glencourse and Polygon Woods, both scenes of fierce fighting. Very little ground was gained at the cost of many casualties. On 16 August, General Gough ordered an attack by XVIII Corps on St Julian and Langemarck and succeeded in holding both positions.

Percival Phillips reported the events of 16 August in the following day's *Daily Express*:

'The battle of Flanders was resumed early this morning, when the British and French armies struck heavily on a wide front north and east of Ypres.

'Considerable ground has already been gained in the region round St Julian and Langemarck. Indications point to our being firmly established in Langemarck village and beyond it, while further south the attack has developed in the direction of Polygon Wood and adjoining patches of woodland strongly held by the enemy. Fighting still continues along this broad front.

'The approaches to Langemarck were mere bogs at the best – actual ponds at the worst. Successive rainstorms had flooded the fields. In some places, wherever there were gullies water lay at the bottom, and the roads of pre-war days have wholly disappeared in a desert of shell-holes and the debris of three years' trench life.'

The nightmarish conditions were no better for the Germans, as Philip Gibbs wrote:

> *'The suffering of all of the German troops huddled together in exposed places, must be as hideous as anything in the agony of mankind, slashed to bits by storms of shells and urged forward to counter-attack which they know will be their death.'*

During the whole month of August, there were only three days in which no rain fell and the total rainfall for the month was almost double the August average. Not only were the conditions extremely difficult for fighting, they had become downright lethal with overburdened soldiers, wounded men, horses and mules slipping into the waterlogged craters and drowning. A sergeant in the Medical Services wrote: *'It requires six men to every stretcher, two of these being constantly employed helping the others out of holes; the mud in some cases up to our waists.'*

For the remainder of the month, there were smaller operations, most of which ended in failure and heavy losses. On one of the few dry days, XIX and XVIII Corps with the support of twelve tanks, managed to capture fortified farmhouses along the St Julien–Poelkapelle road. All efforts to capture the higher ground of the Gheluveld [today Gheluvelt] Plateau east of Ypres were again repulsed with many casualties. Once again the condition of the attacking troops was unconsidered, with some troops standing up to their knees in water for up to ten hours before zero hour.

To quote from Becket and Stevens book *Haig's Generals*:

> *'Gough's command style influenced the planning and execution of the Third Battle of Ypres. Convinced that his approach to assaulting the German positions was correct, he ignored advice from Haig and the director of military operations, Davidson, that he should take the high ground on his right flank near the Gheluveld Plateau first, or that he should consider a form of 'bite and hold' in order to deal with the new type of defence in depth that the enemy had instituted in their positions around Ypres. Gough failed to understand that pressing his advance as far as possible in the initial attack would leave his infantry out of range of their own artillery, vulnerable to counter-attack by the enemy and unable to hold their gains. Following Gough's failure, Fifth Army was relegated to a supporting role and Plumer's Second Army took centre stage.'*

Plumer had some luck on his side. The rains stopped and the ground hardened, only to the extent that it was less boggy. On 20 September, the Second Army began their assault on the Gheluveld Plateau, taking the Menin Road. Due to the churned-up state of the ground, plank roads and even a short length of monorail were quickly constructed. Building these supply routes was essential for the success of the *'bite and hold'* operation.

Then, six days later, two Australian and five British divisions launched their attack on the Polygon Wood. Charles Bean was there to describe the initial barrage:

> *'The most perfect that ever protected Australian troops. It seemed to break out with a single crash. The ground was dry, and the shell-bursts raised a wall of dust and smoke which appeared almost to be solid. So dense was the cloud that individual bursts could not be distinguished. Roaring, deafening, it rolled ahead of the troops "like a Gippsland bushfire".'*

Polygon Wood was taken and defended against counter-attacks, thanks to the heavy artillery barrages which broke up the German attacks.

Plumer's last assault in good weather was to complete the capture of the Gheluveld Plateau and occupy Broodseinde Ridge. This was successfully done and the anticipated counter-attack resulted in devastating losses for the Germans.

Despite the casualties inflicted on the enemy, the British had sustained enormous losses for relatively small gains. This was becoming apparent with the British newspaper-reading public who read with alarm and despondency of the mounting casualty figures as they followed the slow progress of the Ypres battle. Whether or not the High Command suggested to the attendant war correspondents that they should put an optimistic spin in their reports is unproved. Certainly Perry Robinson writing for the *Daily News and Leader* on 20 September made a good attempt as he defended the military:

> *'We here are wondering whether you at home properly appreciate the magnitude of the recent victory. If not it is probably our fault, because we have found it so difficult to explain.*
>
> *'The Germans in their wireless point out as evidence of the significance of our success to the "extraordinarily small amount of positive gains". This is their old game, which perhaps impresses the*

ignorant among their own people and neutrals. For a long time they sought to represent each of our attacks as "an attempt to break through". We have never attempted to break through. It is not that kind of war. But wherever they were strongest, wherever they had their most formidable positions and had most troops assembled to kill we have struck and grasped their positions and killed.

    'It is the same in the recent battle. Here on the end of the ridge on the Menin Road the Germans had staked their best troops to try and avert our menace against that ground. Today we hold that ground, and look down laughingly on all their positions beyond, and no one knows better than the German Higher Command how bitterly their sacrifice has been in vain.

    'Our "extraordinarily small positive gain" is only about one mile deep on a front of five or six. But that one mile, or rather the few acres in the centre of that mile, must have cost the Germans not less than a hundred thousand men in all their fighting here.'

The rather condescending tone of his article blatantly denies that there was any plan for a breakthrough, even though that was Haig's intention until bad weather intervened; from breakthrough to attrition, which is defined as wearing down your opponent. In the case of the Third Ypres, the wearing down applied equally to the British as well as the Germans.

    Yet another effort was made on 9 October to cut the distance to Passchendaele when the French First Army and the British Second and Fifth armies advanced on a 13,500 yard front. The Battle of Poelcapelle was fought in heavy rain and glutinous mud. The German counter-attacks pushed back the advance and prevented a breakthrough but at a high cost. The Germans were finding it harder to replace their heavy losses.

    Three days later, another attempt was made to reach Passchendaele and again heavy rain and mud made movement difficult. It was becoming increasingly hard to bring up supporting artillery to support the infantry. It was recorded that it took six hours to move an artillery piece 250 yards. In this attack, the Allies lost 13,000 men including 2,735 New Zealanders, the greatest daily loss in its history. Finally, even Haig and his commanders agreed that the attacks should stop until the weather improved and supply lines were extended.

    The Canadian Corps played a key role in the so-called Second Passchendaele battle. General Kiggell, Haig's Chief of Staff, advised him to send them to Plumer's Second Army and not to Gough, as he was extremely unpopular with them. After a series of three attacks, what remained of the village of Passchendaele was finally entered by the Canadians on 6 November. Philip Gibbs reported in the *Daily Chronicle* dated 7 November:

'*It is with thankfulness that one can record today the capture of Passchendaele, the crown and crest of the ridge which made a great barrier round the salient of Ypres and hemmed us in the flats and swamps. After an heroic attack by the Canadians this morning they fought their way over the ruins of Passchendaele and into the ground beyond it. If their gains be held the seal is set upon the most terrific achievement of the war ever attempted and carried through by British arms.*

'*For at and all around Passchendaele is the highest ground on the ridge, looking down across the sweep of the plains into which the enemy has been thrust, where he has his camps and dumps, where from this time hence, if we are able to keep the place, we shall see all his roads winding like tapes below us and his men marching up them like ants, and the flash and fire of his guns and all the secrets of his life, as for three years he looked down on us and gave us hell.*

'*What is Passchendaele? As I saw in this morning through the smoke of gun-fire and a wet mist it was less than I had seen before, a week or two ago, with just one ruin there – the ruin of its church – a black mass of slaughtered masonry and nothing else, not a house left standing, not a huddle of brick on that shell-swept height. But because of its position as the crown of the ridge that crest has seemed to many men like a prize for which all these battles of Flanders have been fought, and to get to this place and the slopes and ridges on the way to it, not only for its own sake but for what it would bring with it, great numbers of our most gallant men have given their blood, and thousands – scores of thousands – of British soldiers of our own home stock and from overseas have gone through fire and water, the fire of frightful bombardments, the water of the swamps, of the becks and shell holes, in which they have plunged and waded and stuck and sometimes drowned.*'

The casualty figures are somewhat disputed, but the British suffered about 244,000 killed and wounded. The Germans lost a similar number, but as they did not have the manpower reserves, claimed that the Germany army had been brought nearer to certain destruction by the Flanders battles and that it was, *'the greatest martyrdom of the War'*. In his memoirs written twenty years later, Lloyd George wrote: *'Passchendaele was indeed one of the greatest disasters of the war...No soldier of any intelligence now defends this senseless campaign.'*

Perhaps the most telling reaction to the campaign was when General Sir Launcelot Kiggell, Haig's Chief of Staff, who had spent the battle at GHQ in Cassell, paid his first visit to the front. As his car bumped and slithered over the battlefield, he was reduced to tears, muttering: *'Good God, did we really send men to fight in that?'* It was pointed out to him that conditions were much worse farther up.

The war correspondents had been tamed by their close association with GHQ and the reports they submitted were barely scanned by the new censor, Neville Lytton, who remarked:

'They knew that I had not the smallest wish that they should not tell the truth as fully as possible, and they informed me on several occasions that, had there been no censorship, they would have written in just the same strain.'

Although the reporters kept an upbeat theme in their despatches, it is something of a surprise that the censor allowed the reports of the appalling conditions endured by the soldiers to pass for publication. One man who would agree with that was Field Marshal Haig, who thought some reporters exaggerated the conditions in which his men had fought.

In his book, *Realities of War*, Philip Gibbs reacted:

'As a man who knows something of the value of words, and who saw many of those battle scenes in Flanders, and went out from Ypres many times during those months to Westhoek Ridge, and the Pilkem Ridge, to the Frenzenburg and Inverness Copse and Glencorse Wood, and beyond to Polygon Wood and Passchendaele, where his dead lay in the swamps and round the pill-boxes, and where tanks that had been swallowed into the mire were shot into scrap-iron by German gun-fire (thirty knocked out by direct hits on the first day of battle), and where our guns were being flung up by the harassing fire of heavy shells, I say now that nothing that has been written is more

than a pale image of the abomination of those battlefields, and that
no pen or brush has yet achieved the picture of that Armageddon in
which so many of our men perished.'

The painter, William Orpen, who visited Ypres in 1917, described the effect that the war was having on some of the war correspondents: '*Philip Gibbs was also there – despondent, gloomy, nervy, realising the horror of the whole business; his face drawn very fine, and intense sadness in his very kind eyes...*'

After the war, Gibbs returned many times in print to describe the horrors of Passchendaele which had a profound effect on all those who went through it. In his book *Now It Can Be Told*, he recalled that his courage was at a low ebb:

'I agonised over our losses and saw the suffering of our men and those foul swamps where the bodies of our boys lay in pools of slime, vividly coloured by the metallic vapours of high explosives, beside the gashed tree-stumps; and the mangled corpses of Germans who had died outside their pill-boxes; and when I saw dead horses on the roads out of Ypres, and transport drivers dead beside their broken wagons, and officers of ours with the look of doomed men, nerve-shaken, soul-stricken, in captured blockhouses, where I took a nip of whisky with them now and then before they attacked again; and groups of dazed prisoners coming down the tracks through their own harrowing fire; and always, always, streams of wounded in tens of thousands.'

Gibbs and other reporters wrote of this appalling battle without the constraints of censorship, but it was too late to sway the opinion of the serving soldier. Along with generals, staff officers and politicians, the war reporters, sarcastically referred to as '*literary gents*', came in for particular contempt.

At an army commanders conference on 13 October, General Julian Byng of the Third Army proposed keeping the pressure on the Germans by launching another assault on the Hindenburg Line to keep the enemy troops pinned to Flanders. The area chosen was the rolling downland west of the town of Cambrai, which had been relatively untouched by artillery fire. At the suggestion of Major-General Sir Henry Tudor, Commander Royal

Artillery, it was to be an artillery-infantry attack using new techniques, including the No. 106 shell fuse designed to explode high explosive ammunition without cratering the earth, and sound ranging to locate and silence enemy guns. He also advocated the use of a massed tank attack to clear the extensive barbed wire defences.

The newly-created Tank Corps was keen to have the opportunity to operate on perfect tank terrain – firm and chalky. Every available tank in France and Belgium – a total of 476 tanks including 378 combat tanks – were conveyed by specially constructed railway wagons to the railhead and then driven overnight to an assembly area in Havrincourt Wood. Although the Germans had got wind of an attack, they were caught unawares by the absence of a prolonged artillery barrage. At 6.20am on 20 November in misty conditions, the armada of tanks rumbled forward. The sound belied the speed they could travel, which was only about 1 to 2mph. Nevertheless, the Germans were soon aware that their machine-gun fire was largely ineffective against these 30-ton monsters which kept steadily advancing towards them.

For the war reporters, it was a day largely of guesswork, for there was little they could see. The optimistic official information that they usually received, as with the first day of the Somme battle, turned out to be accurate – the first day was a huge success.

The tanks had flattened channels through the thick barriers of barbed wire, allowing the infantry to follow. Pockets of defenders were dealt with, with most surrendering. Breaking through the Hindenburg Line, the tanks were met by artillery fire and many were knocked out. There were also a large number of mechanical failures, but this did not blunt the incredible feat of the British penetrating the German defences to a depth of five miles by the end of the day. A similar distance had been achieved during Third Ypres, but that had taken three months and a huge casualty bill. When the news reached the British newspapers the following day, there was great rejoicing and church bells were rung throughout the country, the first time since the war began. Sadly, the euphoria was premature.

Although the British infantry and some remaining tanks managed to take the Bourlon Ridge, there were so few reserves that the British could not capitalise on their victory. On 28 November, the Germans, under the command of General Georg von der Marwitz, launched a ferocious barrage on Bourlon Wood and Fontaine, the positions nearest to Cambrai. Two days later, the expected counter-attack pushed the British back three miles, during which they suffered their greatest number of casualties. On 3 December, Haig ordered a retreat from the salient, thus surrendering practically all the British gains. It was a setback and the correspondents had to endure some criticism from the British public for raising their expectations.

Amongst the correspondents, there was a certain amount of professional jealousy and back-biting which the London editors attempted to control. One example involved *The Times* man on the spot. Perry Robinson, curmudgeonly and protective of his senior correspondent status, had fallen out with Herbert Russell of Reuters. He also had an awkward relationship with his editor, Geoffrey Robinson, which went back to a telegram he received on 31 August 1916, relieving him during the Somme battle. It took some smoothing of ruffled feathers before relations between the two men improved. It did not, however, stop Robinson from chiding him in a letter dated 27 November:

> *'I do urge you not to give colour to the idea that there is any instability about Haig's position. It is the kind of thing that Charteris is so fond of doing, and in this particular I think that Charteris, with his devotion and obvious merits, has been one of Haig's worst enemies.'*

He concludes that: *'Intrigues all come from your side of the water.'*

As the close season for battles arrived, most of the correspondents returned to London for the winter to write up their reports and compile them into book form; 1917 had been a terrible year and an end to the war still seemed a distant hope. There was much to reflect on.

Chapter 12

The Eastern Front

It was not only the Western Front that experienced the horrors of war. While Britain and France were attempting to stall the Germans as they swept through Belgium into Northern France, their ally, Russia, was confronting the Austro-Hungarian and German armies on the Eastern Front.

France repeatedly requested her eastern ally to mount an attack against the Germans to help take pressure off the Western Front. Unprepared as they were, the Russians advanced into East Prussia. This was a large salient that jutted into the front line, running from the Baltic Sea to the northern frontier of Russian Poland. On 17 August 1914, the First Army attacked the northern sector, while the Second Army advanced on 22 August in a pincer movement from the south. After making a speedy advance, which saw the German Eighth Army rapidly pull back, the Russian attack stalled due to a poor supply system and a lack of communication between the commanders of the two armies. This was further exacerbated because they were separated from each other by the Masurian Lakes, a complex of water and thick forest that stretched 50 miles north to south, which gave little prospect that they could support each other.

The replacement commanders of the German Eighth Army were Field Marshal Paul von Hindenburg and General Erich Ludendorff, who decided to go on the attack despite being numerically outnumbered. Leaving a small holding force opposite the First Army, they sent the bulk of the Eighth Army south to attack the Russian Second Army. In a fierce and bloody battle fought in the thick forests around the Masurian Lakes, the Russian resistance collapsed and thousands of ill-trained and starving peasant soldiers surrendered or streamed away to the rear. The Battle of Tannenberg, as it came to be known, was the worst defeat suffered by the Russians in the war and their disillusioned army never fully recovered. Of the 150,000 men of the Russian Second Army, only 10,000 managed to escape. There were over 30,000 casualties and 95,000 were taken prisoner. Such was the catastrophe that the British Government made the decision not to allow the newspapers to publish reports of the defeat.

Despite the chaotic way the Russian army was run, they were ahead of the British in accrediting war reporters to accompany their army. One was the New Zealand-born Harold Whitemore Williams, writing for the *Daily Chronicle*. He had attended university in Berlin and Munich before becoming *The Times* special correspondent in Germany. After the Russian uprising in 1905, he became involved with a newspaper called *Ozvobozhdenie* (Liberation) organised by exiled Russian liberals who had been expelled. For the next few years to 1912, he was the St Petersburg correspondent for the *Manchester Guardian* and then the *Morning Post*. During his time with the Russian Army, he managed to take part in a raid by the Cossack cavalry though the Wyszkow Pass and into Hungary.

Although Williams was left-wing in his views, he was staunchly anti-Bolshevik and when they seized power, he was forced to leave Russia. When the Civil War broke out in 1920, he returned to report from Denikin's White Russian army in Southern Russia.

The *Daily News* correspondent was Arthur Ransome, later to become renowned for his children's books, notably *Swallows and Amazons*. Like Harold Williams, he was socialist in his outlook, but this did not stop him joining one of Lord Northcliffe's newspapers in 1916. He recalled:

'Soon after I came back to Petrograd from the northern front, J.L. Garvin (Editor) telegraphed me to become correspondent for the Observer. *I was delighted and found things much easier.*[1] *As correspondent for a Conservative newspaper, I found doors wide open that would have been scarcely ajar for the correspondent of the* Radical Daily News.*'*[2]

One reporter who was able to witness a battle was Basil Clarke of the *Daily Mail*, who had actually been sent not to cover the war, but to write about the political views of Greece, Serbia and Romania. Unable to find much to write about, he decided to visit the frontier to pick up any news of the war. He stayed at a Romanian village which bordered Russia and Austria. On the morning of 18 February 1915, an artillery barrage signalled the start of the Battle of Czernowitz. Clarke was joined by most of the village on a small hill that enabled them to watch the battle unfold from a distance of about 200 yards.

Clarke wrote:

> '*I am now watching the opening of a battle from a hill at Marmornitza. The Cossack cavalry is exchanging shots with Austrian infantry on the Czernowitz road. The artillery is getting into position. I can see more troops advancing. Young Russians are replacing older reserves. We could see the men working their guns and hear their talk and the orders to fire. The Russian shells, on the other hand, exploded right under our gaze not a hundred yards away. We could watch each shell drop, see the upheaval it made, what havoc was caused, and the ensuing commotion among the Austrians among whom it fell.*
>
> '*Through a glass I could watch their eager faces as they* [Russians] *crept among the high grass and brush near the river or lay flat, with eye along rifle barrel, waiting greedily for a favourable chance to shoot.*
>
> '*The Austrians opened the attack from batteries about a hundred yards from the house where I am staying, just across the frontier stream, and fired 30 rounds before the Russians replied. Then the first Russian shrapnel whistled overhead, followed quickly by others. Their shooting was excellent.*'

In the event, the Austrians prevailed and occupied the town of Czernowitz. As luck would have it, there was a telegraph office in the village and Clarke was able to send off his report that appeared in the *Mail* two days later. Afterwards, he was invited to lunch with about twenty Russian soldiers in a nearby village and was somewhat surprised by the absence of vodka, which the Tsar had banned. Another reporter, Stanley Washburn, wrote about this decree in *The Times* dated 5 March 1915:

> '*One cannot write of the Russian mobilization or of the rejuvenation of the Russian Empire without touching on the prohibition of vodka; the first manifest evidence of the increased efficiency was, of course, in the manner and promptness with which the army assembled; but, from that day, the benefits have been increasingly visible, not only in the army, but in every phase of Russian life...At one stroke she freed herself of the curse that has paralyzed her peasant life for generations. This in itself is nothing short of a revolution.*'

American-born Stanley Washburn was one of the most prominent of the war reporters on the Eastern Front. He had covered the Russo-Japanese War for the *Chicago Daily News* and afterwards reported on events in India and the Black Sea area. In 1914, he was sent to Europe by *Collier's Weekly*, but was recruited by Lord Northcliffe to be *The Times* war correspondent with the Russian Army. He witnessed most of the Eastern campaign until July 1917. In May 1917, he was commissioned as a major in the US Cavalry but was allowed to continue as a correspondent until it became impractical. While he was on the Eastern Front, he was often accompanied by George H. Mewes of the *Daily Mirror*, the only English photographer officially attached to the Russian Army.

At the invitation of the Russian General Staff, the accredited reporters travelled to the eastern border of Russian Poland. To their surprise they found that the command and staff were living on a special train, the Nord Express, that had run between Berlin and St Petersburg. He found that after the trauma of Tannenberg, the Russians were cockahoop about their gains in Galicia and particularly the victory at the Battle of Lemberg [Lvov].

Washburn wrote of the many Austrian prisoners who had been captured:

> *'Cossacks on their shaggy ponies were herding about 300 prisoners like cowboys herding cattle...Civilian onlookers threw pieces of bread to the starving men who struggled as hens scramble for a few crumbs thrown by their feeder...The prisoners looked sad and sick. It is hard to believe that any I have seen have had any heart or interest in the present campaign.'*

He wrote later about prisoners captured at Przemysl:

> *'As nearly as I could estimate, there are about one Russian to a hundred prisoners...Usually one discovers the guard sitting with a group of prisoners, talking genially, his rifle leaning against the trunk of a tree nearby...They have been driven into a war for which they care little, they have been forced to endure the hardships of a winter in the trenches with insufficient clothing, a winter terminating with a failure in food supplies that brought them all to the verge of starvation.'*

The journalists were shown a lot of wounded soldiers and military hospitals, which prompted Washburn to speculate:

'Possibly the Russian authorities hope that if they show us enough of human wrecks that war has created, we shall lose our present strong desire to get to the front and that we shall all go peacefully home and forget that we ever asked to be led to the firing line.'

After six weeks campaigning in Galicia, the Russians had pushed the Austrians back to the Carpathian Mountains. So far, the German army had not become involved, having their hands full on the Western Front, but they regarded their ally's collapse with alarm. The Austro-Hungarian army, although large, was poorly equipped, badly led and, as a consequence, low on morale. With many regiments comprising nationalistic Hungarians, Czechs, Slovenians, Bosnians, Croatians, Serbs and Romanians, they had little enthusiasm for the war and all wished to be rid of Austrian rule. The empire that had set in motion the war was itself in no state to go to war. Otto von Bismarck once remarked that a closer association with the declining Habsburg Empire would be: *'to tie the trim Prussian frigate to a worm-eaten Austrian galleon'.*

One of the victories that the Russians were proud of was the surrender on 22 March 1915 of the huge fortress town of Przemysl on the northern slopes of the Carpathians. It served as the Austro-Hungarian Army's Headquarters, but the High Command managed to leave the day before the fortress was invested on 16 September 1914. The Russians began with a week-long bombardment, but lack of siege guns made little impact on the thick walls. Frustrated, the Russians attempted to overwhelm the defenders with a rush of infantry and consequently suffered 10,000 casualties. Learning from this abortive attack, the Russians settled down to a siege that dragged on for another six months. Starving and low on ammunition, the Austrians attempted to break out, only to be repulsed by the Russians. With no alternative but to surrender, 119,000 Austrian troops went into captivity.

Stanley Washburn arrived shortly after the surrender and wrote in *The Times* dated 30 March:

'The siege started with a total population within the lines of investment of approximately 200,000...It is probable that such supplies as there were uneconomically expended, with the result that when the push came the situation was at once acute, and the suffering of all classes, save the officers, became general. First the cavalry and transport horses were consumed. Then everything

available. Cats were sold at eight shillings, and fair-sized dogs at a sovereign.

'While the garrison became thin and half-starved, the mode of life of the officers in the town remained unchanged. The Café Sieber was constantly well filled with dilettante officers who gossiped and played cards and billiards and led the life to which they were accustomed in Vienna. Apparently very few shared any of the hardships of their men or made any effort to relieve their condition...

'The Russians were utterly amazed at the casual reception which they received. The Austrian officers showed not the slightest sign of being disconcerted or humiliated at the collapse of their fortress.'

When word of the victory reached Petrograd, the inhabitants rejoiced. Despite the biting wind and snow, the citizens filled the streets to celebrate. Washburn's hope for Russia's future would be dashed in two years:

'If ever a people genuinely rejoiced over good news it was the citizens of Russia's capital when it became known that Przemysl was at last in Russian hands...This is the great hope for the war. It is also Russia's hope for the future. In another generation it is destined to bring forth greater progress and unity than the Empire of the Czar has ever known.'

It was impossible for Washburn and the other reporters to cover the whole Russian Front, where movement was still fluid. He wrote in 1915 from the Polish front: *'This war is primarily a motor-car war, and it is difficult to imagine what the staff, the Red Cross and the journalists over here would do on this extended front without this conveyance.'* Although he was taken to see the front-line trenches, just 250 yards from the enemy lines, and watched Russian artillery in action, it was a different war from the set-piece battles of the fully-entrenched Western Front. There, despite the restrictions, the war reporters were able to observe a battle.

A fellow reporter on this trip was Perceval Gibbon of the *Daily Chronicle*, who wrote from the demolished village of Bartniki:

'The army, whose trenches are on the river bank just beyond the high trees, whose batteries, faked with green branches to look to the scouting aeroplanes like clumps of thicket, shout from the fields, has

taken it over. There is no place left for any man whose business is not the killing of Germans...'

He went on to describe the killing of a Russian peasant soldier, just one of the millions who became statistics in this cruellest of wars:

'Upon the road there were few people; the morning's shelling had warned them off it; but toward the end of the village a few soldiers came out of a garden and walked along perhaps fifty yards in front of us. Then, of a sudden, the air creaked and rattled with the bursting of a beautifully timed shrapnel, exploding, as it should, not more than twenty feet above the road. The noise of a fagot of sticks broken across a giant's knee, the sudden appearance like a mean miracle, of the little balloon of bomb-smoke overhead, and a group of soldiers ahead of us burst asunder with queer, tiny cries, mere startled squeaks.

'Two fell; one, as we ran towards him, rose to his feet, cursing in a slow, monotonous voice like a man who has recently cursed a great deal; he had merely tripped over his own feet in trying to run. But the other did not rise. The shrapnel had taken him along the side of his face, ploughing him down through the cheek and descending into that nest of arteries and vital parts which is situated in the base of the neck; but he was not dead. A sanitar, with the Red Cross brassard on his left arm came running from somewhere...Do you know the colour of blood – that startling red that not only looks but smells red and feels red when you touch it? He was on one elbow, his head drooping, and around him the mud of the road was reddening with the very essence of his life that spouted from him, that dyed his shoulder to the hue of horror – the awful, copious blood of a man...

'Have you seen a man die? That queer hardening of the man into a corpse, that terrifying metamorphosis that with a gasp, a gurgle in the throat, and a slackening of the jaw, makes a man dead flesh? No? Then you don't know war. War is death pervading humanity like an odour; it is the spirit of horrible burlesque working upon the dignity of mankind; it is abrupt catastrophe intruding like a robber upon the sanctity of life. War is hell – I know all that; but war is an insult to man, insult to the stuff man is made of, insult to the image of God.'

Welsh-born Perceval Gibbon was also a novelist best remembered for his short stories. He was widely travelled and counted Joseph Conrad as a close friend. He went on to cover the Italian Front before being commissioned as a major in the Royal Marines in 1918.

In order to prop up their failing Austrian ally, the German command decided to make its main effort on the Eastern Front and transferred considerable forces there. The command of both the German and Austro-Hungarian forces was given to General August von Mackensen, who concentrated an overwhelming number of divisions against the unprepared Russians in what became known as the Gorlice-Tarnów Offensive, south east of Krakow. Starting with a massive barrage on 1 May 1915, his army pushed the Russians out of Galicia and Poland and back to the border of their own country. In what they called the Great Retreat, the Russian lost 750,000 prisoners.

Stanley Washburn, ever supportive of the Russian cause, wrote encouragingly of the retreat, claiming that the Russians were now in a much better position than before. He repeated this to Charles Repington when they met in London in December on his way home to America. Repington wrote in his diary:

> 'Went to see Stanley Washburn in a private hospital. He is on his way home to America on leave for a few weeks. He told me that he thought that the Russians had 1 million rifles and would have 2 million combatants next spring...The Germans are well dug in all along the Russian Front. Had the Russians 500,000 more rifles they could drive the enemy away. It is all a question of rifles, but Washburn says that the Armies are not stiff with guns, and have lost a lot.'

To exacerbate matters, there was much wrangling and jealousy amongst the Army commanders; 1915 had been a bad year for the Tsar's Army, but Washburn was optimistic about the coming year. As Washburn was reporting to his *Times* colleagues in London, a meeting was taking place in Chantilly where it was agreed that Russia, France, Britain and Italy would commit themselves to simultaneous attacks against the Central Powers in the summer of 1916.

Honouring their part of the agreement, the *Stavka*, the Russian High Command, approved a plan by one of Russia's ablest commanders, General

Aleksei Brusilov, to mount an *en masse* attack against the Austrians in Galicia. On 4 June, the Russians opened the offensive with a brief but intense bombardment followed by a massive attack.

Henry Hamilton Fyfe had moved from France to the Russian Front where, despite the vast distances, he found that journalists were still able to report the war without restrictions. He wrote:

'Brusilov was the ablest of the army group commanders. His front was in good order. For that reason we were sent to it. The impression I got in April was that the Russian troops, all the men and most of the officers, were magnificent material who were being wasted because of the incompetence, intrigues, and corruption of the men who governed the country.

'In June Brusilov's advance showed what they could do when they were furnished with sufficient weapons and ammunition. But that effort was wasted, too, for want of other blows to supplement it, for want of any definite plan of campaign.'

Arthur Ransome also recalled this period:

'It was March 1916 before I was given my first limited permission to visit the Russian Front as a war correspondent. We went to Kiev and thence to the South Western Army Headquarters at Berditchev, where we met for the first time General Brusilov, the smartest-uniformed and most elegant of all Russian generals, later to be famous for his break-through in the west and for the disasters his armies suffered in retreat.

'I remember interminable driving in vehicles of all kinds along roads that war had widened from narrow cart-tracks to broad highways half a mile wide. Drivers had moved out of the original road to ground on either side of it not yet churned to mud. As each new strip turned to bog, the drivers steered just outside it, so that in many places two carts meeting each other going in opposite directions would be out of shouting distance.'

General Brusilov's offensive broke the Austrians' lines, enabling three of his four armies to advance sixty miles on a wide front. The Austrians were in full retreat and the Russians captured 350,000 prisoners. Although his lines were extended and his troops short of supplies, Brusilov's armies regained Galicia and reached the foothills of the Carpathians. Like many victorious commanders before him, Brusilov did not know when to stop.

Arthur Ransome wanted to view the front from the air and to take some photographs. His flight was not without incident as he recalled:

'In August, I had flown along the front in one of the old two-seater Voisin machines in which the passenger was as in an open canoe with a foot on each side of the pilot, in whose stupidity he had the utmost confidence. It was cold in the air and I well remember beating my hand against the outside of the canoe to get my fingers warm enough to take a photograph.

'Our real trouble, such as it was, began when just before dusk we flew back to the place from which we started. We began to spiral down and instantly there appeared puff after puff of smoke from shells sent up to meet us. The pilot suddenly turned the nose of the machine up, pointing with a grin to a small tear in one wing. Presently he spiralled down again and again was greeted with shells from below. Once more we sheered off, this time with curses, and on coming back yet again we were, at last, recognised as friends and allowed to land.

'I dined that night with the battery that had done the shooting, and sat next to the officer in charge. I complained that I did not think he had given me a very hospitable reception. "Perhaps not", he replied, "I'm very sorry, but really you ought to count yourself lucky, for usually when we fire at our own machines we hit it." He explained that the aeroplanes had been given to the Russian army because they were not good enough for the French. They were very slow and therefore easy targets.'

By late September, Brusilov's forces were suffering from supply problems, including a shortage of water. They had also lost a million casualties in what was the most lethal campaign of the war. This terrible figure when added to the other casualties suffered during the war resulted in a staggering five million. Now the demoralised Austro-Hungarians had the full support of Germany and began making gains in Romania. Russia's impressive offensive had run out of steam and the dormant seeds of discontent would soon grow into a full-scale revolution.

The economy was breaking down and it became increasingly difficult to buy food, which led to riots in the major cities. The State Duma warned the Tsar that a constitutional form of government should be put in place, but he ignored them. As a consequence, the Tsarist regime was toppled by the revolution in February 1917. Although the provisional government led by Alexander Kerensky did their best to keep Russia in the war they were fighting a battle that was already lost. When Kerensky's government was displaced by the Bolsheviks in October 1917, the Russians sued for peace with Germany.

In the Brest-Litovsk Treaty signed on 3 March 1918, Russia accepted Germany's unpalatable terms, which included the surrendering of the Ukraine, Finland, the Baltic provinces, the Caucasus and Poland.

With no war to report about, the Western war reporters moved, either back to France or to the latest front involving the Allies – Italy.

Notes

1 The name of the city changed in 1914 from St Petersburg to Petrograd, because it sounded too German. In 1924, it was again changed to Leningrad before reverting to St Petersburg in 1991.

2 After the Bolshevik Revolution in late 1917, Arthur Ransome remained in Russia and became friendly with Lenin, Leon Trotsky and other Bolshevik leaders. In 1924, he married Trotsky's secretary, Evgenia Shelepina. When they left the Soviet Union, his wife smuggled out two million roubles in diamonds and pearls to help fund Trotsky's cause.

Chapter 13

Other Fronts Part 1

Italy

Although she was a member of the Triple Alliance with Austria-Hungary and Germany, Italy did not join them in declaring war in August 1914. Several things held her back. Firstly, a large and vociferous radical political movement called *Italia Irredente* (Unredeemed Italy) called for the return of Italian-inhabited territories forming part of the Austro-Hungarian empire. In the main, these were the Austrian Littoral on the Dalmatian coast with its important port of Trieste, and the South Tyrol. She also wanted to wait until she could see how her rival, Austria, would fare. With news of the 1915 Russian victories in Galicia and Przemysl in the Carpathians, she signed the Treaty of London on 26 April and joined the Entente.

Another factor not appreciated by the politicians was that Italy was not prepared for an offensive campaign. They had been so secretive in their negotiations that the Italian military command was not informed of the change of Italy's alliance until 5 May 1915. This gave them less than three weeks to prepare for war against Austria.

They were poorly equipped, lacking in sufficient artillery, adequate clothing, and led by a commander, Field Marshal Luigi Cadorna, who was loathed and feared by his soldiers. His lack of concern for them extended to the belief that they would only fight if terrorized. When men were reluctant to go over the top, he would order the artillery to fire on them until they moved. During the Battle of Caporetto, he ordered the execution of officers whose units had retreated. In all, about 750 soldiers were executed, the highest number in any army during the whole war. It was small wonder that morale in the Italian army was so low.

In spite of their unpreparedness, the Italians began their campaign by attacking the Isonzo River region in the north-east with the aim of taking Trieste. This would be the start of eleven battles of the Isonzo fought between 1915 and 1917. Driven by their desire to reunite this Italian-speaking region with the motherland, Italy battered away at the enemy's defence resulting in some 250,000 casualties without any appreciable gains.

For the Austrians, the Italian Front was an irritating diversion from the main enemy – Russia. The Austrian commander, Conrad von Hotzendorf, decided to attack from the Trentino mountain region in the north-west and onto the Venetian Plain. Once into the lowlands, the Austrians would cut off the Italian army on the Isonzo front from the rest of Italy and force a surrender. Much of this plan depended on considerable German support, but as their army was engaged in the Verdun battle, von Hotzendorf still decided to go ahead with his plan. Unfortunately for the Austrians, the plan became an open secret and the Italians had plenty of time to divert troops to the Trentino region. The resultant attack resulted in a stalemate.

Both the Isonzo and Trentino fronts were completely unsuited for offensive warfare, being broken and mountainous. In truth, there was little combat in the Alpine front in winter; just surviving nature was enough of a struggle. Deep snow severely limited movement and brought its own version of terror. During the three years of war in the Austro-Italian Alps, at least 60,000 soldiers died in avalanches. 'The sigh of the avalanche', brought millions of cubic metres of snow, rushing at speeds up to 120mph, sweeping away batteries, men and animals. Both sides observed ceasefires as they combined in their attempts to find survivors.

In 1915, 40-year-old Alice Schalek became the first woman photo-journalist in the Austro-Hungarian war information office. She undertook dangerous journeys to the Alpine front to interview soldiers and to take photographs. Her presence was welcome, not least because it was guaranteed that the Italians would not shoot. When she remarked: *'Are they so gallant?'*, an officer explained that gallantry had nothing to do with their decision not to fire; when the Italians saw a woman on the front, they assumed that the activities across the line could not possibly be military in purpose. To her annoyance, the officer added that it was not worth the cost of a bullet to fire at a female.

In 1917, the Austrian Government awarded her the Golden Cross with Crown for Bravery. Not everyone, however, was uncritical. She came under attack for glorifying war and one writer described her as a 'hyena of the battlefield'.

Although there were Italian journalists in the back areas, Cadorna absolutely forbade them to approach the forward areas. The most prominent

Italian reporter was Luigi Barzini of the *Corriere della Sera*, who was the official correspondent with the Italian army. An account of his experiences was published in the British weekly magazine, *The War Illustrated*. The British newspapers had to rely on the official version for their reports.

In October 1917, a combined force of 400,000 Germans and Austrians launched a surprise attack on the Isonzo near the village of Caporetto. The Italian line was broken, which precipitated a chaotic retreat back across the Venetian Plain to the Piave River. In what was one of the war's worst defeats, the Italians suffered 11,000 dead and over a quarter of a million captured. They also lost half of all their artillery.

Yet in the midst of this unmitigated disaster, some good emerged. The government collapsed and was replaced by a more competent Prime Minister, Vittorio Orlando. Cadorna was dismissed, along with many of his staff, and replaced by General Diaz who had an entirely different way of treating his men. Germany withdrew her troops back to the Western Front in preparation for her major March offensive, leaving the Austrians to keep in check the Italian army.

Italy also received help from Britain and France who sent infantry divisions and squadrons of aircraft to stiffen the line along the Piave River. Now that Britain and France were involved, the newspapers took an interest and sent their war reporters. *The Times* wanted to recall Gerald Campbell from his long-term attachment with the French Army in France and send him to the Italian Front. As if to demonstrate just how the relationship between the military and war reporters had changed, the French Army refused to part with him, arguing that they had grown to trust him. Only when the French troops arrived in Italy was he allowed to join them. He then spent a miserable, but fortunately, brief time with them. He endured harsh winter conditions that had already defeated two other *Times* personnel, W.K. McClure, the Rome correspondent, and Avis Dolora Waterman, the Milan correspondent.

Charles Repington mentions the latter in his journal of June 1916, when he visited Italy:

'Dined at the Roma and met Mrs Waterman, a rather good-looking American woman aged about thirty-five, who is The Times *Milan correspondent and occasional visitor to the front.'* He did accompany her to the front near Asiago with some reservation: *'I was very much bored with taking a lady to the battlefield, which was*

no place for her, and also she had velvet shoes on, but she insisted on coming.'

This turned to admiration when he commented that their guide: '[Colonel] *Claricetti was furious with us when we exposed ourselves. Mrs Waterman was as brave as a lioness, and paid absolutely no attention to the shooting.'*

The *Daily Mail* war correspondent, G. Ward Price, had spent most of the First World War reporting from Gallipoli and Salonika. Now he had been assigned to the Italian Front and reported on 20 June:

'The bridges over the Piave are so constantly cut by shell-fire that the Austrians are actually having to use aeroplanes to bring supplies across the river. Last evening I watched the Italian and British airmen as they bombed and fired on the Austrians on the slopes of the Montello. One British airman, I heard later, having dropped all his bombs and emptied every drum of cartridges, came down to within a score or two feet and pelted with his spare parts and tools in his repair outfit the Austrians cowering under the banks and among bushes.'

In mid-1918, the Austrians launched another offensive but it was becoming clear that it was the last throw of the dice. Food-riots at home, nationalist uprising throughout the Empire and general war-weariness signalled that the end was in sight for the army.

Italy seemed to gain in confidence, and when she went on the offensive, the Austrians crumbled. The retreat degenerated into a rout and on 30 October 1918, the Habsburg Empire sued for an armistice.

Salonika

'When you step out of Salonika you step into a virtual desert, roadless, treeless, uncultivated, populated only by scattered villages of the most primitive kind, inhabited by a low grade peasantry...Two roads, in a condition quite inadequate to support heavy traffic, three single lines of railway ran, at the most divergent angles possible, from Salonika towards the enemy's territory. Apart from these there was hardly even a track which in winter was possible for wheeled traffic.

'A handicap that has weighed heavily upon the Balkan Army is a climate unpropitious for soldiering, cold and wet in winter, hot feverish in summer. Winter, right up to the beginning of April, is a season of snow, rain, and, above all, mud. Tracks dissolve into quagmires, main roads break up into holes and ridges impassable for motor-traffic.'

So wrote George Ward Price, the *Daily Mail*'s official reporter with the British Salonika Force, which landed at the Macedonian port of Salonika on 5 October 1915. This first impression did not improve over the next three years.

The reason British troops were sent to this outpost in the Balkans was in response to pleas from Serbia for the Allies to support them against the combined attacks of Austria-Hungary, Germany and Bulgaria. The French Prime Minister, Viviani, had wanted to send 400,000 men but this was quickly ruled out. Sir Edward Carson spoke of the folly of detaching any troops from France: *'Serbia is done for'*. He was right, for by the time the Allies had decided to send troops, the Serbian army had been beaten and forced to retreat to the Adriatic coast so severing the link with Salonika.

The French, supported by the British 10th Division transferred from Gallipoli, pushed up the Vardar Valley to the Greco-Serbian border.[1] In this mid-winter mountainous region, the troops suffered terribly. Ward Price wrote:

'But these Irish brigades were still imperfectly installed on the barren inhospitable Dedeli Ridge, they were savagely smitten by that cruel three-day blizzard which caused bitter suffering to our troops not only in the Balkans but at the Dardanelles. It began on 27 November with torrents of rain which soon turned to snow. Then it froze so quickly that the drenched skirts of greatcoats would stand out stiff like a ballet-dancer's dress...In that terrible weather our patrols and those of the Bulgars, which used both to visit the unoccupied village of Ormanli, would be driven to shelter and light fires in houses so close together that each could hear the other talking, and each by tacit agreement left the other undisturbed. It was too cold to fight.'

The 10th Division had been transferred from Suvla Bay on the Gallipoli

Peninsula and were already in poor physical condition. At the start of that ill-starred campaign they had gone ashore at the most bloody of the landings – V Beach – and suffered terrible losses. Most had faces that were gaunt and all were under-weight when this severe ordeal was imposed on them. Heavily out-numbered by the Bulgarians who shelled their positions without reply, the Irish brigades were unable to put up much resistance. Ward Price wrote:

> *'The hill had originally been held by a battalion of Irish Fusiliers. But there was no cover there; it was nothing but a treeless, shelterless, boulder-strewn height, and the battalion had suffered so severely during the blizzard in that isolated position that it was withdrawn and only one company and one machine-gun were left to hold it... Our first encounter with the Bulgars as enemies had not been one to fill us with unmingled satisfaction.'*

With a major German-Bulgarian attack imminent, the French and British were forced to retreat and dig in on the outskirts of Salonika. It was hoped that the Allied presence would dissuade the Bulgarians from attacking Greece and also tie up their troops. There were many in Britain who wanted the British to pull out altogether but both the French and British commanders, Generals Maurice Sarrail and Mahon respectively, persuasively argued the case to stay.[2] For many, Salonika was like an eel-trap: easy to enter but not easy to quit.

The French were much more ambitious as they wished for influence in the Balkans after the war. Charles Repington repeatedly writes in his diary of the folly of the Salonikan campaign:

> *'It is extraordinary that the French should want to burden us with this expedition when they are being heavily attacked since Feb 21 at Verdun and nine French provinces are in German hands.'*

The Greeks were also posing a problem with the pro-Entente prime minister, Eleftherios Venizelos, being driven from office by the pro-German King Constantine. In 1916, Venizelos regained power and Constantine abdicated in favour of his pro-Entente son, Alexander.[3]

With the Gallipoli Campaign being wound down, those war correspondents still in the area were instructed to follow the British force to

Salonika. Amongst them was Fergus Ferguson of Reuters, William Massey of the *Daily Telegraph* and G.T. Stevens of the *Daily Chronicle*. The latter was the Athens correspondent and had covered the Greco-Turkish War and the Balkan Wars and had been with the Serbs during 1914–15. He then survived the trials of the Salonika Front only to be killed during an air raid on London on 24 September 1917. In recognition of his service to Greece, the Greek Government granted a pension to be paid to his widow.

For the first four months of 1916, the Allies were occupied in the construction of their entrenched camp around the surrounding ground behind Salonika. Eight miles to the north of the port was a high ridge running east to west which acted as a rampart dominating the broad plain beyond. Along this perimeter, a continuous and elaborate barrier of wire was strung which became known as 'The Birdcage'. A steady stream of reinforcements arrived to bolster the French and British presence, which included French Colonials, Serbians, Russians and Italians. By early 1917, there were some 300,000 troops on the Salonika front. Small wonder that the Germans sarcastically called it their 'largest prisoner of war camp'. Even the Allies referred to it as their 'biggest internment camp'. For the troops it was a cheerless posting. After the freezing winter, they had to endure baking hot winds, plagues of flies and the ever-present threat of endemic malaria.

General Sarrail, now in overall command, had a considerable army and could occupy a wider front about forty miles around Salonika. The British, now commanded by General G.F. Milne, covered the Allied front from the east to the north-east, roughly along the River Struma. The Allies set about building an infrastructure of roads, bridges and a water supply. The port was improved with piers, docks and warehouses, which made it an aerial target for the Germans. Ward Price wrote of a raid on 6 May 1916:

'In the small hours of 6 May, the town was awakened by the crash of anti-aircraft guns from the hills behind and from ships in the harbour, and there, floating yellow in the glare of the searchlights over the heart of Salonika, was a Zeppelin, the first the townspeople had set eyes on. A characteristically silly panic started, the people rushing out of their houses, and scurrying in contrary directions along the streets. The Zeppelin made for the harbour as if to bomb the warships there. At first it was too vertically above them for the naval gunners to fire, but a moment later the airship altered course, and a 12-pounder mounted on a high carriage on the forward bridge

146

of HMS Agamemnon *brought it down in a long slant onto the marshes at the mouth of the Vardar, where, a moment later after it had touched, the Zeppelin burst into flames. A startling, long-drawn out cheer rang from the silent English and French warships at the sight and echoed through the darkness across the frightened town.'*

For the opposing sides, the summer of 1916 was largely spent staring at each other. Then in September, the Serbs mounted a strong attack towards their border town of Monastir, which they finally took in November. The British on the Struma kept the Bulgarians pinned down with a series of attacks on some fortified villages, which they occupied. With the onset of winter, all fighting ceased and the soldiers suffered in the bleak weather. Ward Price wrote about the stalemate and the German view:

'Hitherto they have had considerable reason to be satisfied with the existing state of affairs. The Salonika Expedition is not doing them any vital harm; it is Bulgars, not Germans, who are being killed in our attacks...Moreover, the German General Staff knows that Salonika is a heavy drain upon the resources of the Allies.'

Hostilities commenced with the coming of spring 1917 with attacks in the mountains around Lake Doiran. Despite capturing enemy trenches and strongpoints, counter-attacks had pushed the British back to their original lines. Ward Price, who witnessed the battle, noted:

'One satisfactory feature of the fighting was the chivalrous way in which the Bulgarians allowed our stretcher parties to go out in broad daylight and pick up wounded who were left lying there after the night attack. So steep were the rocky slopes of the Jumeaux ravine and so completely swept by enemy fire that it would have been extremely difficult to bring in the unfortunate fellows who had been left behind when we retired from the enemy trenches. But the morning after the fighting our doctors and stretcher-bearers with great gallantry stepped out into the open, trusting to no other protection than the Red Cross. For a moment fire was opened upon them from the Bulgar trenches, but almost immediately an enemy officer jumped up on the parapet, waving a blue flag. The fire at once ceased, and a message was evidently telephoned back to the

Bulgarian batteries, for there was no shelling while our stretcher parties were at work. The Bulgars even allowed one of them to walk through a gap in their wire and pick up a man who was lying within ten yards of the enemy's parapet.'

Another example of co-operation and understanding between the sides was when the British decided to leave their front line along the River Struma in mid-summer and retreat to the surrounding hills. This was to avoid the malaria-carrying mosquitoes that thrived along the river and had caused so many casualties. Ward Price wrote:

'the Bulgar is as well aware of the unhealthiness of the Struma as we are. He put out placards: "We know you are going back to the hills: so are we", and now he, too, only has a strong outpost line in the plain. The only forces that hold the Struma in strength are the mosquitoes, and their effectives may be computed by thousands of millions.'

Another event that summer was the great fire of Salonika, which started on 18 August. Fanned by the strong hot wind that tormented the troops, the fire spread rapidly destroying some 4,000 houses and making 100,000 homeless. The Allies combined to drive these refugees to safety but there was little more that could be done for them. As H. Collinson Owen, the editor of the soldier newspaper *The Balkan News*, observed:

'Salonika never recovered during the occupation of the Allies. It remained a "washed-out" city; the wreckage was too big to repair.'

When Greece finally joined the Allies in June 1917, it enabled Britain to reduce her force by several divisions who were sent to Palestine and France.

Ward Price was moved from Salonika in June 1918 to report on the British involvement in Italy and so missed the only major battle of the Salonika campaign. In September 1918, the Allies launched an attack along the whole line. Although there was no contemporary account in the British newspapers of the Third Battle of Doiran, later reports from participants reveal that the British part in the attack resulted in terrible losses. In an ill-conceived frontal attack on a bare ridge against a well-entrenched enemy, two brigades were wiped out by machine-gun fire. Still more men were thrown into what was a suicidal assault and the attack ended as a bloody disaster. It was all for nothing as Bulgaria asked for an armistice a few days later.[4]

Notes

1 British 10th Division came from Gallipoli consisting of 6/7 Dublins, 6/7 Munster Fusiliers, 5/6 Inniskillings, 5/6 Irish Fusiliers, 5th Connaught Rangers, Irish Rifles, Leinsters and 10th Hampshires.

2 General Maurice Sarrail, a socialist, had been dismissed by Marshal Joffre which caused a political uproar from the Left. He was given command of the Salonikan Expedition and it was felt expedient to continue with the campaign for political reasons rather than risk opposition from the Left. Even his political connections could not save him from being dismissed in December 1917.

3 His disagreement with Venizelos over whether Greece should enter the War led to the National Schism. Constantine forced Venizelos to resign twice, but in 1917 he left Greece after threats from the Entente forces to bombard Athens, and his second son, Alexander, became king.

4 The Battle of Doiran was an Anglo-Greek assault which resulted in the loss of about 7,000 men.

Chapter 14

Other Fronts Part 2

Mesopotamia
In November 1915, the American magazine *The Independent* published an article about the British involvement in Mesopotamia. It began:

> *'In the earlier months of the Great War attention was concentrated upon central Europe, for it was thought that whatever took place elsewhere would have no influence upon the final issue of the struggle. But now it seems likely that the deadlock in France may remain unbroken and the war and its terms of settlement be decided by what is done in the Balkans, Asia, Africa and the Pacific. When the final history comes to be written it is quite conceivable that more consideration will be given to the anabasis of the eleven thousand British who fought their way up from the sea to Baghdad than to the fruitless fighting of millions in France and Flanders. There is another reason why the outside world has paid little attention to the campaign in Mesopotamia, and that is because little has been heard of it. No war correspondents infest this field...'*

At the beginning of November 1914, the Ottoman Empire decided to ally itself with the Central Powers and war was declared on Britain. In a pre-emptive strike, Whitehall decided to send a force from India to protect the pipeline from the oil fields at Abadan in Persia, to the mouth of the Shatt-al-Arab on the Persian Gulf.[1] Mesopotamia, 'the land between two rivers', was a sleepy backwater province of the Ottoman Empire and a more difficult theatre in which to fight would be hard to imagine. Flies and mosquitoes tormented the troops causing malaria and dysentery. The nights were freezing and the days were unbearable hot. In the rainy season the dust turned to mud and the Tigris River caused flooding.

The Mesopotamian campaign was almost entirely an Indian Government affair. On 21 November 1914, they sent the Anglo-Indian 6th (Poona) Division, who occupied the town of Basra on the west bank of the Shatt-al-Arab. This became the base for the Indian Expeditionary Force D (IEFD), from where they continued their advance, winning the Battle of Quirna and ensuring the protection of the oilfields. A further success at the Battle of Shaiba on 12 April 1915 encouraged the British command to advance on Baghdad and Kut. Although the IEFD was small in numbers, Lord Kitchener still advised the Dardanelles Committee that Baghdad should be seized for the sake of prestige and then abandoned.

On 22 November, General Sir Charles Townsend led his small force against a reinforced Turkish army at the Battle of Ctesiphon, a town just 25 miles south of Baghdad. After two days of fierce fighting, it ended in a stalemate. Townsend withdrew his force to Kut-al-Amara, on the left bank of the Tigris, and prepared to defend it. The Turkish army quickly surrounded the town and sent other forces down the river to prevent any relief reaching the besieged garrison. Several attempts by land and river were made to relieve Townsend but all failed. Finally, on 29 April 1916, the starving defenders of Kut were forced to surrender – 13,164 soldiers went into a terrible captivity, losing nearly 5,000 through brutal treatment.

After this humiliating defeat, coming soon after the Gallipoli debacle, the British sent reinforcements and built up a more efficient supply system. All the previous commanders were replaced and a more thorough offensive was planned.

Although there had been no war correspondents present during the first year, the disaster at Kut had alerted the newspapers to how important was this distant campaign. At the end of 1915, Edmund Candler of *The Times* was appointed correspondent to represent British and Indian newspapers. An agreement was made that his salary of £1,500 would be shared fifty-fifty between the Indian Government and the Newspapers Proprietors' Association. The one-armed Candler had spent the previous decade in India and was a sympathetic observer.

A government enquiry into the defeat at Kut and the general condition of the IEFD revealed a scandalous deficiency in medical treatment. This was graphically revealed by Major R. Markham Carter of the Indian Medical Services.

After the Battle of Ctesiphon, the wounded were sent down river to Carter's hospital ship at Basra, from where he observed:

'I was standing on the bridge in the evening when the Medjideh *arrived. She had two steel barges, without any protection against the rain, as far as I remember. As this ship, with two barges, came up to us I saw that she was absolutely packed, and the barges too, with men...The patients were so huddled and crowded together on the ship that they could not perform the offices of nature clear of the edge of the ship, and the whole of the ship's side was covered with stalactites of human faeces...'*

There was more of this distressing detail and he concludes with:

'In my report I describe mercilessly to the Government of India how I found men with their limbs splinted with wood strips from "Johnny Walker" whisky boxes, "Bhoosa" wire and that sort of thing.'

The findings of the enquiry were reported in the British newspapers:

'The Mesopotamian Report continues to excite national interest... particularly the medical scandal which Major Carter did so much to bring to light. Carter was a well-known footballer and director of the Pasteur Institute in India. He is now in charge of a Royal Hospital ship in Mesopotamia.'

The reports pointed out that the revelations would shatter public confidence in the Gallipoli and Mesopotamian campaigns. The *Daily Telegraph* wrote*:*

'Those responsible for the publication of the findings are assuming a great responsibility if they continue this system of revelation which affects many actually directing the forces of the State at the present moment...A highly unsatisfactory feature of the report is the evidence of General Sir Beauchamp Duff and Surgeon General Hathaway, as to suppressing evidence that things are going badly. The Commission emphasize the active intolerance of all criticism or for suggestions of reform. When Major Carter disclosed the medical debacle of Ctesiphon he was treated with great rudeness. General Cowper, who himself had been rebuked by General Duff, threatened Carter with arrest, and said he would get his hospital ship taken from him as he (Carter) was a meddlesome faddist.'[2]

The commander, General Sir John Nixon, and most of his staff had overseen a badly conducted campaign and were relieved of their duties.

The new commander was General Stanley Maude, who spent six months training and organising his army. The new offensive was launched on 13 December 1916 with an advance up both banks of the Tigris, destroying Turkish positions along the way. Outmanoeuvring the Turkish army, the British occupied Kut and continued their advance up the river. On 11 March 1917, the British entered Baghdad.

Edmund Candler's report appeared in the newspapers dated 16 March:

'Our vanguard entered Baghdad soon after nine o'clock this morning. The city is approached by an unmetalled road between palm groves and orange gardens.

'Crowds of Baghdadis came out to meet us: Persians, Krabe, Jew, Armenians, Chaldeans and Christians of diverse sects and races. They lined the streets, balconies and roofs, hurrahing and clapping their hands. Groups of school children danced in front of us, shouting and cheering, and the women of the city turned out in their holiday dresses.

'The people of the city have been robbed to supply the Turkish army for the last two years. The oppression was becoming unendurable, and during the last week it degenerated into brigandage. I am told that the mere mention of the British was punishable, and the people were afraid to talk freely about the war. It appears that the enemy abandoned all hope of saving the city when we effected the crossing of the Tigris on 22 February...

'The German Consul left weeks ago, and the Austrian two days since. The bridge of boats, the Turkish army clothing factory and Messrs Lynch's office were blown up or otherwise destroyed last night, and the railway station, the Civil Hospital and most British property except the Residency, which had been used as a Turkish hospital, were either gutted or damaged.

'As soon as the gendarmerie left at two o'clock this morning, Kurds and others began looting. As we entered from the east this morning, they were rifling, and among the first citizens we met were merchants who had run out to crave our protection.

'Regiments were detailed to police the bazaar and houses and pickets and patrols allotted, but there was much that it was too late

to save. Many shops had been gutted, and the valuables had all been cleared. The rabble was found busily engaged in dismantling the interiors, tearing down bits of wood and iron and carrying off bedsteads. They had even looted the seats from the public parks.

'Our entry was very easy and unofficial, and it was clear that the joy of the people was genuine. No functionaries came out to meet us. There is still fear of reprisals. Our own attitude was characteristic. There was no display or attempt at creating an impression. The troops entered, dusty and unshaven after several days hard fighting. Fighting between the 7th and 10th had been heavy, and extraordinary gallantry was shown in crossing the Diala river.'

Wisely, General Maude halted his advance as he felt his supply lines were too stretched. The British settled down for the summer in the capital. Sadly Maude died of cholera on 18 November; his place was taken by General William Marshal who now commanded a large army. Apart from capturing three towns, the army was largely one of occupation. With the campaign in Palestine still to be resolved, troops were transferred to Sinai and Palestine to help Allenby's advance.

The battle for Mesopotamia was all but finished. For Edmund Candler, it had been an unsatisfactory campaign to report, which he voiced in a letter dated 3 August 1918 to *The Times* editor: '*I am only sorry for the meagreness of the material I was allowed to send. I regret that the NPA should have saddled themselves with my full salary and expenses.*' He returned to India where he was appointed Director of Publicity to the Punjab Government.

Palestine
When the Ottoman Empire entered the war, it sought to attack a target that was vital to Britain – the Suez Canal. In January 1915, a German-led Turkish army invaded the Sinai Peninsula, then part of the British Protectorate of Egypt, in an attempt to take the Suez Canal or at least disrupt its traffic. The 30,000 strong British-Indian force, under the command of General Sir John Maxwell, concentrated their defences along the canal and managed to repulse the Turks. Little happened during the rest of the year until the arrival of nearly 400,000 men evacuated from Gallipoli to Egypt. Most were sent to France, but the remainder stayed.

In March 1916, this enlarged army was formed into the Egyptian Expeditionary Force (EEF) under the command of General Sir Archibald

Murray. One of the first things he did was to build a freshwater pipeline that extended to positions near the Palestine border. He also ordered the construction of a railway and the building of roads to ensure a flow of supplies.

The EEF was largely made up of British infantry and Anzac mounted troops. Also, the Royal Flying Corps and the Australian Flying Corps made their mark flying many bombing missions against concentrations of Turks.

Another confrontation that occupied the Turks was the start of the Arab Revolt in the south-western Arabian Peninsula. Already the Amir of Mecca had caused the Ottoman garrisons at Mecca and Jeddah to capitulate and was moving on Medina. The British were keen for the Arab Revolt to de-stabilise the Turks and in October 1916, they sent several Intelligence officers, including Thomas Edward Lawrence, to liaise with the Arab forces. Lawrence's main task was to persuade the Arab leaders, Faisel and Abdullah, to co-ordinate their actions in support of British strategy in Sinai and Palestine. During the campaign, Lawrence donned Arab dress and fought alongside the Arab irregular troops, most notably in the capture of Aqaba on the Red Sea.[3]

It was at the end of 1917 that the British campaign really got under way. It had already made two unsuccessful attempts to take Gaza, leading to General Murray being replaced by General Sir Edmund Allenby, who had himself suffered being dismissed from his command after the Somme. He met the newly-promoted Major Lawrence, who explained his strategy for the revolt. Allenby was impressed and paid tribute to him in 1935, after Lawrence's death:

'I gave him a free hand. His co-operation was marked by utmost loyalty, and I never had anything but praise for his work, which, indeed, was invaluable throughout the campaign. He was the mainspring of the Arab movement...'

The newspapers began to take an interest in the campaign, in what had been considered a backwater, now that events were moving towards a probable victory. There was, however, hardly a rush to send a crowd of journalists, so the NPA settled on selecting William Thomas Massey of the *Daily Telegraph* as their accredited war correspondent.

The British resumed active operations in October 1917 and won a string of stunning victories. Massey was on hand to witness the taking of Beersheba on 31 October and reported:

'By a rapid and well-developed surprise blow, General Allenby's army has smashed the western end of the Turks' entrenched line in Southern Palestine and wrested one of the most ancient Biblical towns from the enemy. In the early moonlight hours of Oct. 31 Beersheba was occupied by Australian mounted troops and British infantry after a stern day-long fight, in which our troops displayed great endurance and courage, doing everything planned for them, and working out the Staff scheme as if by the clock...

'Our movements were all done by night. At dawn yesterday the cavalry were south of the town, and the infantry were facing the northern, western and south-western defences, which were cut in the range of hills hiding Beersheba from view...On the night of Oct. 30-31, under a beautiful moon, our horsemen made a wide, rapid sweep round from the south to south-east, ready at dawn to rush up and cover the town from the east and get astride the Hebron road to prevent a retirement in that direction. The infantry were to attack the trenches on the south-east, but before that could be done, Hill 1070, about three miles to the south had to be taken. This hill had been made into a very strong redoubt, commanding a wide stretch, but an extremely heavy fire was brought to bear against it, and the gallant infantry carried it with an irresistible rush within half an hour of the attack. There was a German machine-gun section on the hill, but prisoners admitted that every machine-gun was knocked out by our fire...

'The advance against the south-western trench system was a great achievement. The Turks held on desperately, and time would not permit more than an hour's bombardment to cut the wire. The advance, too, was over exposed ground and, but for an extremely clever scheme, the infantry must have sustained serious loss...During the morning the shells were tearing up so much earth that a dense sand pall hid the line of entanglements they were cutting. Our infantry made rushes across the open, heeding neither the enfilade fire of the guns nor the spasmodic machine-gun fire. In a few places the shells had broken down the wire, and into these the bombers dashed, while others tore down the wire from the iron supports with their hands and

were upon the Turks before they realised that resistance was futile...
Fighting for more than ten hours had not lessened their
determination, and, moving steadily and methodically on the same
well thought out plan which had been so successful throughout the
day, they proceeded to capture one length of defences after another,
until at 9.30 all the Beersheba stronghold was ours.'

A week later, Massey reported from Gaza: *'This Philistine stronghold has*
been captured.' When Beersheba had been taken it made the fall of Gaza
inevitable and the Turks started to pull back, leaving behind a token force.

'Gaza, framed in a deep margin of field fortifications, was taken at
a cost of few casualties; yet, if it had been defended with the tenacity
which the Turks usually show, and we had to assault it, the cost of
victory would have been heavy.'

Allenby's army continued to move north and fought a series of actions
against the Turkish rearguard, particularly at Tel el Khuweife and Mughar
Ridge in the southern part of the Judean Hills. As a consequence of victory
at the latter, Jaffa was occupied on 19 November. Massey wrote of the
Turkish retreat:

'I have been over many miles of battlefield, and saw everywhere
many wagons and an enormous amount of under destroyed gun
ammunition, in places of field and heavy gun shells in boxes and
wicker crates.'

Allenby was now anxious to consolidate his position and to capture
Jerusalem before the onset of winter rains brought a halt to the advance. In
the event, the holy city fell after a single day's fighting. Massey managed to
get into the city before the official entry and found the population in a poor
state having been deprived of food by corrupt Turkish officers, who had
demanded extortionate prices for the release of grain. Despite their hunger,
Massey found...

'when we got into Jerusalem there were people willing to make flat
loaves of unleavened bread for sale to our troops. The soldiers had
been living for weeks on hard biscuit and bully beef and many were

willing to pay a shilling for a small cake of bread. They did not know that by buying this bread they were also taking it out of the mouths of the poor.'

On 11 December, General Allenby displayed a fine political sensibility as reported by a slightly-over-the-top Massey:

'By omitting to make a great parade of his victory...General Allenby gave Britain her best advertisement. The simple, dignified and, one may say, humble order of ceremony was the creation of a truly British mind...The General who by capturing Jerusalem helped us so powerfully to bring Germany to her knees and humble her before the world, entered on foot by an ancient way, the Jaffa Gate...A small, almost meagre procession, consisting of the Commander-in-Chief and his Staff, with a guard of honour, less than 150 all told, passed through the gate unheralded by a single trumpet note; a purely military act with a minimum of military display told the people that the old order had changed, yielding place to new.'

The Turkish army, now commanded by General Erich von Falkenhayn, made determined counter-attacks which were thrown back with heavy losses. For the Turks, the loss of Jerusalem was a grave blow to their prestige in the region. For the Allies, its capture offset the disappointments of Cambrai and Caporetto.

There was now a hiatus and progress north was effectively stalled. This was due to the 1918 March Offensive by the Germans, which meant the hasty transfer of troops from Allenby's army to the Western Front. At this time the EEF's front line stretched from the Mediterranean coast to the valley of the River Jordan by the Dead Sea. The Arabs to the east, with Lawrence's contribution, were still raiding and blowing up the only supply route, the Hajez Railway, which tied down thousands of Ottoman troops. While he was on one of his visits to HQ in Jerusalem, he met an American journalist and his cameraman. They would both have a profound effect on his post-war life.

As mentioned in Chapter 7, the photographer Frank Hurley had been sent to Palestine to cover the Australian contribution to the Palestine expedition. He was now joined by Henry Somer Gullett, who had been reporting on the Western Front in 1915 with the French army. Gullett had returned to

Australia to enlist as a gunner in the Australian Imperial Forces. When he was sent to England, he met Charles Bean, who was organising the Australian War Records. Bean persuaded Gullett to help, had him commissioned and sent him to Egypt to compile the War Records of the Australian forces serving in the EEF. His tenure was brief for the AIF saw in him what they had been denied – an experienced war correspondent – and Bean was happy for him to act as an accredited journalist with the Anzacs. He took up his new appointment in August 1918 – just in time for the launch of Allenby's final offensive.

With the dry season approaching and a build-up of reinforcements, the British resumed their campaign with a stunning victory at Megiddo on 19 September. At that moment, Allenby had some 12,000 cavalry, 57,000 infantry and nearly 500 guns, all fit and well equipped. The Turks were greatly weakened and could only muster 2,000 cavalry, 32,000 infantry and 400 guns. Allenby's plan was to fool the Turks about his intention to launch his attack up the Jordan Valley. Instead, he moved the bulk of his cavalry to the west, from where they would ride north along the coast before swinging east behind the Turkish army. The cavalry had to cover the distances of between 45 and 60 miles in one sweep. The intention was to capture the Turkish communication centres and attack their headquarters at Nazareth. In order to convince the enemy that his main force was positioned in the east, he had dummy camps erected with lines of dummy horses made of wood and canvas. The same few soldiers would march back and forth creating the impression of a build-up of troops. Mules trailing sleds were led about continuously to stir up clouds of dust. Finally, the Air Force flew constantly to keep the enemy's aircraft from the skies.

The ruse worked perfectly and the Turks moved men from the west to the east of their line. Allenby ordered a division to attack up the Jordan Valley, to confirm the Turks' belief that the main thrust of the attack was in the east. In the west, a brief bombardment heralded the vastly superior British force overwhelming the depleted Turkish defences and a wide front opened allowing the 9,000-strong cavalry to sweep behind the enemy lines. It was just what old cavalry commanders like French and Haig would love to have ordered. Massey wrote:

'It was General Allenby's cavalry that was responsible for the complete overthrow of the Turk. The infantry was able at any time to break through any line of defences the Turks might occupy after the

entrenched line from the sea to the Jordan had been carried, but alone they could not prevent a more or less methodical retirement. Nothing but the splendid mobility of the cavalry could have closed all the roads by which the enemy might have escaped, and, while it is equally true that without the infantry and artillery the cavalry could not have gained a passage through the entrenched line, the big results of the last months of the campaign were obtained by mounted troops.'

Some of the Gloucestershire Hussars did reach Nazareth, taking the enemy by surprise. Dressed in his pyjamas, the German commander, General Liman von Sanders only just managed to evade capture. The yeomanry searched the town, taking documents and some prisoners. As the Turkish armies fell back in confusion, they were repeatedly attacked by the Air Force, which bombed the fleeing columns.

In conjunction with this sweeping victory west of the Jordan River, the Arabs in the east were adding to the total disruption of the retreating Turks. Massey wrote:

'The sheiks of the Ruwalla tribe, one of the most powerful in Arabia, brought 3,000 horsemen and Haurani peasantry others, so that near Deraa there was a force of 11,000 camelry, horsemen and Arab irregulars with the column, which on September 16th got to the Hejaz Railway, south of Deraa, and blew up the line.

'Next day the north town was destroyed, with six kilometres of railway and an important bridge. On the night of the 18th they cut the line between Deraa and Nabulus, in the Yarmuk Valley, burning the station of Mezerib and the rolling stock, with six German lorries.

'The following day they moved south of Deraa, having made a complete circle round the town, and blew up the bridge. An armoured car saw two airplanes and riddled them with bullets. As the line was repaired it was again destroyed, so that the enemy's railway communication between Damascus and the main Turkish Army was broken for five days. The Amman garrison was cut off for eight days.

'Wherever the Arabs camped enemy planes bombed them, flying low and using machine guns. At one period near Deraa the enemy planes made frequent bombing raids, but were ineffectual to prevent the complete disorganisation of the railway service.

'The work of the Air Service has been most praiseworthy...Our planes south of Amman secured the surrender of 2,000 Turks. The pilot, seeing a long-drawn-out column, dropped a message to say if they did not surrender they would be bombed. He returned to the aerodrome and six machines shortly afterward were sent out with bombs, and while circling the ground the signal was laid out recalling them; the Turks had hoisted a white flag.'

Major T.E. Lawrence took part in much of the Arab raiding and he had attracted the attention of an American journalist named Lowell Jackson Thomas. When America entered the war, Thomas was asked by the War Department to gather material and stories that would encourage the American public's support. In other words, he wrote as a propagandist and even signed his correspondence, 'Lowell Thomas, Propagandist'.

While working for the *Chicago Daily News,* Thomas had exposed a conman who had stolen millions from the city of Chicago. In gratitude, some of the leading businessmen funded Thomas so he could visit the war fronts and submit patriotic reports. He was able to purchase the contract of a leading cameraman, Harry Chase, and together they travelled to Europe to cover the war. The trenches and mud of France were hardly rousing, so they moved to the Italian Front, where they learned of the capture of Jerusalem. Using his connection with fellow-propagandist John Buchan, he managed to get accreditation to move to Palestine. Buchan saw the value of throwing a spotlight on the recent victories in what: ' *...heretofore was an obscure struggle in the Middle East...*' and he sent a telegram to the HQ in Alexandria requesting that they do everything to help Thomas.

Leaving his wife in Italy to work with the Red Cross, Thomas with Chase travelled to Jerusalem, where he met T.E. Lawrence. Sensing a whiff of glamour, Thomas followed Lawrence to Aqaba, now the Northern Arabs' headquarters, on the understanding that they photograph and interview Arab leaders like Feisal. Spending two weeks with the Arab forces, Thomas wrote copious notes in his field journal on the conversations he had with Lawrence. Meanwhile, Harry Chase took hundreds of photographs and shot reels of 35mm film.

By the time Thomas returned to America, the war was over and there was no longer any need to build support for it. With all the excellent material he and Chase had collected on Lawrence and the Arab Revolt, Thomas set about putting together a film documentary entitled, *With Lawrence in Arabia.* Initially, Lawrence did not object, as the publicity would help the sales of his new book, *Seven Pillars of Wisdom.* As the film gained in popularity, so the relationship became strained, with Lawrence describing Thomas as a 'vulgar man'. It cannot be denied that in a war of many heroic men, the one that most people readily recall is T.E. Lawrence – *Lawrence of Arabia*.[4]

After the Battle of Megiddo, Allenby's advance was irresistible. By 1 October, Damascus was in British hands with the Ottoman Army in full retreat. On 14 October, Turkey requested an armistice and surrendered on 30 October.

Ward Price was on board a destroyer accompanying a troop transport to the Ottoman capital, Constantinople, on 10 November to witness its occupation:

'There was no demonstration of any kind. It seemed as if no one had even noticed the arrival of this herald of the British fleet. But as we drew near to the quay one saw the houses and the windows were thronged with people. The crowd had an unusual tone of red about it, derived from all the crimson fezzes bobbing to and fro as their wearers strained for a glimpse. And a few waved handkerchiefs.

'A German officer stood on the quay close to where the destroyer gradually came alongside. He was more interested than anyone, but affected indifference and yawned with care from time to time. A little group of German soldiers and sailors gradually formed behind him as if for mutual support. For years they had been the self-ordained military gods of this place, but now their altars are overthrown and they see Turkish naval officers of high rank hurrying past them to pay their respects to representatives of a nation they once thought they could despise.

'We are indeed, much surrounded by an unwelcome neighbourhood of Germans... Here in my bedroom at the Pera Palace Hotel there are Germans talking in the rooms on either side of me as I write. I gather from fragments overhead that they are packing up. One is pleased to think that their compatriots throughout Turkey are doing the same. As we drove up from the quay, too, there seemed a considerable number of Germans and also Austrians, in the streets. The Austrians saluted the party of British officers. The Germans swaggered by with a stare, the non-commissioned officers and men smoking cigars, which give them, to English eyes, a peculiar appearance of pretentiousness.'

An unpleasant sequel to the Palestine victory was the Surafend affair, which caused both horror and resentment amongst the Anzac Mounted Division. In early December, a New Zealand trooper was woken by a thief attempting to steal a bag he was using as a pillow. The soldier gave chase and as he caught up with him, the thief turned and shot him dead. The camp was roused and traced the footprints to the nearby village of Surafend. The Military Police were called in and made a thorough search of the village and could find no trace of the culprit or the stolen bag. On the night of 11 December, around 200 men of the Mounted Division and some Scottish soldiers, entered the village and expelled the women and children. They then attacked all the men with heavy sticks and bayonets and set fire to the houses. About 40 people were killed and upwards of 100 injured.

General Allenby was outraged and refused to acknowledge the Anzacs their considerable part played in the defeat of the Turkish Army. It was only when Henry Gullett spoke to the general about the great resentment felt by the Mounted Division, that Allenby relented and lavished praise on them for their service.[5]

Notes

1 The oilfields were essential to the Royal Navy, who had recently converted from coal-fired to oil-fired boilers.

2 General Sir Beauchamp Duff was the Commander-in-Chief of the Indian Army. After the humiliation of Kut and the Mesopotamian Report, he was relieved of command. Unable to live with the shame, he committed suicide on 20 January 1918.

3 T.E. Lawrence was one of several British and French officers serving in Arabia. Lieutenant-Colonel Stewart Newcombe, Captain Henry Hornby and Major H.Garland also led many attacks.

4 Lowell Thomas made T.E. Lawrence a household name when he toured the world narrating his film. To strengthen the emphasis on Lawrence, more shots of him were needed than had been taken in Palestine. Lawrence agreed to a series of posed shots in Arab dress which were taken in London. The film played to packed houses in London and about four million people saw the film around the world. It made Thomas $1.5 million.

5 No one was charged and the Anzacs refused to reveal names. Two years later, the governments of the three nations involved paid compensation to the authorities in Palestine.

Chapter 15

1918

T he dawn of the fourth year of the Great War found the opposing armies similarly gloomy about the prospects for 1918. On the Allied side, the British were only just coming to terms with the enormity of their losses at Passchendaele which had sapped their strength and morale. The army in 1918 was smaller than in 1917 and half the infantry were 19 or younger. Enlistments fell from 1.28 million in 1915 to 820,000 in 1917. Healthy manpower was not there any more. In 1917–18 only thirty-six per cent of men examined were suitable for full military duties.

Charles Repington was outraged when he found that the government were to add only 100,000 fit men to the Army.[1] His mood was not helped by what he saw as the misleading editorials that appeared in *The Times*. After a heated exchange, he left *The Times* on 16 January 1918 and joined the *Morning Post* a week later. Soon after, he attended a War Council conference in Paris and felt sufficiently appalled by its conclusions that he wrote an article exposing Lloyd George's failure to support the Army. His new editor, Howell Gwynne, supported him and managed to get it passed by the censor. The result was that Repington and Gwynne were charged under the Defence of the Realm Act, but got away with just fines of £100 each.

Another correspondent who fell foul of the authorities was Robert Dell of the *Manchester Guardian*. Based mostly in Paris, he wrote an account of the secret session of the French Chamber, at which an Austrian proposal for separate peace was discussed. As a result, Prime Minister Clemenceau expelled him and he was banned from France for several years.

The French army, too, was exhausted and running out of replacements for its enormous list of casualties. To the Allies it seemed that Germany was on the front foot.

From a German perspective, the prospects were less than rosy. True, she was now able to transfer fifty divisions from the Eastern Front now that

Russia had withdrawn from the war. If she had one less enemy to deal with, it was about to be replaced by another – the United States. The Royal Naval blockade of German imports was causing severe hardship and there were rumblings of civil unrest. Faced with the prospect of the war dragging on and further weakening the country, the two key German commanders, Field Marshal von Hindenburg and General Ludendorff, decided to launch an all-out offensive against the weakened Anglo-French defenders before the Americans arrived in force.

Dubbed the *Kaiserschlacht* – Kaiser's Battle – the Spring Offensive consisted of four major assaults code-named *Michael, Georgette, Blücher-Yorck* and *Gneisenau*. It was, in effect, the last throw of the dice, for German manpower was depleted and losses could not be effectively replaced.

In February 1918, Allied intelligence learned of the build-up of German forces opposite perceived weak points on the British front. These were aimed specifically at the Fifth Army commanded by General Hubert Gough and General Sir Julian Byng's Third Army, who together held a 40-mile front between Arras and La Fère. The goal was to cut the BEF off from the French in the south and to wheel north-west to the Channel ports. With the prospect of a rare German offensive, the military gave the war correspondents permission to warn the British public of the impending attack.[2]

Most of the divisional commanders dismissed the reports as *'GHQ, has the wind up'*, convinced that they could contain the German attack. This over-confidence was thrown into relief when Philip Gibbs was summoned to the headquarters of General Gough, who explained:

'We're holding this line very thinly in comparison with the great strength the enemy has massed against us. We may have to give ground. We may have to fall back on our main battle zone...Our real line of defence is the Somme. It will be nothing like a tragedy if we hold that. If we lose the Somme crossings it will, of course, be serious...It will only be a tragedy if we lose Amiens, and mustn't do that.'

It was a bitter pill to swallow; the prospect of surrendering all those hard-fought-for objectives for which so many had paid with their lives. Field Marshal Haig's call for more reinforcements was not well received by the British Government who were loath to send any more after the Passchendaele slaughter. Haig also called upon General Philippe Pétain to send troops but he was refused as the French were more concerned about protecting Paris. With no prospect of additional men, Haig was forced to tell Gough that he had to make do with what he had.

On 20 March, a raiding party from the Warwickshire Regiment took prisoners, who revealed that the long-anticipated attack would start the next day. Unbelievably, this piece of intelligence was ignored and no general alarm raised.

Operation Michael, the main German attack, began at 4.40am with a two-hour barrage of gas and HE shells. The infantry advanced in dense fog, smashed through the British lines and, in the misty confusion, captured pockets of defenders who found themselves cut off from the main body. In spite of the seeming ease with which they advanced, the Germans were sustaining heavy casualties from the British rearguard actions as they fought over the old battlefields of the Somme. For the reporters, they were as blind as the defenders and their reports conveyed their confusion.

Philip Gibbs reported in the *Daily Chronicle* on 23 March:

'Thursday's offensive was on a colossal scale. The Germans flung on the British the full weight of their great army, closely crowded with supporting troops, advancing mass after mass. At least fifty divisions (over half a million men, counting German divisions of 10,000) were engaged, of which forty were identified.

'We were much outnumbered, so the troops had extremely hard fighting. The obstinacy of their resistance was a wonderful feat of courage. Their discipline was splendid under the fiercest ordeal the British soldiers have yet faced.

'All the Germans were storm troops, including the Guards, who had been trained for many months for the great assault. They wore brand new uniforms, and did not falter, until they were shattered by our machine-gun fire. It was a return to the old methods of Mons and Le Cateau.

'Though continually mown down by our fire, the supporting waves advanced over the bodies of the dead and wounded, the German commanders ruthlessly sacrificing life in the hope of overwhelming the British defence.

'During the four hours' bombardment the Germans poured in gas shells, and they also concentrated gas on our batteries, reserves, and trenches all day long. The defenders had many weeks' training with

gas masks, which were a priceless help. Many of the men wore them for eight hours. The new respirators proved quite efficacious, there being only six cases of gassing at one of the large clearing stations.

'The main object of the enemy's attack on the left was probably to bite off the Bullecourt salient and pierce the three main lines of defence between Croiselles and St Leger, thus turning the line to enable him to capture Hennesle and the old Hindenburg tunnel trench.

'A little to the right lay the Bullecourt salient, which was smothered in flame, smoke and earth. No one could withstand such a storm and no men could hold on, but eventually, as was long foreseen, the outposts had merely to fall back. It was a battle for positions, where the stronger positions were aimed at in order to rally a counter-attack.

'The withdrawal was carried out in good order and with magnificent courage, in view of the intense enemy barrage. When the enemy followed up, bringing forward his light artillery, our guns smashed his ranks and left masses of dead on the field. The airmen say that large numbers of German dead were heaped in the debris of our wire, but others came on with fanatical courage, filling the gaps.

'Our guns and machine guns could not kill fast enough. After hard fighting at Bullecourt, Ecoust, and Noreuil, 3,000 of the enemy were seen in a sunken road between Noreuil and Lagnicourt. Apparently this would mean that the defenders at Noreuil had been pushed back, and that the survivors, after a strong, heroic defence, had been obliged to retire to the line Beaumetz – Morchies – Vaulx.

'Another enemy attack was made in the afternoon, in massed formation, down the slopes of the Sensee valley, from the Cherisy-Fontaine wood. Our guns fired with open sights, cutting down swathes and checking the assault. There was fierce fighting at St Leger, where we took prisoners and machine guns.

'The fighting was equally intense from Noreuil to Lagnicourt, on the bend of the Cambrai salient. The outposts were withdrawn in good order. The enemy, by great sacrifices, penetrated our defensive system near Lagnicourt, Boursies and Hargicourt, after which they were held by tanks. We brilliantly counter-attacked on Thursday evening, recapturing some of the ground at Doignies.

'Owing to our withdrawal behind the canal between St. Quentin and the Oise, the enemy is now confronted by a watery, marshy waste *in that sector. The spirit of our troops, despite the hard fighting, and they are proud that they have broken the backbone of the massed attacks, whereon the German hopes were fastened.'*

Despite the bullish tone of Gibbs's report, it was hardly a cause for optimism. By the end of the first day, the British had suffered 20,000 dead and 35,000 wounded. Gough's Fifth Army was all but destroyed and the unpopular general was replaced by General Sir Henry Rawlinson.

By 5 April, the German army had advanced some 40 miles and was within range of Amiens. Philip Gibbs recalled that the town was thinly defended as he and a small group of fellow correspondents sat down for a meal at the Hotel du Rhin. Their dinner was interrupted by a shell that landed nearby and Captain Cadge, the military minder, raised the question whether…

'we should go or stay that night. The enemy might come into Amiens at any hour and we might all be captured. Was there any sense in that? There seemed to be a diversity of opinion amongst us. Cadge wrote out seven ballot papers and suggested we should put an X against the alternative Stay or Go. I voted for staying. So did the majority of the others. We stayed the night in Amiens. It was not an amusing night. Until 4.40 in the morning the enemy sent over squadrons of aeroplanes and bombed this small town mercilessly.'

The raid caused large fires and over 2,000 houses were destroyed. The following morning, Gibbs noted that the body of a British officer lay at the entrance of the Hotel du Rhin. He had been killed as he banged on the door.

The Germans failed to take Amiens thanks in no small part to the Australian Brigade, who made a surprise attack on Villers-Bretonneux, a village to the east of the town. They had just joined the front after a period of rest behind the lines and had not taken part in the exhaustion of retreat. They were the ideal reserves and as Gibbs observed:

'They were great fighters who had developed a marvellous team-work of their own, differing from our English discipline – they were the bad boys behind the lines – but magnificent and grim in action.'

The German advance had run out of steam. There was still fighting for strategic objectives but the forward momentum had been lost. One significant fight was the German attempt to retake Villers-Bretonneux. Percival Phillips of the *Daily Express* reported the battle on 26 April:

'For the first time British and German tanks have met in battle, and the victory is ours. They fought yesterday in the open fields around Villers-Bretonneux, east of Amiens, where the enemy made a determined and, for the moment, a successful attack on that town and high ground round it.

'The German tanks [the A7V] led the attack, swinging on the town from the north-east and from the south, and in their wake came infantry with their machine-guns and heavy mortars and light artillery.

'Although there were four or five tanks, they were bulky, ungainly creatures, quite unlike the British tank in appearance, with a broad, squat turret containing quick-firing guns. Hidden in the thick mist until very close to our trenches, they crawled up in the wake of an intense barrage about six o'clock in the morning.

'They concentrated their guns on one British tank [Mark IV], but others came to the rescue, and in a brief duel that followed one enemy tank was put out of action by an opponent of less bulk and lighter armament and the others scuttled away.

'The lesson of this first engagement between German and British tanks seems to be that we have nothing to fear from the enemy despite the greater size and armament of his machine. The crews plainly showed their unwillingness to stand when invited to fight out to a finish.'[3]

With the British sending men south to protect Amiens, it left the Ypres sector vulnerable to attack. This was just what Ludendorff planned and he was now ready to launch Operation Georgette, the Lys offensive.

At dawn on 9 April, the German guns opened up with a four-hour barrage of HE and gas shells. The first objective was the area around Neuve Chapelle. Once again, the dense fog favoured the attackers, who by-passed strongpoints and caused panic when they appeared behind the defenders. Guarding this sector was the Portuguese 2nd Division, under strength, partly-trained and totally unprepared for the German attack. It was little wonder that a large part of the Portuguese force fled the field. In just eight hours, the Germans had punched a hole in the British positions that was ten miles wide and five miles deep.

The following day, the defenders were pushed further back across the River Lys, surrendering Armentières, Ploegsteert and the hard-fought-for Messines Ridge. On 12 April, the most bitter pill of all was swallowed when General Plumer ordered that Passchendaele should be abandoned. Percival Phillips wrote in the 18 April edition of the *Daily Express:*

> *'Our withdrawal from Passchendaele and the ground for which so many men of the Empire have died causes the deepest regret, but it has not discouraged the soldiers, who know that in open warfare trench positions lose their former value, and that the people at home will regard the sacrifice in the same sensible way.'*

One wonders which soldiers Phillips spoke to, to conclude they were not discouraged about evacuating a position which had just a few months before had cost the lives of thousands.

For the British war correspondents it was a frustrating time. They had been accustomed to responding to the timetable of British offensives when they could get a grandstand view of the battle. Now that the BEF was in retreat, they found themselves driving for hours in the hope of making sense of the ever-changing front lines. Small wonder that their reports were heavily reliant on official communiqués. Their composition changed with Hamilton Fyfe covering for Beach Thomas, who was on a lecture tour of the United States. The latter would return to see out the war. The absence of Philip Gibbs, who was taken sick and had to return to England, was filled by Henry Nevinson.

By 30 April the front line was perilously close to Ypres town, swinging south-west towards the railhead at Hazebrouck and finishing just above Béthune. Haig issued his 'backs to wall' message to his troops, which was aimed equally at the British public. Despite these gains made at a casualty cost of 109,300 men, the German advance ran out of steam causing Ludendorff to halt the operation. Philip Gibbs summed it up: '*Well, the agony passed. The frightful menace frustrated. The great German offensive wilted and failed and stopped.*' For the time being, the BEF was able to lick its wounds, while the Germans consolidated their gains.

The French had been highly critical of the British for failing to hold their front line and it must have been with a certain amount of *schadenfreude* that the British watched while the Germans launched their third operation, Blücher-Yorck. Although a few British units were involved, it was in the French sector of Aisne that Ludendorff launched his offensive on 27 May. The main thrust was against the French Sixth Army holding the line between Rheims and Soissons. As with the previous two operations, the Germans smashed through the French defences, pushing the Allies back to the River Marne.

This brought the capital in range of the Germans' heaviest artillery in the shape of the rail-mounted 'Paris gun'.[4] One of these monsters was captured during the British attack outside Amiens on 9 August. General Foch, the new Allied army supreme commander, had ordered the securing of the lateral railways vital for moving troops up and down the front. Men of the 1st Cavalry Brigade, made up of the Queen's Bays, 5th Dragoon Guards and the 11th Hussars, had been ordered forward into open country and came upon a train drawing a massive train gun. It had been attacked by a Royal Air Force Sopwith Camel, which had set one of the wagons alight.[5] As the Germans attempted to steam away, the cavalry galloped into action, and after a stiff fight, captured the gun which was later put on show in Paris.

With the American Army (AEF) arriving in increasing numbers, they were soon thrown into the front line. On 28 May, the AEF fought its first battle at the hamlet of Cantigny, about 15 miles from Amiens. The battle commenced at 6.45am and on hand was the war reporter Jimmy Hopper of *Collier's Weekly*, who accompanied the 26th Infantry. They were supported by twelve tanks of the French 5th Battalion and it took just 45 minutes for the Americans to take Cantigny for the loss of 100 men. As they entered Cantigny, Hopper was taken aback when he was mistaken for an American officer and accepted the surrender of fifteen Germans. Regaining his composure, Hopper marched them back to the American lines. Two days later, the Germans counter-attacked but were beaten back. This small battle showed the French and British that the AEF could fight and win.

In June 1917, Frederick Palmer had been persuaded by the American commander, General John 'Black Jack' Pershing, to take on the task of press censor for the AEF, as he was the only American reporter who had been accredited to the BEF and was conversant with British and French press policies. Palmer had been accredited to represent the three American wire services, AP, UP and INS, which made him the official reporter for all American newspapers. He had spent nearly fifty years reporting wars, including the Greco-Turkish War of 1897, the Boxer Rebellion, the Boer

War, the Russo-Japanese War and the 1912 Balkan War. He became the first war correspondent to be awarded the US Army Distinguished Service Medal. President Teddy Roosevelt called Palmer *'our best war correspondent'*. He was still reporting in the Second World War and was at Dunkirk as the BEF was evacuated.

General Pershing decided to allow twelve accredited war correspondents to accompany the AEF. Each press association and newspaper had to deposit $3,000 with the War Department to ensure payment for any expenses incurred by the Army, e.g. transport. It was also held as a forfeit for any reporter who broke the censorship.

American censorship was no less stringent than its British equivalent. When the first Americans arrived, they suffered during the winter of 1917–18 because of chronic shortages of equipment, with men dying of pneumonia for want of dry clothing and shelter. When this was reported by Heywood Broun in the *New York World*, he lost his accreditation and his paper was fined $10,000.

Another American correspondent who had an eventful war was Floyd Gibbons, who was sent by the *Chicago Tribune* to cover the war in Europe. In fact, he secured his first story before he even reached the Continent. His ship, the Cunard SS *Laconia*, was torpedoed off southern Ireland on 25 February 1917. Fortunately, all but twelve of the passengers and crew managed to take to the lifeboats and were saved. For a journalist, this was manna from heaven, and he gained fame through his despatches about the sinking:

> *'It is a little over thirty hours since I stood on the slanting decks of the big liner, listened to the lowering of the lifeboats, heard the hiss of escaping steam and the roar of ascending rockets as they tore lurid rents in the black sky and cast their red glare over the roaring sea...'*

He recalled that a small group of male passengers had been in the first-class lounge discussing the odds of being torpedoed, when:

> *'At this moment the ship gave a sudden lurch sideways and forward. There was a muffled noise like the slamming of some large door at a good distance away. The slightness of the shock and the meekness of the report compared with my imagination were disappointing. Every*

man in the room was on his feet in an instant. I looked at my watch. It was 10.30 pm...

'The torpedo had hit us well astern on the starboard side and had missed the engines and the dynamos...Steam began to hiss somewhere from the giant grey funnels that towered above...There was a tilt to the deck. It was listing to starboard at just the angle that would make it necessary to reach for support to enable one to stand upright...'

Gibbons related the difficulty they had in lowering his lifeboat:

'The list of the ship's side became greater, but, instead of our boat sliding down it like a toboggan, the taffrail caught and was held. As the lowering continued, the other side dropped down and we found ourselves clinging on at a new angle and looking straight down on the water. Many hands and feet pushed the boat from the side of the ship, and we sagged down again, this time smacking squarely on the pillowy top of a rising swell. It felt more solid than in mid-air, at least. But we were far from being off. The pulleys stuck twice in their fastenings, bow and stern, and the one axe passed forward and back, and with my flashlight, as the entangling ropes that held us to the sinking Laconia *were cut away...*

'As we pulled away from the side of the ship, its receding terrace of lights stretched upwards. The ship was slowly turning over...We rested on our oars, with all eyes on the still lighted Laconia*...It was thirty minutes afterward that another dull thud, which was accompanied by a noticeable drop in the hulk, told its story of the second torpedo that the submarine had dispatched through the engine room and the boat's vitals from a distance of two hundred yards. We watched silently during the next minute, as the tiers of lights dimmed slowly from white to yellow, then to red, and nothing was left but the murky mourning of the night, which hung over all like a pall.'*

The occupants of the lifeboats endured a bitter cold six hours adrift before they were rescued by a Royal Navy mine sweeper and taken to the port of Queenstown.

In June 1918, Gibbons was present at the Third Battle of the Aisne, when the 5th US Marine Corps gained their battle honour for the battle of Belleau Wood, just to the east of Château-Thierry. His part was painfully brief as he, and his military minder, Lieutenant Oscar Hartzel of the Intelligence Division, persuaded the battalion commander, Major Berry, to allow them to accompany the attack.

The Marines were poised on the edge of a V-shaped field of oats, bordered on all sides by thick woodland. Gibbons later recalled that Berry gave the order to advance, stepping out first himself, with each man following at ten to fifteen yard intervals. Gibbons and Hartzel were next in line to Berry. Gibbons related the events to his brother Edward, who wrote:

> '*As they reached the middle of the field, German machine-gunners a hundred yards to their left, opened up. Berry ordered everybody down, and they flattened themselves in the young oats as best they could. Floyd looked up to see Major Berry, his right hand holding the stump of what had been his left hand, still standing.*
>
> '*Floyd yelled for him to get down, and started inching towards him. Trying to hide his movements from the German machine-gunners, Floyd crawled along, his left cheek hugging the ground and his helmet pushed over the right, partly covering his face on that side. He had only gotten but a few feet when a bullet hit him in the left arm, just above the elbow, going in one side and out the other. He continued to push himself forward. A few moments later, another bullet hit him in the left shoulder blade, still he inched on. Another five feet along, a third bullet hit him, it ricocheted off a rock in the ground, and with an upward course ripped out his left eye, continuing on, making a compound fracture of the skull, and finally coming out on the right side of his helmet where it blew a hole three inches long.*
>
> '*Remarkably, Floyd did not lose consciousness, he was dazed, and experienced a sensation of a lot of glass crashing around him, everything turning white in his mind's eye. His eyeball was lying on his cheek split in half. His left hand and arm were numb and out of commission. He wondered if he was dead...*
>
> '*Movement in any direction was now impossible. A mortally wounded Marine near him lay thrashing about, bringing machine-gun spray just inches from Floyd. Floyd watched the bullets rip apart the young man's body, buttons and parts of his uniform flying off, 'til finally he lay still.*
>
> '*A short time later Floyd looked up to see Major Berry jump to his feet, and in a hail of bullets, get back to the woods. Floyd learned*

later the major was able to get word back to a light artillery unit,
enabling the unit to wipe out the German machine-gun nest holding
up the advance.'[6]

Floyd Gibbons was helped back to a field hospital by Lieutenant Hartzel
and then to a base hospital where he was operated on. Apart from the loss
of his left eye, he made a good recovery and, in August, received the French
Croix de Guerre with Palm.

For a month, Germany had pushed back the British and French until
exhaustion and larger-than-expected losses forced another stalemate.
Ludendorff's Operation Blücher-Yorck had been brought to a standstill. The
Germans had punched three large holes in the Allied defences but had been
unable to deliver the killer blow. The arrival of the Americans and the fact
that they had made an immediate impact made a German victory
unobtainable. There was one more offensive that might achieve a
breakthrough and that was Operation Gneisenau.

On 15 July, Ludendorff opened the Second Battle of the Marne, attacking
both sides of Rheims. Initially, the Germans made great progress pushing
east towards Epernay. Foch and General Pétain then ordered a counter-stroke
which threatened to encircle the Germans in the salient they had created.
Realising the danger, Ludendorff ordered a withdrawal, so ending
Germany's Hundred Days Offensive. The effort had cost the Germans
200,000 casualties. The initiative had clearly passed to the Allies.

On 8 August, the Allied fight-back commenced with General
Rawlinson's Fourth Army and the French First Army attacking the Germans
in an early morning mist and taking the enemy by complete surprise. In two
days about eight to ten miles had been taken with 24,000 prisoners and some
300 guns. The attack began with a four-minute hurricane barrage, followed
by the infantry and tanks under a creeping barrage. The momentum was with
the Allies and by the 27 August, they were back to their former line on the
Somme. Ludendorff called it *'the blackest day of the German Army'*.

William Beach Thomas had returned in time for the Allied Offensive
after his lecture tour of America. Losing none of his flowery rhetoric, he
wrote in the *Daily Mail*, 9 August:

'From dawn to midday we watched along the cliff of the Somme one
of the greatest single feats of arms in the annals of the British Army,
and the arms were of the strangest and most varied sorts.

'On the ground were our iron horses on caterpillar feet; 300ft above flew airmen whose impudent audacity has never been equalled. Seldom did an adventure end more triumphantly or begin in greater strain...'

Perry Robinson wrote in the *Daily News* on 10 August:

'I have spent much of the day, from early morning until noon, walking over parts of the battlefield, having first the extraordinary experience of being able to pass in a motor-car not only over what yesterday was No Man's Land, but over trenches of the front German system, and from my seat look down on the enemy dead below. When the road became impassable by reason of the shell-holes made by our guns, one could stray at large over the great deserted plain, while the guns thudded intermittently and our aeroplanes wheeled overhead.'

On 27 August, as he approached the village of Pozières on the Somme battlefield, Henry Nevinson spotted some small pockets of Germans approaching. He was joined by a New Zealand officer armed with a pistol, but no bullets, and together they called for the Germans to surrender. The demoralised enemy raised their hands and Nevinson took them back to the British lines.

Two days later, Nevinson was in the thick of some fighting when he was pinned down with the remains of the Middlesex Regiment, who had lost 200 men. With some difficulty, the veteran reporter managed to crawl back to safety and enjoyed a reviving drink in an officer's dug-out. This was the last action he witnessed, as Philip Gibbs returned to resume his long-held role.

Gibbs reported on the Battle of Amiens of 27 August:

'In July, it was Rupprecht's army that was the chief threat against us, and it was an army of perhaps 250,000 fresh troops, apart from those in line waiting to be hurled against us if the German Crown Prince could do without them...After that the tide turned in an astonishing way. It is now the enemy who is on the defensive, dreading the hammer blows that fall upon him day after day, and the initiative of attack is so completely in our hands that we are able to strike him at many different places.

'Since 8 August, we have taken nearly 50,000 prisoners and 500 guns...Many of them...admit they do not care how peace comes as long as there is peace. They are sullen with their own officers, and some of those whom I saw today were more than sullen...

'The success of our infantry is the more remarkable because in this battle very few tanks have been used, and machine-gun nests had to be taken in many cases without their help. The advance gives a sense of the enormous movement behind the British lines, and there is not a man who is not stirred by the motion of it. They are feeling that they indeed are getting on with the war. It is like a vast tide of life moving slowly but steadily.'

The Allies were now advancing over familiar territory and re-occupying towns that had been largely reduced to rubble: Albert, Peronne, Merville, Amentières and passing over the Hindenburg Line. Between 27 September and 1 October a most decisive battle was won by the British, French and Americans when they managed to cross the St. Quentin Canal, one of the most formidable strongpoints on the Hindenburg Line.

Germany's allies, the Austro-Hungarians, the Turks and Bulgarians had sued for peace and the Central Powers alliance was no more. On 29 September, Ludendorff demanded that the German Government seek an armistice with the Allies.

More victories followed in quick succession including the Second Battle of Cambrai. Between 14–19 October the Second Battle of Belgium saw the Army Group of Flanders, comprising British, Belgian and French divisions, recapture the Belgian towns of Menin, Courtrai, Roulers, Ostend, Bruges, Zebrugge and the French towns of Lille and Douai.

Philip Gibbs had followed the advance into Belgium and recalled the joy of the civilians in those liberated towns. He remembered particularly the entry into Lille:

'For more than four years the inhabitants of Lille had been under German rule, which had been harsh and intolerable. Everything had been taken from them – the mattresses of their beds, their linen, their brass pots and candlesticks, their silver and pewter, the machinery out of their factories. The greatest outrage against them was the forcible levy of young girls sent behind the German line for slave labour, and the seizure of able-bodied young men for the same

purpose. They had suffered, these people of Lille, and for years they had heard the guns, and the noise of great battles, as the British Army fought towards Lens and Vimy Ridge. They had seen the flash of gunfire and had lived on hope, year after year, that one day we should come. At last we had come. Their joy delirious.

'So it was in Bruges...Beach Thomas and I, taking a chance, went into that lovely old city before we were quite sure the Germans had left it. But they had gone that morning...I had a special reason for getting into Bruges. I had a sister-in-law – my wife's sister, Beryl – who was a nun in a convent there. We had heard nothing from her during the years of war. We did not know whether she was alive or dead. I found my way to the convent of St André and saw a nun walking down the path.

"Hullo, Beryl", I called out.

'She looked at me as though she saw a ghost. Then she gave a cry and ran towards me and flung her arms round my neck. To her it was like a miracle from Heaven. She did not know that the Germans had left Bruges. That very morning they had been in the convent grounds.'

Charles Repington expressed in his diary on 5 November 1918 the absence of jubilation at the prospect of victory:

'We have most of us lost by custom the capacity for surprise, joy or sorrow. A dead, numb, implacable feeling of seeing the thing through fills our minds. There has not been a flag raised, nor a bell rung, for all the victories of these past four months, unequalled though they may be. The feeling is so strong that most people have shut it up in their hearts and give little open expression to it...'

On the morning of 11 November 1918, Gibbs was making his way to Mons, where the war had begun for the BEF. Men and guns were still trudging through the mist towards the retreating Germans, when he came upon an officer who told him that hostilities would cease at eleven o'clock:

'We knew it was coming. For several days there had been talk of a German surrender...Now it had come, and it seemed unbelievable. Peace? Could it be possible? No more blood! No more casualties! No more mutilated, blinded, and shell-shocked men. No more

sacrifice of boys, too young to die...I followed behind our transport wagons on the way to Mons. We looked at our wrist-watches – 11am.
'Through the white woolly mist, a bugle sounded. It was Cease Fire to a world war.'

In contrast to the jubilation expressed at home, the soldiers' reaction was generally muted and dazed. They knew that they and the rest of the world would never be the same.

Notes

1 Charles Repington wrote that Prime Minister Lloyd George feared a social revolution if more men were sent to France. *'The absurdity of this argument was shown later. Between our defeat in March 1918 and the Armistice of November, we sent 740,624 men to France, including 112,738 Dominion troops, and there was not one murmur, still less a social revolution.'*
2 This was the first offensive mounted by the Germans since Mons and Verdun.
3 The commander of the British tank was Lieutenant Frank Mitchell who, after several attempts, managed to put three 6-pound shells into his adversary causing it to keel over. He then fired on two other German tanks, which retreated. For this action, Mitchell received the Military Cross.
4 With its 130 ft long barrel, the railway gun could hurl its missile 80 miles. Between 23 March and 9 August, it fired around 350 HE shells at the city. Near panic gripped Paris and more than a million people fled the city.
5 The Royal Air Force came into being on 1 April 1918, replacing the Royal Flying Corps.
6 *Floyd Gibbons –Your Headless Hunter* by Edward Gibbons. Exposition Press NY 1953.

Chapter 16

An Uneasy Peace

D ates can be misleading. True, the First World War ended in November 1918, but the previous four years had seen regimes tumble and empires disappear, leaving a huge vacuum to be filled by competing forces. The Austro-Hungarian Empire fell apart and its components declared themselves either independent republics, like Hungary, Czechoslovakia and Yugoslavia, or were united with their ethnic brethren in Poland, Ukraine and Romania. The Habsburg dynasty, which had ruled since 1273, ended in a whimper for Charles I when a new Austrian republican government took power in 1919. Ironically, the opening sentence of the Habsburg motto states 'Leave the waging of wars to others!' Words it had been unwise to ignore.

Over the decades, the Ottoman Empire had been steadily eroded until all that was left was its homeland, Turkey. The Middle East lands it lost were to become a huge headache for the world, from Palestine and Iraq, to more recently, Syria. In the aftermath, a former army officer, Mustafa Kemal, created the Republic of Turkey and accorded the surname Atatürk (meaning 'Father of the Turks'). Under his leadership, Turkey gained from its defeat by transforming itself into a modern, secular and democratic nation-state.

Russia, which had withdrawn from the war with the signing of the Brest-Litovsk Treaty on 3 March 1918, descended into a long civil war which resulted in both famine and the iron grip of Soviet Russia. The Tsar and his family did not get to go into comfortable exile, but were murdered at Yekaterinburg in July 1918.

Exactly five years after Gavrilo Princip fired those fatal shots in Sarajevo, the Treaty of Versailles was signed on 28 June 1919, formally ending the state of war between the Allies and Germany. The treaty forced Germany to disarm, pay reparations and concede territories – conditions that many regarded as too harsh. The country went through a harrowing decade with hyper-inflation, hunger, near-civil war and the emergence of Adolf Hitler and the Nazi Party. It also saw the demise of the Hohenzollern dynasty with Kaiser Wilhelm II forced into exile in the Netherlands.[1]

The euphoria the world enjoyed at the end of 1918 was countered by a devastating influenza pandemic. It had swept through the German Army during its long retreat contributing to its demise. Even the Kaiser caught it but survived. Dubbed the Spanish Flu, it affected most nations throughout the world, ranging from remote Pacific islands to the Inuits in the Arctic. Lasting from January 1918 to December 1920, the epidemic killed between 50 and 100 million, making it one of the deadliest natural disasters in human history.

For the war correspondents, there was no longer any fighting to follow, but there was a peace to report. The newspapers wanted to know of conditions in Germany and how the population were coping with defeat. In June 1919, Philip Gibbs and his colleagues followed the British Army through Liège, Spa and across the German border into the town of Malmédy. They accompanied a patrol of Dragoon Guards, whose young lieutenant was apprehensive: *'We shall probably get sniped'*, he said. In the event, the town was welcoming and just relieved that they had been spared the ordeal of being fought over.

A few days later, they reached Cologne and the bridge over the Rhine. One of the conditions of the Versailles Treaty was that the Allies occupied Germany west of the Rhine. Gibbs wrote:

'On the morning of our arrival, a British Tommy walked on to the Hohenzollern Bridge and drew a line across it half way with a bit of white chalk. It was the line and limit of our military occupation of the German Fatherland. Sir Douglas Haig came riding onto the bridge with an escort of lancers. He dismounted and spoke to a small group of men standing there in the dank mist of a November day. They were a little group of war correspondents whom he summoned to meet him.

'"Gentlemen", he said, "you know as well as I do all the sacrifices, and all those losses, and all the valour of our men on the way to the Rhine which we have now reached. I hope we shall make a just peace and not a peace of vengeance which will lead us to a new war".'

'He thanked us for our services. "You have been the chroniclers of this war," he said, "You have done fine work".'

Gibbs and his colleagues found the population of Cologne very friendly towards the British presence. This had probably more to do with the threat that came from the sailors and marines of the German High Seas Fleet who had mutinied and formed themselves into marauding militias. They had marched into Cologne and other cities, looting shops and stores. With the breakdown of law and order, they released the inmates from the prison, who joined them in their orgy of pillaging. With the arrival of the British Army, order was quickly restored.

Gibbs later wrote:

'So the occupation of the Rhineland began under British, French and American command in different zones. In our zone there was immediate fraternisation to which commanding officers and the civil administration turned a blind eye... Our men liked the Germans and the German way of life. They liked them far better than the French among whom they had lived.'[2]

In the French zone, the occupation was far tougher, with the French, who had suffered the most, exacting petty revenge and humiliation. There were between 25,000 and 40,000 French colonial troops, mostly Senegalese, based in Rhineland, who committed rape and other atrocities against the civilian population. This led to considerable racial tensions, which was further stoked up by the right-wing press. The Armies of Occupation remained until the last of the French departed in 1929.

In 1920, the accredited war reporters were offered knighthoods. Henry Fyfe Robinson saw it as a bribe to keep quiet about the inefficiency and corruption he had witnessed. He believed that Britain's political and military leaders had made fatally bad decisions during the war. He was also a strong critic of the Versailles Peace Treaty, which he felt would force Germany into another war. He was joined by his fellow radical Henry Nevinson, who also predictably turned down the award.

The war reporters who did accept the honour were Philip Gibbs, William Beach Thomas, Percival Phillips and Herbert Russell. Both Thomas and Gibbs were conscience-stricken and considered refusing their honours but, in the event, they both bent their knees.

Gibbs wrote of his investiture:

'I was in a tall hat and a tail coat, and on the side of my coat, according to instructions, a little loop had been sewn. There was a

queue of naval and army officers, airmen, military nurses and others...When my turn came, I knelt down on one knee on a velvet cushion – it could be frightful, I thought, if I had a touch of cramp – held my top hat in one hand and saw the King take a step in my direction. He touched me on the shoulder with a sword, hung a silver star on the loop of my tail coat, and put a cross and ribbon round my neck...'

Later, a friend told Gibbs that a result of his elevation would be that his meals would cost more. In common with other war reporters, Gibbs also became a Chevalier of the Legion d'Honneur.

Gibbs undertook a trip to report on the conditions in the capital cities of the former enemies. In Berlin, he found a city untouched by the war, where life was attempting to get back to normal. He noted young men who had recently been wearing field grey now dressed in civilian clothes:

'They all carried black attaché cases filled with papers, diagrams and blueprints...They were getting back to business much more quickly than our officers were doing in England.'

But elsewhere, he saw the dismal effects of war on the population: *'In the streets the crowds looked shabby, but not stricken by defeat...'*

Also noted was a sight that would be all too common on the streets of Europe:

'On street corners stood blinded men licenced by the police, motionless, with match-boxes on trays. Cripples without legs wheeled themselves about on bits of board. They were the men who fought in Flanders and on the Somme. This was their reward – to stand sightless listening to the passing crowds, or showing their limbless bodies to passers-by who turned their heads away, The Glory of War!'

Travelling to Vienna, Gibbs found the city:

'more stricken than Berlin. It was utterly stricken...There was no gaiety now but only misery. Along Kärntnerstrasse emaciated people passed, and in the days that followed thin hands clawed at me and

begged for charity. There was in Vienna, at that time in winter, no fuel in the houses, and no lighting because there was no fuel, and very little food anywhere, even for foreigners like myself who had the means to pay for it.'

He found more than 60 per cent of children were suffering from rickets and malnutrition. A group of doctors and scientists from the Lister Institute in London had arrived to set up clinics in an effort to treat these sick children. He also met an English woman named Eglantyne Jebb, who had raised money for a new fund to bring relief to the starving children of Austria and Germany. She had been arrested in Trafalgar Square for handing out leaflets that had not been passed by the government censors showing photos of starving children. Despite this, she raised £10,000 and was able to deliver aid to Vienna within just ten days. So began the charity Save the Children Fund.[3]

Philip Gibbs returned to England and then embarked on a long lecture tour of the USA. When he returned, he resigned from the *Daily Chronicle* over its support for the government's Irish policy.[4] Instead, he concentrated on adding to his series of books about the Great War with *The Realities of War* (1920) – a chance to air his frustration at wartime censorship, at incompetent generals, and to write truthfully what he knew about life on the frontline but had been unable to have published.[5]

He was a prolific writer and produced over fifty novels over the next thirty years. In 1946, he completed his biography in which he returned to his experiences in the First World War, which still had a profound effect on him. He died on 10 March 1962, aged 82.

Gibbs's colleague and friend, William Beach Thomas, also wrote a book in 1925 entitled *A Traveller in Time*. Like Gibbs, he used it as a confessional for the misleading reports he and the other reporters submitted to their newspapers. He wrote about the Somme battle:

'A great part of the information supplied to us by [British Army Intelligence] *was utterly wrong and misleading. The despatches were largely untrue so far as they deal with concrete results. For myself, on the next day and yet more on the day after that, I was thoroughly and deeply ashamed of what I had written, for the very good reason that it was untrue. Almost all the official information was wrong. The vulgarity of enormous headlines and the enormity of one's own name did not lessen the shame.'*

A cynical observer might point to the fact that both outspoken books were published after the authors had received their knighthoods, but at least they tried to offer an explanation for the biased reporting.

Beach Thomas went on to write articles on foreign affairs and resumed a weekly column on country matters. Appropriately, his last book published in 1944, was entitled *The Way of a Countryman* – a fitting memorial to a man out of his depth.

Percival Phillips also attended the Paris Peace Conference in 1919 before being sent to Ireland to cover the start of the war for Irish Independence. He also accompanied the Prince of Wales on many royal tours including Canada (1921) India and Japan (1921–22) and Africa (1928 and 1930). He covered all the major stories around the world, which probably prevented him from writing a book about his experiences as a war reporter. In 1936, he was invalided home while covering the Spanish Civil War and died soon after in January 1937.

Charles Montague, the newspaper editor turned censor, returned to the *Manchester Guardian* until his retirement in 1925. He wrote several books, including novels and a collection of essays, one of which was *Disenchantment* (1922), in which he argued:

> *'The freedom of Europe, The war to end all war, The overthrow of militarism, The cause of civilization – most people believe so little now in anything or anyone that they would find it hard to understand the simplicity and intensity of faith with which these phrases were once taken among our troops, or the certitude felt by hundreds of thousands of men who are now dead that if they were killed their monument would be a new Europe not soured or soiled with the hates and greeds of the old.*
>
> *'So we had failed – had won the fight and lost the prize; the garland of war was withered before it was gained. The lost years, the broken youth, the dead friends, the women's overshadowed lives at home, the agony and bloody sweat – all had gone to darken the stains which most of us had thought to scour out of the world that our children would live in. Many men felt, and said to each other, that they had been fooled.'*

Charles Repington, the brilliant diarist and correspondent, experienced mixed fortunes in the post-war years. After the war, he joined the *Daily*

Telegraph and wrote several books, including two volumes of his war-time diaries, which sold well. In them he divulged private conversations and correspondence which alienated many former friends, who felt he had betrayed them. Repington is credited with coining the phrase 'First World War' in 1919 and used in the title of his war diary published in 1920. Repington and his long-suffering wife, moved to Brighton where he died in 1925.

After the Armistice, people learned more about what had happened during the war. It was clear that the world had gone through a revolution which had changed society. Britain, France, Germany and the other warring nations seemed to be populated by black-garbed spinsters and widows and men who were physical and mental cripples. Peoples' attitude had changed towards authority and what they read. Indeed, by the late 1920s, when much of the truth was told, the public reacted with anger and cynicism about anything the government and newspapers had to say.

For the war correspondents, the war had been a shaming experience. They were no longer the stars of journalism and gone were the days when what they wrote sold newspapers. Henry Nevinson wrote nostalgically:

> *'In the old days of "scoops" and "beats", I have sat at meals with a group of correspondents all silent for fear of giving away some piece of information which we all knew. But during the Great War a complete change was developed...We pooled our knowledge and submitted our composite reports to a body of censors to be dispatched by special messenger. We lived chirping together like little birds in a nest, and thought of weary days when a war correspondent spent half his time in seeking food and shelter for himself, his horses and his man, or wandering far and wide in search of a censor and telegraph office.'*

The reporters have been castigated for misleading the British public, and later several wrote of their shame in passing on falsely optimistic statements and slavishly writing what they were told by the military. Their employers, the newspapers, were also complicit in the censoring of critical reports and their proprietors enjoyed the confidence of the government, often leading to an elevation to the peerage.

In truth, the war reporters had very little option but to comply with the new ground rules. Those that did not, such as Ellis Ashmead-Bartlett, and reported anything that was critical about how the war was being conducted, would find that their war reporting days were over. As Harold Evans wrote in his essay *'Reporting in the Time of Conflict'*:

> *'far more frequent than* [such] *journalistic excesses, have been the excesses of censorship and harassment of the press – not to save the lives of men but to protect the careers of military brass and politicians. The public has no "need to know" the date and route of a troopship sailing, but it does need to know when scandals are being covered up.'*

With some exceptions, the reports printed in the daily press during the First World War are interesting as period pieces – a sort of background to what was really going on at the sharp end – observers from afar, rather than rubbing shoulders with the men doing the fighting. The reporters were, in the main, gifted writers, and several, like Philip Gibbs, wrote eloquently and truthfully after the conflict.

Despite the debate on the part played by the war correspondents reporting from the front, their role had been changed for ever.

Notes

1 Wilhelm enjoyed a peaceful and comfortable exile at a country house near Doorn. When the Germans invaded the Netherlands in May 1940, Winston Churchill offered asylum, which the old Kaiser declined. He died on 4 June 1942 aged 82.

2 Belgium also supplied an occupying force of five divisions based at Aachen.

3 One of the reasons for the near-famine was that the British Government refused to lift its blockade until the actual signing of the peace in June.

4 Gibbs was a Roman Catholic and the first journalist to interview the Pope.

5 During the war, Gibbs had written *The Battle of the Somme, From Bapaume to Passchendaele, Open Warfare –The Way to Victory* and *The Soul of War*.

Bibliography

Realities of War by Philip Gibbs 1920
The Pageant of the Years 1946
In Flanders Fields – Before Ypres There Was Yser by Paul Van Pul 2006
1918 – The Year Of Victories by Martyn Marix Evans 2004
Haig's Generals Edited by Ian F.W. Beckett & Steven J. Corvi 2006
News From The Front – War Correspondents on the Western Front 1914–18 by Martin J. Farrar 1999
I Was There – The Human Story of the Great War Edited by Sir John Hammerton
What Did You Do In The War Daddy A Visual History of Propaganda Posters by Peter Stanley 1983
The First Casualty by Phillip Knightley 1979
1915 by Lyn Macdonald 1993
To Conquer Hell by Edward G. Lengel 2008
The Wipers Times
Damn The Dardenelles – The Agony of Gallipoli by John Laffin 1980
The Neglected War: Britain's Mesopotamian Campaign 1914–1918 by A.J. Barker 1967
The First World War 1914–1918 Vols 1 & 2 by Charles Repington 1920
The Uncensored Dardenelles by Ellis Ashmead Bartlett 1928
From the Frontline – The Extraordinary Life of Sir Basil Clarke by Richard Evans
Field Notes from the Russian Front by Stanley Washburn 1915
The Russian Campaign by Stanley Washburn 1915
Victory into Defeat by Stanley Washburn 1916
WW1 Short History by Norman Stone 2007
The Story of the Salonica Army by G. Ward Price 1918
War Wanderings – A Record of War and War Travels 1914–1916 by George Renwick 1916
The Great War in the Middle East – Allenby's final triumph by W.T. Massey
Verdun to The Vosges by Gerald Campbell 1916
An Onlooker in France by William Orpen 1921
The Fire of Life by H.W. Nevinson 1929

BIBLIOGRAPHY

A Traveller in News by William Beach Thomas 1925
To End All Wars: How the First World War Divided Britain by Adam
  Hochschild 2011.
Horsemen in No Man's Land – British Cavalry and Trench Warfare by
  David Kenyon 2011

INTERNET SOURCES
www.scoop-database.com
http://spiderbites.nytimes.com
www.cairogang.com
www.gutenberg.org
http://coffeecuphistory.wordpress.com
www.kingsacademy.com
http://militaryhistory.about.com
http://llsa.revues.org
http://paperspast.natlib.govt.nz
www.54warcorrespondents-kia-30-ww2.com
www.usaww1.com

Index

INDEX

INDEX